AMERICAN POLITICAL, ECONOMIC, AND SECURITY ISSUE

FREE TRADE AGREEMENTS

SELECTED ANALYSES FROM NAFTA TO THE TRANS-PACIFIC PARTNERSHIP

American Political, Economic, and Security Issue

Additional books in this series can be found on Nova's website under the Series tab.

Additional e-books in this series can be found on Nova's website under the e-book tab.

AMERICAN POLITICAL, ECONOMIC, AND SECURITY ISSUE

FREE TRADE AGREEMENTS

SELECTED ANALYSES FROM NAFTA TO THE TRANS-PACIFIC PARTNERSHIP

JENELL GALLO
EDITOR

nova publishers
New York

Library of Congress Cataloging-in-Publication Data

ISBN: 978-1-63117-366-0

Published by Nova Science Publishers, Inc. † New York

CONTENTS

PREFACE

The North American Free Trade Agreement (NAFTA) entered into force on January 1, 1994. The overall economic impact of NAFTA is difficult to measure since trade and investment trends are influenced by numerous other economic variables, such as economic growth, inflation, and currency fluctuations. NAFTA continues to be of interest to Congress because of the importance of Canada and Mexico as U.S. trading partners, and also because of the implications NAFTA has for U.S. trade policy. This book provides an overview of North American trade liberalization before NAFTA, an overview of NAFTA provisions, the economic effects of NAFTA, and policy considerations. It also examines the provisions of the U.S.-South Korea Free Trade Agreement (KORUS FTA) in the context of the overall U.S.-South Korean economic relationship, U.S. objectives, and South Korean objectives. The book examines some of the issues that have arisen during the implementation of KORUS FTA, and analyzes the issues related to the proposed Trans-Pacific Partnership (TPP), the state and substance of the negotiations, the specific areas under negotiation, the policy and economic contexts in which the TPP would fit, and the issues for Congress that the TPP presents.

Chapter 1 - The North American Free Trade Agreement (NAFTA) entered into force on January 1, 1994. The agreement was signed by President George H.W. Bush on December 17, 1992, and approved by Congress on November 20, 1993. The NAFTA Implementation Act was signed into law by President William J. Clinton on December 8, 1993 (P.L. 103-182). The overall economic impact of NAFTA is difficult to measure since trade and investment trends are influenced by numerous other economic variables, such as economic growth, inflation, and currency fluctuations. The agreement may have accelerated the trade liberalization that was already taking place, but many of these changes may have taken place with or without an agreement. Nevertheless, NAFTA is significant because it was the most comprehensive free trade agreement (FTA) negotiated at the time and contained several groundbreaking provisions. A legacy of the agreement is that it has served as a template or model for the new generation of FTAs that the United States later negotiated and it also served as a template for certain provisions in multilateral trade negotiations as part of the Uruguay Round.

The 113th Congress faces numerous issues related to international trade. Canada and Mexico are the first and third largest U.S. trading partners, respectively. With the two countries participating in the negotiations to conclude a Trans-Pacific Partnership (TPP) free trade agreement among the United States and 10 other countries, policy issues related to NAFTA continue to be of interest for Congress. If negotiations progress, a TPP agreement could affect the rules and market access commitments governing North American trade and investment since NAFTA entered into force. A related trade policy issue in which the effects of NAFTA may be explored is the possible renewal of Trade Promotion Authority (TPA; formerly known as "fast-track authority") to provide expedited procedures for the consideration of bills to implement trade agreements.

NAFTA was controversial when first proposed, mostly because it was the first FTA involving two wealthy, developed countries and a developing country. The political debate surrounding the agreement was divisive with proponents arguing that the agreement would help generate thousands of jobs and reduce income disparity in the region, while opponents warned that the agreement would cause huge job losses in the United States as companies moved production to Mexico to lower costs. In reality, NAFTA did not cause the huge job losses feared by the critics or the large economic gains predicted by supporters. The net overall effect of NAFTA on the U.S. economy appears to have been relatively modest, primarily because trade with Canada and Mexico account for a small percentage of U.S. GDP. However, there were worker and firm adjustment costs as the three countries adjusted to more open trade and investment among their economies.

The rising number of bilateral and regional trade agreements throughout the world and the rising presence of China in Latin America could have implications for U.S. trade policy with its NAFTA partners. Some proponents of open and rules-based trade maintain that a further deepening of economic relations with Canada and Mexico will help promote a common trade agenda with shared values and generate economic growth. Some opponents argue that the agreement has caused worker displacement and that NAFTA needs to be reopened. One possible way of doing this is through the proposed TPP. The ongoing TPP negotiations, launched in the fall of 2008, may not result in a reopening of NAFTA, but could alter some of the rules and market access commitments governing North American trade and investment.

Chapter 2 - On October 3, 2011, President Obama submitted draft legislation (H.R. 3080/S. 1642) to implement the U.S.-South Korea Free Trade Agreement (KORUS FTA) to both houses of Congress. On October 6, the House Ways and Means Committee reported out H.R. 3080 (H.Rept. 112-239). The Senate Finance Committee reported out S. 1642 (without written report). On October 12, the House passed H.R. 3080 (278-151) and sent it to the Senate which passed it (83- 15). The President signed the legislation on October 21, 2011 (P.L. 112-41). In South Korea, after a contentious battle, the Korean National Assembly passed the agreement on November 22. On March 15, 2012, the KORUS FTA entered into force.

The KORUS FTA is the second-largest U.S. FTA (next to NAFTA). South Korea is the seventh-largest trading partner of the United States, and the United States is South Korea's third-largest trading partner. The KORUS FTA covers a wide range of trade and investment issues and, therefore, could have substantial economic implications for both the United States and South Korea.

Congress approved the KORUS FTA implementing legislation using expedited procedures authorized by the Trade Promotion Authority (TPA). Under TPA, the President had the discretion on when to submit the implementing legislation to Congress. The KORUS FTA was negotiated and signed on June 30, 2007, by President George W. Bush. However, President Bush did not submit the legislation because of differences with the Democratic leadership over treatment of autos and beef, among other issues. On December 3, 2010, after a series of arduous negotiations, President Obama and President Lee announced that they had reached an agreement on addressing the outstanding issues related to the KORUS FTA. As a result, U.S. and South Korean negotiators agreed, in the form of an exchange of letters and agreed minutes, to modifications to the commitments made in the 2007 agreement. These modifications included changes in phase-out periods for tariffs on autos and pork, a new safeguard provision on autos, and concessions by South Korea on allowing a larger number of U.S. cars into South Korea under U.S. safety standards than was the case under the original KORUS FTA provisions. The modifications were included in the implementing legislation.

A broad swath of the U.S. business community supported the KORUS FTA. With the modifications in the commitments reached in December 2010, this group also included the three Detroit-based auto manufacturers and the United Auto Workers (UAW) union. It still faced opposition from some labor unions and other groups, including Public Citizen. Many U.S. supporters view the KORUS FTA as important to secure new opportunities in the South Korean market, while opponents claimed that the KORUS FTA does not go far enough to break down South Korean trade barriers or that the agreement will encourage U.S. companies to move their production offshore at the expense of U.S. workers. Other observers suggested the KORUS FTA could have implications for the U.S.-South Korean alliance as a whole, as well as on U.S. Asia policy and U.S. trade policy.

Chapter 3 - The Trans-Pacific Partnership (TPP) is a proposed regional free trade agreement (FTA) being negotiated among the United States, Australia, Brunei, Canada, Chile, Japan, Malaysia, Mexico, New Zealand, Peru, Singapore, and Vietnam. U.S. negotiators and others describe and envision the TPP as a "comprehensive and high-standard" FTA that aims to liberalize trade in nearly all goods and services and include commitments beyond those currently established in the World Trade Organization (WTO). The broad outline of an agreement was announced on the sidelines of the Asia-Pacific Economic Cooperation (APEC) ministerial in November 2011, in Honolulu, HI. If concluded as envisioned, the TPP potentially could eliminate tariff and non-tariff barriers to trade and investment among the parties and could serve as a template for a future trade pact among APEC members and potentially other countries. Congress has a direct interest in the negotiations, both through influencing U.S. negotiating positions with the executive branch, and by passing legislation to implement any resulting agreement.

The 19th round of negotiations was held in Bandar Seri Begawan, Brunei, on August 23-30. TPP leaders, with Vice President Biden representing the United States, met on the sidelines of the APEC meetings on October 8, reaffirming their objective to conclude the negotiations in 2013. Issue-specific intercessional meetings continue, and a ministerial meeting is reportedly scheduled for December 7-10 in Singapore. For the year-end deadline to be achieved, outstanding issues involving sensitivities for the participants will likely require political decisions to be made. The negotiating dynamic itself is complex: decisions on key market access issues such as dairy, sugar, and textiles and apparel may depend on the outcome of rules negotiations such as intellectual property rights or state-owned enterprises.

Twenty-nine chapters in the agreement are under discussion. The United States is negotiating market access for goods, services, and agriculture with countries with which it does not currently have FTAs: Brunei, Japan, Malaysia, New Zealand, and Vietnam. Negotiations are also being conducted on disciplines to intellectual property rights, trade in services, government procurement, investment, rules of origin, competition, labor, and environmental standards and other issues. In many cases, the rules being negotiated are intended to be more rigorous than comparable rules found in the WTO. Some topics, such as state-owned enterprises, regulatory coherence, and supply chain competitiveness, may break new ground in FTA negotiations. As the countries that make up the TPP negotiating partners include advanced industrialized, middle income, and developing economies, the TPP, if implemented, may involve substantial restructuring of the economies of some participants.

The TPP serves several strategic goals in U.S. trade policy. First, it is the leading trade policy initiative of the Obama Administration, and is a manifestation of the Administration's "rebalance" to the Asia-Pacific. If concluded, it may serve to shape the economic architecture of the Asia- Pacific region by harmonizing existing agreements with U.S. FTA partners, attracting new participants, and establishing regional rules on new policy issues facing the global economy— possibly providing impetus to future multilateral liberalization under the WTO.

As the negotiations proceed, a number of issues important to Congress are emerging. One is whether the United States can balance its vision of creating a "comprehensive and high standard" agreement with a large and expanding group of countries, while not insisting on terms that other countries will reject. Another issue is how Congress will consider the TPP, if concluded. The present negotiations are not being conducted under the auspices of formal trade promotion authority (TPA)—the latest TPA expired on July 1, 2007—although the Administration informally is following the procedures of the former TPA. If TPP implementing legislation is brought to Congress, TPA may need to be considered if the legislation is not to be subject to potentially debilitating amendments or rejection. In addition, Members of Congress may wish to consider whether the current chapters included in the agreement appropriately address their trade policy concerns, as well as the potential agreement's impact on the multilateral trading system.

Chapter 4 - Free trade areas (FTAs) are arrangements among two or more countries under which they agree to eliminate tariffs and nontariff barriers on trade in goods among themselves. However, each country maintains its own policies, including tariffs, on trade outside the region.

In the last few years, the United States has engaged or has proposed to engage in negotiations to establish bilateral and regional free trade arrangements with a number of trading partners. Such arrangements are not new in U.S. trade policy. The United States has had a free trade arrangement with Israel since 1985 and with Canada since 1989, which was expanded to include Mexico and became the North American Free Trade Agreement (NAFTA) effective in January 1994.

U.S. interest in bilateral and regional free trade arrangements surged, and the Bush Administration accelerated the pace of negotiations after the enactment of the Trade Promotion Authority in August 2002. U.S. participation in free trade agreements can occur only with the concurrence of Congress. In addition, FTAs affect the U.S. economy, with the impact varying across sectors.

The 112th Congress and the Obama Administration faced the question of whether and when to act on three FTAs pending from the Bush Administration—with Colombia, Panama, and South Korea. Although the Bush Administration signed these agreements, it and the leaders of the 110th Congress could not reach agreement on proceeding to enact them. No action was taken during the 111th Congress either.

After discussion with congressional leaders and negotiations with the governments of Colombia, Panama, and South Korea to assuage congressional concerns regarding treatment of union officials (Colombia), taxation regimes (Panama), and trade in autos (South Korea), President Obama submitted draft implementing legislation to Congress on October 3, 2011. The 112th Congress approved each of the bills in successive votes on October 12, along with legislation to renew an aspect of the Trade Adjustment Assistance (TAA) program. President Obama signed the bills into law on October 21, 2011.

In the meantime, on November 14, 2009, President Obama committed to work with the current and partners in the negotiations to form a Trans-Pacific Partnership (TPP) Agreement. The TPP is a free trade agreement that includes nations on both sides of the Pacific. The TPP negotiations emerged from an FTA that included Brunei, Chile, New Zealand, and Singapore and that entered into force in 2006. Besides the United States, Australia, Canada, Malaysia, Peru, Mexico, and Vietnam have joined the negotiations. In addition, Japan has expressed interest in joining. Furthermore, the United States has announced its intention to launch negotiations with the European Union for form an FTA—the Transatlantic Trade and Investment Partnership (TTIP).

FTAs raise some important policy issues: Do FTAs serve or impede U.S. long-term national interests and trade policy objectives? Which type of an FTA arrangement meets U.S. national interests? What should U.S. criteria be in choosing FTA partners? Are FTAs a substitute for or a complement to U.S. commitments and interests in promoting a multilateral trading system via the World Trade Organization (WTO)? What effect will the expiration of TPA have on the future of FTAs as a trade policy strategy?

In the last few years, the United States has considered bilateral and regional free trade areas (FTAs) with a number of trading partners. Such arrangements are not new in U.S. trade policy. The United States has had a free trade arrangement with Israel since 1985 and with Canada since 1989. The latter was suspended when the North American Free Trade Agreement (NAFTA) that included the United States, Canada, and Mexico went into effect in January 1994.

U.S. interest in bilateral and regional free trade arrangements surged, and the Bush Administration accelerated the pace of negotiations after the enactment of the Trade Promotion Authority in August 2002. U.S. participation in free trade agreements can occur only with the concurrence of Congress. In addition, FTAs affect the U.S. economy, with the impact varying across sectors.

The 112th Congress and the Obama Administration faced the question of whether and when to act on three pending FTAs—with Colombia, Panama, and South Korea. Although the Bush Administration signed these agreements, it and the leaders of the 110th Congress could not reach agreement on proceeding to enact them. No action was taken during the 111th Congress either. In addition, the Trade Promotion Authority (TPA) expired on July 1, 2007, meaning that any new FTAs agreed to would not likely receive expedited legislative consideration, unless the authority is renewed.

After discussion with congressional leaders and negotiations with the governments of Colombia, Panama, and South Korea to assuage congressional concerns regarding treatment of union officials (Colombia), taxation regimes (Panama), and trade in autos (South Korea), President Obama submitted draft implementing legislation to Congress on October 3, 2011. The 112th Congress approved each of the bills in successive votes on October 12, along with legislation to renew an aspect of the Trade Adjustment Assistance (TAA) program.

In the meantime, on November 14, 2009, President Obama committed to work with the current and prospective partners to form the Trans-Pacific Partnership (TPP) Agreement. The

TPP is a free trade agreement that includes nations on both sides of the Pacific. The TPP grew out of an FTA that included Brunei, Chile, New Zealand, and Singapore. Besides the United States, Australia, Canada, Malaysia, Mexico, Peru, and Vietnam have also joined the negotiations, and Japan has expressed interest in participating as well. Furthermore, The United States has announced its intention to launch negotiations with the European Union to form an FTA—the Transatlantic Trade and Investment Partnership (TTIP).

FTAs raise some important policy issues: Do FTAs serve or impede U.S. long-term national interests and trade policy objectives? Which type of an FTA arrangement meets U.S. national interests? What should U.S. criteria be in choosing FTA partners? Are FTAs a substitute for or a complement to U.S. commitments and interests in promoting a multilateral trading system via the World Trade Organization (WTO)? What effect will the expiration of TPA have on the future of FTAs as a trade policy strategy?

Chapter 5 - Since 1993, the Administration has negotiated and Congress has approved 13 free trade agreements (FTAs) that contain labor provisions with different degrees of enforceability. This report identifies two types of labor enforcement issues: (1) those that relate to the FTA provisions themselves, including their definitions and their enforceability, and (2) those that relate to executive branch responsibilities, such as resource availability and determining dispute settlement case priorities. This report does not address other labor issues in the various free trade agreements, including cooperative consultation provisions.

In: Free Trade Agreements
Editor: Jenell Gallo
ISBN: 978-1-63117-366-0

Chapter 1

NAFTA AT 20: OVERVIEW AND TRADE EFFECTS*

M. Angeles Villarreal and Ian F. Ferguson

SUMMARY

The North American Free Trade Agreement (NAFTA) entered into force on January 1, 1994. The agreement was signed by President George H.W. Bush on December 17, 1992, and approved by Congress on November 20, 1993. The NAFTA Implementation Act was signed into law by President William J. Clinton on December 8, 1993 (P.L. 103-182). The overall economic impact of NAFTA is difficult to measure since trade and investment trends are influenced by numerous other economic variables, such as economic growth, inflation, and currency fluctuations. The agreement may have accelerated the trade liberalization that was already taking place, but many of these changes may have taken place with or without an agreement. Nevertheless, NAFTA is significant because it was the most comprehensive free trade agreement (FTA) negotiated at the time and contained several groundbreaking provisions. A legacy of the agreement is that it has served as a template or model for the new generation of FTAs that the United States later negotiated and it also served as a template for certain provisions in multilateral trade negotiations as part of the Uruguay Round.

The 113th Congress faces numerous issues related to international trade. Canada and Mexico are the first and third largest U.S. trading partners, respectively. With the two countries participating in the negotiations to conclude a Trans-Pacific Partnership (TPP) free trade agreement among the United States and 10 other countries, policy issues related to NAFTA continue to be of interest for Congress. If negotiations progress, a TPP agreement could affect the rules and market access commitments governing North American trade and investment since NAFTA entered into force. A related trade policy issue in which the effects of NAFTA may be explored is the possible renewal of Trade Promotion Authority (TPA; formerly known as "fast-track authority") to provide expedited procedures for the consideration of bills to implement trade agreements.

---

* This is an edited, reformatted and augmented version of a Congressional Research Service Publication, CRS Report for Congress R42965, dated February 21, 2013.

NAFTA was controversial when first proposed, mostly because it was the first FTA involving two wealthy, developed countries and a developing country. The political debate surrounding the agreement was divisive with proponents arguing that the agreement would help generate thousands of jobs and reduce income disparity in the region, while opponents warned that the agreement would cause huge job losses in the United States as companies moved production to Mexico to lower costs. In reality, NAFTA did not cause the huge job losses feared by the critics or the large economic gains predicted by supporters. The net overall effect of NAFTA on the U.S. economy appears to have been relatively modest, primarily because trade with Canada and Mexico account for a small percentage of U.S. GDP. However, there were worker and firm adjustment costs as the three countries adjusted to more open trade and investment among their economies.

The rising number of bilateral and regional trade agreements throughout the world and the rising presence of China in Latin America could have implications for U.S. trade policy with its NAFTA partners. Some proponents of open and rules-based trade maintain that a further deepening of economic relations with Canada and Mexico will help promote a common trade agenda with shared values and generate economic growth. Some opponents argue that the agreement has caused worker displacement and that NAFTA needs to be reopened. One possible way of doing this is through the proposed TPP. The ongoing TPP negotiations, launched in the fall of 2008, may not result in a reopening of NAFTA, but could alter some of the rules and market access commitments governing North American trade and investment.

INTRODUCTION

The North American Free Trade Agreement (NAFTA) has been in effect since January 1, 1994. Signed by President George H.W. Bush on December 17, 1992, and approved by Congress on November 20, 1993, the NAFTA Implementation Act was signed into law by President William J. Clinton on December 8, 1993 (P.L. 103-182). NAFTA continues to be of interest to Congress because of the importance of Canada and Mexico as U.S. trading partners, and also because of the implications NAFTA has for U.S. trade policy. This report provides an overview of North American trade liberalization before NAFTA, an overview of NAFTA provisions, the economic effects of NAFTA, and policy considerations.

The 113th Congress, in both its legislative and oversight capacities, faces numerous issues related to international trade. The Obama Administration has made the proposed Trans-Pacific Partnership (TPP) free trade agreement one of its top trade priorities.[1] The United States, Canada, and Mexico, along with eight other countries, are participating in the TPP negotiations. If negotiations continue to move forward, it may affect the rules and market access commitments governing North American trade since NAFTA entered into force. A related trade policy issue in which the effects of NAFTA may be explored is the possible renewal of Trade Promotion Authority (TPA; formerly known as "fast-track authority") to provide expedited procedures for the consideration of bills to implement trade agreements.[2]

Many trade policy experts give credit to free trade agreements (FTAs) for enhancing economic linkages between countries, creating more efficient production processes, increasing the availability of lower-priced consumer goods, and improving living standards and working conditions.[3] Others have blamed FTAs for disappointing employment trends and for not having done enough to improve competitiveness, labor standards, and environmental conditions abroad.[4]

A legacy of NAFTA is that it has served as a model for other FTAs that the United States later negotiated and also for multilateral negotiations. NAFTA initiated a new generation of trade agreements in the Western Hemisphere and other parts of the world, influencing negotiations in areas such as market access, rules of origin, intellectual property rights, foreign investment, dispute resolution, worker rights, and environmental protection. The United States currently has FTAs with 20 countries. As with NAFTA, these trade agreements have often been supported or criticized on similar arguments related to jobs.

MARKET OPENING PRIOR TO NAFTA

The concept of economic integration in North America was not a new one at the time NAFTA negotiations started. In 1911, President William Howard Taft signed a reciprocal trade agreement with Canadian Prime Minister Sir Wilfred Laurier. After a bitter election, Canadians rejected free trade and ousted Prime Minister Laurier, thereby ending the agreement. In 1965, the United States and Canada signed the U.S.-Canada Automotive Products Agreement that liberalized trade in cars, trucks, tires, and automotive parts between the two countries.[5] The Auto Pact was credited as a pioneer in creating an integrated North American automotive sector. In the case of Mexico, the government had been implementing reform measures since the mid-1980s, prior to NAFTA, to liberalize its economy. By 1990, when NAFTA negotiations began, Mexico had already taken significant steps towards liberalizing its protectionist trade regime.

The U.S.-Canada Free Trade Agreement of 1989

The United States and Canada recently marked the 25th anniversary of the October 3, 1987 signing of the U.S.-Canada Free Trade Agreement (FTA). The FTA was the first economically significant bilateral FTA signed by the United States.[6] Implementing legislation[7] was approved by both Houses of Congress under "fast-track authority"—now known as trade promotion authority (TPA)—and signed by President Ronald Reagan on September 28, 1988. While the FTA generated significant policy debate in the United States, it was a watershed moment for Canada. Controversy surrounding the proposed FTA led to the so-called "free trade election" in 1988, in which sitting Progressive Conservative Prime Minister Brian Mulroney, who negotiated the agreement, defeated Liberal party leader John Turner, who vowed to reject it if elected. After the election, the FTA was passed by Parliament in December 1988, and it came into effect between the two nations on January 1, 1989. At the time, it probably was the most comprehensive bilateral FTA negotiated worldwide and contained several groundbreaking provisions. It:

- Eliminated all tariffs by 1998. Many were eliminated immediately, and the remaining tariffs were phased-out in 5-10 years.

- Continued the 1965 U.S.-Canada Auto Pact, but tightened its rules of origin. Some Canadian auto sector practices not covered by the Auto Pact were ended by 1998.
- Provided national treatment for covered services providers and liberalized financial services trade. Facilitated cross-border travel for business professionals.
- Committed to provide prospective national treatment for investments originating in the other, although established derogations from national treatment such as for national security or prudential reasons were allowed to continue. Banned imposition of performance requirements, such as local content, import substitution, or local sourcing requirements.
- Expanded the size of federal government procurement markets available for competitive bidding from suppliers of the other country. It did not include sub-federal government procurement.
- Provided for a binding binational panel to resolve disputes arising from the agreement (a Canadian insistence).
- Prohibited most import and export restrictions on energy products, including minimum export prices. This was carried forth in NAFTA only with regard to Canada-U.S. energy trade.

Many of these provisions were incorporated into, or expanded in, NAFTA. However, the FTA did not include, or specifically exempted, some issues that would appear in NAFTA for the first time. These include

- **Intellectual property rights (IPR).** The FTA did not contain language on intellectual property rights. NAFTA was the first FTA to include meaningful disciplines on IPR.
- **Cultural exemption.** It exempted the broadcasting, film, and publishing sectors. This exemption continues in NAFTA.
- **Transportation services and investment** in the Canadian energy sector were excluded from the FTA. These exclusions were limited in NAFTA.
- **Trade remedies.** Neither the FTA nor NAFTA ended the use of trade remedy actions (anti-dumping, countervailing duty, or safeguards) against the other. This was a key Canadian goal of the FTA. NAFTA did create a separate dispute settlement mechanism to adjudicate trade remedy disputes, but this mechanism has not been replicated in other FTAs.
- **Softwood lumber.** The FTA grandfathered in the then-present 1986 Memorandum of Understanding (MOU) governing softwood lumber trade. Over time, the MOU has been replaced by other agreements—such as the current Softwood Lumber Agreement (SLA)—and, at times, by resort to trade remedy actions.
- **Agricultural supply management.** Canada was able to exempt its agriculture supply management system, although it committed to allow a small increase in imports of dairy, poultry, and eggs, which carried over into the NAFTA. The United States was also able to exclude certain products from liberalization commitments under the FTA and the NAFTA.

Mexico's Pre-NAFTA Trade Liberalization Efforts

Well before NAFTA negotiations began, Mexico was already liberalizing its protectionist trade and investment policies that had been in place for decades (see **Appendix B** for more information on Mexico's pre-NAFTA protectionist policies). The restrictive trade regime began after Mexico's revolutionary period and remained until the early- to mid-1980's when the country was facing a debt crisis. It was at this time that the government took unilateral steps to open and modernize its economy by relaxing investment policies and liberalizing trade barriers. The trade liberalization measures that began in the mid-1980s shifted Mexico from one of the world's most protected economies into one of the most open. Mexico now has 12 FTAs involving 44 countries.[8]

Mexico's first steps in opening its closed economy focused on reforming its import substitution policies in the mid-1980s. Further reforms were made in 1986 when Mexico became a member of the General Agreement on Tariffs and Trade (GATT). As a condition of becoming a GATT member, for example, Mexico agreed to lower its maximum tariff rates to 50%. Mexico went further by reducing its highest tariff rate from 100% to 20%. Mexico's trade-weighted average tariff fell from 25% in 1985 to about 19% in 1989.[9]

Although Mexico had been lowering trade and investment restrictions since 1986, the number of remaining barriers for U.S. exports remained high at the time of the NAFTA negotiations. Mexico required import licenses on 230 products from the United States, affecting about 7% of the value of U.S. exports to Mexico. Prior to its entry into GATT, Mexico required import licenses on all imports. At the time of the NAFTA negotiations, about 60% of U.S. agricultural exports to Mexico required import licenses. Mexico also had numerous other nontariff barriers, such as "official import prices," an arbitrary customs valuation system that raised duty assessments.[10]

For Mexico, an FTA with the United States represented a way to lock in the reforms of its market opening measures from the mid-1980s to transform Mexico's formerly statist economy after the devastating debt crisis of the 1980s.[11] The combination of the severe economic impact of the debt crisis, low domestic savings, and an increasingly overvalued peso, put pressure on the Mexican government to adopt market-opening economic reforms and boost imports of goods and capital to encourage more competition in the Mexican market. An FTA with the United States was a way of blocking domestic efforts to roll back Mexican reforms, especially in the politically sensitive agriculture sector. NAFTA helped deflect protectionist demands of industrial groups and special interest groups in Mexico.[12] One of the main goals of the Mexican government was to increase investment confidence in order to attract greater flows of foreign investment and spur economic growth. Since the entry into force of NAFTA, Mexico has used the agreement as a basic model for other FTAs Mexico has signed with other countries.[13]

For the United States, NAFTA represented an opportunity to expand the growing export market to the south, but it also represented a political opportunity for the United States and Mexico to work together in resolving some of the tensions in the bilateral relationship.[14] An FTA with Mexico would help U.S. businesses expand exports to a growing market of almost 100 million people. U.S. officials also recognized that imports from Mexico would likely include higher U.S. content than imports from Asian countries. In addition to the trade and investment opportunities that NAFTA represented, an agreement with Mexico would be a way to support the growth of political pluralism and a deepening of democratic processes in Mexico. NAFTA also presented an opportunity for the United States to spur the slow progress on the Uruguay Round of multilateral trade negotiations.[15]

OVERVIEW OF NAFTA PROVISIONS

At the time that NAFTA was implemented, the U.S.-Canada FTA was already in effect and U.S. tariffs on most Mexican goods were low. NAFTA opened up the U.S. market to increased Mexican imports and the Mexican market to the United States and Canada, creating a single market with 400 million people and accounting for one-third of the world's output of approximately $1 trillion per year.[16] Some of the key NAFTA provisions included tariff and non- tariff trade liberalization, rules of origin, services trade, foreign investment, intellectual property rights protection, government procurement, and dispute resolution. Labor and environmental provisions were included in separate NAFTA side agreements.

Removal of Trade Barriers

The market opening provisions of the agreement gradually eliminated all tariffs and most non- tariff barriers on goods produced and traded within North America over a period of fifteen years after it entered into force. Some tariffs were eliminated immediately, while others were phased out in various schedules of five to fifteen years. U.S. import-sensitive sectors, such as glassware, footwear, and ceramic tile, received longer phase-out schedules.[17] NAFTA provided the option of accelerating tariff reductions if the countries involved agreed.[18] The agreement included safeguard provisions in which the importing country could increase tariffs, or impose quotas in some cases, on imports during a transition period if domestic producers faced serious injury as a result of increased imports from another NAFTA country. It terminated all existing drawback programs by January 1, 2001.[19]

Given that the U.S.-Canada FTA was already in place, most of the market opening measures resulted in the removal of U.S. tariffs and quotas applied to imports from Mexico, and Mexican trade barriers applied to imports from the United States and Canada. At the time that NAFTA went into effect, about 40% of U.S. imports from Mexico entered duty-free and the remainder faced duties of up to 35%, with a trade-weighted average rate of about 7%. Mexico's trade- weighted tariff on U.S. agricultural products averaged about 11%. Also affecting U.S.-Mexico trade were both countries' phytosanitary rules, Mexican import licensing requirements, and U.S. marketing orders.[20]

Some of the more significant changes took place in the textiles, apparel, automotive, and agricultural industries. Elimination of trade barriers in these key industries are summarized below.

- **Textiles and Apparel Industries.** NAFTA phased out all duties on textile and apparel goods within North America meeting specific NAFTA rules of origin[21] over a 10-year period. Prior to NAFTA, 65% of U.S. apparel imports from Mexico entered duty-free and quota-free, and the remaining 35% faced an average tariff rate of 17.9%. Mexico's average tariff on U.S. textile and apparel products was 16%, with duties as high as 20% on some products.[22]

- **Automotive Industry.** NAFTA phased out Mexico's restrictive auto decrce. It phased out all U.S. tariffs imports from Mexico and Mexican tariffs on U.S. and Canadian products as long as they met the rules of origin requirements of 62.5% North American content for autos, light trucks, engines and transmissions; and 60% for other vehicles and automotive parts. Some tariffs were eliminated immediately, while others were phased out in periods of 5 to 10 years. Prior to NAFTA, the United States assessed the following tariffs on imports from Mexico: 2.5% on automobiles, 25% on light-duty trucks, and a trade-weighted average of 3.1% for automotive parts. Mexican tariffs on U.S. and Canadian automotive products were as follows: 20% on automobiles and light trucks, and 10-20% on auto parts.[23]
- **Agriculture.** NAFTA set out separate bilateral undertakings on cross-border trade in agriculture, one between Canada and Mexico, and the other between Mexico and the United States. As a general matter, U.S.-Canada FTA provisions continued to apply on trade with Canada.[24] Regarding U.S.-Mexico agriculture trade, NAFTA eliminated most non-tariff barriers in agricultural trade, either through their conversion to tariff-rate quotas (TRQ's)[25] or ordinary tariffs. Tariffs were phased out over a period of 15 years with sensitive products such as sugar and corn receiving the longest phase-out periods. Approximately one-half of U.S.-Mexico agricultural trade became duty-free when the agreement went into effect. Prior to NAFTA, most tariffs, on average, in agricultural trade between the United States and Mexico were fairly low though some U.S. exports to Mexico faced tariffs as high as 12%. However, approximately one-fourth of U.S. agricultural exports to Mexico (by value) were subjected to restrictive import licensing requirements.[26]

Services Trade Liberalization

NAFTA services provisions established a set of basic rules and obligations in services trade among partner countries. The agreement expanded on initiatives in the U.S.-Canada FTA and the Uruguay Round of multilateral trade negotiations to create internationally-agreed disciplines on government regulation of trade in services.[27] The agreement granted services providers certain rights concerning nondiscriminatory treatment, cross-border sales and entry, investment, and access to information. However, there were certain exclusions and reservations by each country. These included maritime shipping (United States), film and publishing (Canada), and oil and gas drilling (Mexico).[28] Although NAFTA liberalized certain service sectors in Mexico, particularly financial services, which profoundly altered its banking sector, other sectors were barely affected.[29] In telecommunications services, NAFTA partners agreed to exclude provision of, but not the use of, basic telecommunications services. NAFTA granted a "bill of rights" for the providers and users of telecommunications services, including access to public telecommunications services; connection to private lines that reflect economic costs and available on a flat-rate pricing basis; and the right to choose, purchase, or lease terminal equipment best suited to their needs.[30] However, NAFTA did not require parties to authorize a person of another NAFTA country to provide or operate telecommunications transport networks or services. NAFTA did not bar a party from maintaining a monopoly provider of public networks or services, such as Telmex, Mexico's dominant telecommunications company.[31]

Other Provisions

In addition to market opening measures through the elimination of tariff and non-tariff barriers, NAFTA incorporated numerous other provisions, including foreign investment, intellectual property rights (IPR), dispute resolution, and government procurement.

- **Foreign Investment.** NAFTA removed significant investment barriers, ensured basic protections for NAFTA investors, and provided a mechanism for the settlement of disputes between investors and a NAFTA country.[32] NAFTA provided for "non-discriminatory treatment" for foreign investment by NAFTA parties in certain sectors of other NAFTA countries.[33] The agreement included explicit country-specific liberalization commitments and exceptions to national treatment. Exemptions from NAFTA investment provisions include the energy sector in Mexico in which the Mexican government reserved the right to prohibit foreign investment. It also included exceptions related to national security and to Canada's cultural industries.[34]
- **IPR.** NAFTA built upon the then-ongoing Uruguay Round negotiations that would create the Trade Related Aspects of Intellectual Property Rights (TRIPS) agreement in the World Trade Organization and on various existing international intellectual property treaties. The agreement set out specific enforceable commitments by NAFTA parties regarding the protection of copyrights, patents, trademarks, and trade secrets, among other provisions.
- **Dispute Settlement Procedures.** NAFTA's provisions for preventing and settling disputes were built upon provisions in the U.S.-Canada FTA. NAFTA created a system of arbitration for resolving disputes that included initial consultations, taking the issue to the NAFTA Trade Commission, or going through arbitral panel proceedings.[35] NAFTA included separate dispute settlement provisions for addressing disputes over antidumping and countervailing duty determinations.
- **Government Procurement.** NAFTA opened up a significant portion of federal government procurement in each country on a nondiscriminatory basis to suppliers from other NAFTA countries for goods and services. It contains some limitations for procurement by state-owned enterprises.[36]

NAFTA Side Agreements on Labor and the Environment

The NAFTA text did not include labor or environmental provisions, which was a major concern to many in Congress at the time of the agreement's consideration. Some policymakers called for additional provisions to address numerous concerns about labor and environmental issues, specifically in Mexico. Other policymakers argued that the economic growth generated by the FTA would increase Mexico's resources available for environmental and worker rights protection. However, congressional concerns from policymakers, as well as concerns from labor and environmental groups, remained strong.

Shortly after he began his presidency, President Clinton addressed labor and environmental concerns by joining his counterparts in Canada and Mexico in negotiating formal side agreements. The NAFTA implementing legislation included provisions related to the side agreements, authorizing U.S. participation in NAFTA labor and environmental commissions and appropriations for these activities. The North American Agreement on Labor Cooperation (NAALC) and the North American Agreement on Environmental Cooperation (NAAEC) entered into force on January 1, 1994, the same day as NAFTA.[37] NAFTA implementing legislation also included two adjustment assistance programs, designed to ease trade-related labor problems: the NAFTA Transitional Adjustment Assistance (NAFTA-TAA) Program and the U.S. Community Adjustment and Investment Program (USCAIP).

The labor and environmental side agreements included language to promote cooperation on labor and environmental matters as well as provisions to address a party's failure to enforce its own labor and environmental laws. Perhaps most notable were the side agreements' dispute settlement processes that, as a last resort, may impose monetary assessments and sanctions to address a party's failure to enforce its laws.[38] NAFTA marked the first time that labor and environmental provisions were associated with an FTA. For many, it represented an opportunity for cooperating on environmental and labor matters across borders and for establishing a new type of relationship among NAFTA partners.[39]

In addition to the two trilateral side agreements, the United States and Mexico entered into a bilateral side agreement to NAFTA on border environmental cooperation.[40] In this agreement, the two governments committed to cooperate on developing environmental infrastructure projects along the U.S.-Mexico border to address concerns about the degradation of the environment along the U.S.-Mexico border due to increased economic activity. The agreement established two organizations to address these concerns: the Border Environment Cooperation Commission (BECC), located in Juárez, Mexico, and the North American Development Bank (NADBank), located in San Antonio, Texas. The sister organizations work closely together and with other partners at the federal, state and local level in the United States and Mexico to develop, certify, and facilitate financing for water and wastewater treatment, municipal solid waste disposal, and related projects on both sides of the U.S.-Mexico border region. Both organizations also have ongoing efforts to measure the results of the projects on the border region. From 1995 to 2011, BECC certified 189 projects (86 in the United States and 103 in Mexico), representing nearly $4.3 billion in environmental infrastructure investment, directly benefiting 14 million border residents. NADBank has financed 152 of these projects with approximately $1.33 billion in loans and grants.[41] These projects have provided border residents with more access to drinking water, sewer and wastewater treatment. They also include water conservation, air quality, and renewable energy projects.[42]

TRADE TRENDS AND ECONOMIC EFFECTS

Many economists contend that trade liberalization promotes overall economic growth and efficiency among trading partners, although there are short-term adjustment costs. NAFTA was unusual in global terms because it was the first time that an FTA linked two wealthy, developed countries with a low-income developing country. For this reason, the agreement received considerable attention by U.S. policymakers, manufacturers, service providers, agriculture producers, labor unions, non-government organizations, and academics. Proponents argued that the agreement would help generate thousands of jobs and reduce income disparity between Mexico and its northern neighbors. Opponents warned that the agreement would create huge job losses in the United States as companies moved production to Mexico to lower costs.[43]

Estimating the economic impact of trade agreements is a daunting task due to a lack of data and important theoretical and practical matters associated with generating results from economic models. In addition, such estimates provide an incomplete accounting of the total economic effects of trade agreements.[44] Numerous studies suggest that NAFTA achieved many of the intended trade and economic benefits.[45] Other studies suggest that NAFTA has come at a cost to U.S. workers.[46] This has been in keeping with what most economists maintain, that trade liberalization promotes overall economic growth among trading partners, but that there are both winners and losers from adjustments.

Not all changes in trade and investment patterns within North America since 1994 can be attributed to NAFTA because trade has also been affected by a number of factors. The sharp devaluation of the peso at the end of the 1990s and the associated recession in Mexico had considerable effects on trade, as did the rapid growth of the U.S. economy during most of the 1990s and, more recently, the economic slowdown caused by the 2008 financial crisis. Trade-related job gains and losses since NAFTA may have accelerated trends that were ongoing prior to NAFTA and may not be totally attributable to the trade agreement.

U.S. Trade Trends with NAFTA Partners

U.S. trade with its NAFTA partners has more than tripled since the agreement took effect. It has increased more rapidly than trade with the rest of the world. In 2011, trilateral trade among NAFTA partners reached the $1 trillion threshold. Trade between the United States and Mexico contributed considerably to growth in North American trade, accounting for 49% of the increase in regional trade since NAFTA enactment in 1994.[47] Between 1993 and 2012, total U.S. trade with Mexico increased by 506%. In comparison, U.S. trade with Canada increased by 192%, while trade with non-NAFTA countries increased by 279%. In 2012, Canada was the leading market for U.S. exports, while Mexico ranked second. The two countries accounted for 32% of total U.S. exports in 2012. In imports, Canada and Mexico ranked second and third, respectively, as suppliers of U.S. imports in 2012. The two countries accounted for 26% of U.S. imports.[48]

Most of the trade-related effects of NAFTA may be attributed to changes in trade and investment patterns with Mexico because economic integration between Canada and the United States had already been taking place. As mentioned previously, while NAFTA may have accelerated U.S.- Mexico trade since 1993, other factors, such as economic growth patterns, also affected trade. As trade tends to increase during cycles of economic growth, it tends to decrease as growth declines. The economic downturns in 2001 and 2009, for example, likely played a role in the decline in both U.S. exports to and imports from Canada and Mexico, as shown in **Figure 1**.

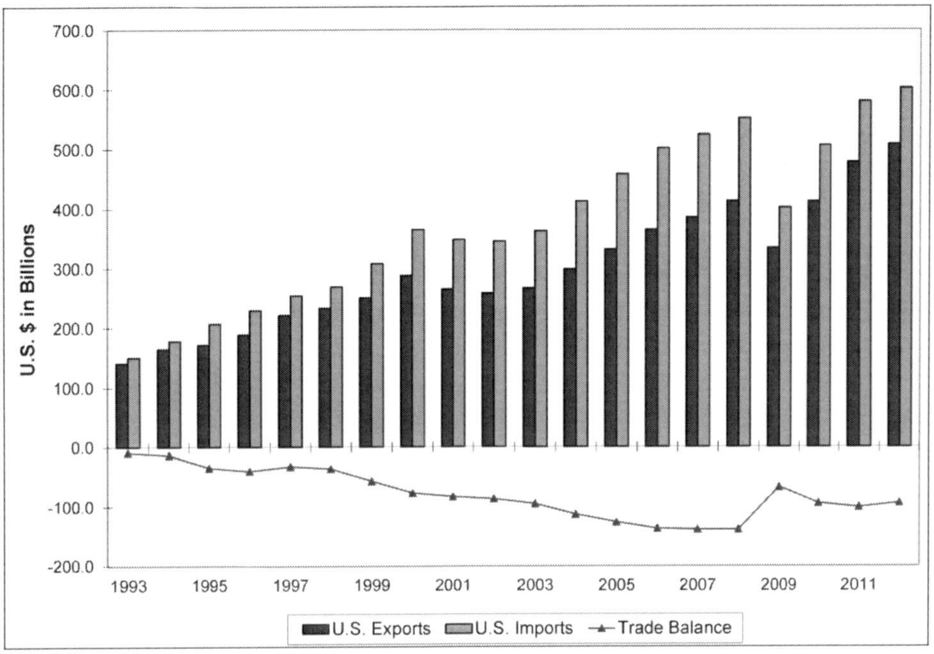

Source: Compiled by CRS using trade data from the U.S. International Trade Commission's Interactive Tariff and Trade Data Web, at http://dataweb.usitc.gov.

Figure 1. U.S. Trade with NAFTA Partners: 1993-2012 (billions of nominal U.S. dollars).

The United States is, by far, Mexico's leading partner in merchandise trade. U.S. exports to Mexico increased rapidly since NAFTA, increasing from $41.6 billion in 1993 to $216.3 billion in 2012, an increase of 420% (see **Table A-1** in **Appendix A**). U.S. imports from Mexico increased from $39.9 billion in 1993 to $277.7 billion in 2012, an increase of 596%. The trade balance with Mexico went from a surplus of $1.7 billion in 1993 to a deficit of $61.4 billion in 2012. In 2012, 14% of total U.S. merchandise exports were destined for Mexico and 12% of U.S. merchandise imports came from Mexico.[49] In services, the United States had a surplus of $11.5 billion in 2011 in trade with Mexico. U.S. private services exports to Mexico increased from $10.4 billion in 1993 to $25.2 billion in 2011. U.S. private services imports from Mexico increased from $7.4 billion in 1993 to $13.7 billion in 2011, as shown in **Table A-2**.[50]

U.S. trade with Canada more than doubled in the first decade of the FTA/NAFTA (1989-1999) from $166.5 billion to $362.2 billion. U.S. exports to Canada increased from $100.2 billion in 1993 to $291.8 billion in 2012, an increase of 191%. U.S. imports from Canada increased from $110.9 billion in 1993 to $324.2 billion in 2012, an increase of 192% (see **Table A-1**). After falling off during the recession of 2001, total trade with Canada reached a new high of $596.5 billion in 2008, only to fall victim to the financial crisis in 2009 when it fell to $429.6 billion. In 2011, total trade had returned to 2008 levels at $597.3 billion. The United States has run a trade deficit with Canada since the FTA/NAFTA era, increasing from $9.9 billion in 1989 to $74.6 billion in 2008, before falling back during the 2009 recession. In 2012, the trade deficit with Canada was $32.4 billion. While the increase in the trade deficit with Canada has been attributed to the FTA/NAFTA, the increase has been uneven and may also be attributed to other economic factors, such as energy prices.[51]

Effect on the U.S. Economy

The overall net effect of NAFTA on the U.S. economy has been relatively small, primarily because total trade with both Mexico and Canada was equal to less than 5% of U.S. GDP at the time NAFTA went into effect. Because many, if not most, of the economic effects came as a result of U.S.-Mexico trade liberalization, it is also important to take into account that two-way trade with Mexico was equal to an even smaller percentage of GDP (1.4%) in 1994. Thus, any changes in trade patterns would not be expected to be significant in relation to the overall U.S. economy. A major challenge in assessing NAFTA is separating the effects that came as a result of the agreement from other factors. U.S. trade with Mexico and Canada was already growing prior to NAFTA and it likely would have continued to do so without an agreement. A 2003 report by the Congressional Budget Office observed that it was difficult to precisely measure the effects of NAFTA. It estimated that NAFTA likely increased annual U.S. GDP, but by a very small amount – "probably no more than a few billion dollars, or a few hundredths of a percent."[52] In some sectors, trade-related effects could have been more significant, especially in those industries that were more exposed to the removal of tariff and non-tariff trade barriers, such as the textile, apparel, automotive, and agriculture industries.

Studies by the U.S. International Trade Commission (USITC) on the effects of NAFTA pointed out the difficulty in isolating the agreement's effects from other factors. Although the effects of NAFTA are not easily measured, the USITC provided some estimates over the years. A 2003 study estimated that U.S. GDP could experience an increase between 0.1% and 0.5% upon full implementation of the agreement.[53] Another USITC study that was congressionally mandated in 1997 offered a comprehensive assessment of the operation and effects of NAFTA after three years.[54] The report estimated that NAFTA had a small, but positive, effect on the overall U.S. economy. Some of the findings include the following: data inadequacies at the industry level made it difficult to isolate the effects of NAFTA on absolute trade flows; U.S. trade with NAFTA partners increased more rapidly than U.S. trade with the rest of the world; the share of U.S. exports in the Mexican market increased by a higher percentage than the share of total imports from other countries; industries such as autos, chemicals, textiles, and electronics benefitted by achieving synergies across the North American market.[55]

U.S. Industries and Supply Chains

Many economists and other observers have credited NAFTA with helping U.S. manufacturing industries, especially the U.S. auto industry, become more globally competitive through the development of supply chains.[56] Much of the increase in U.S.-Mexico trade, for example, can be attributed to specialization as manufacturing and assembly plants have reoriented to take advantage of economies of scale. As a result, supply chains have been increasingly crossing national boundaries as manufacturing work is performed wherever it is most efficient.[57] A reduction in tariffs in a given sector not only affects prices in that sector but also in industries that purchase intermediate inputs from that sector. The importance of these direct and indirect effects is often overlooked, according to one study. The study suggests that these linkages offer important trade and welfare gains from free trade agreements and that ignoring these input-output linkages could underestimate potential trade gains.[58]

Much of the trade between the United States and its NAFTA partners occurs in the context of production sharing as manufacturers in each country work together to create goods. The expansion of trade has resulted in the creation of vertical supply relationships, especially along the U.S.-Mexico border. The flow of intermediate inputs produced in the United States and exported to Mexico and the return flow of finished products greatly increased the importance of the U.S.-Mexico border region as a production site.[59] U.S. manufacturing industries, including automotive, electronics, appliances, and machinery, all rely on the assistance of Mexican manufacturers. One report estimates that 40% of the content of U.S. imports from Mexico and 25% of the content of U.S. imports from Canada are of U.S. origin. In comparison, U.S. imports from China are said to have only 4% U.S. content. Taken together, goods from Mexico and Canada represent about 75% of all the U.S. domestic content that returns to the United States as imports.[60]

NAFTA was instrumental in the integration of the North American auto industry, which experienced some of the most significant changes in trade following the agreement. U.S. auto parts producers may use inputs and components produced by another NAFTA partner to assemble parts, which are then shipped to another NAFTA country where they are assembled into a vehicle that is sold in any of the three NAFTA countries.[61] NAFTA provisions consisted of a phased elimination of tariffs and the gradual removal of many non-tariff barriers to trade. It provided for uniform country of origin provisions, enhanced protection of intellectual property rights, adopted less restrictive government procurement practices, and eliminated performance requirements on investors from other NAFTA countries. NAFTA established the removal of Mexico's restrictive trade and investment policies and the elimination of U.S. tariffs on autos and auto parts.

Table 1. U.S. Trade in Vehicles and Auto Parts: 1993 and 2011 (billions of U.S. dollars)

	1993			2011			% Change 1993-2011	
	Exports	Imports	Total	Exports	Imports	Total	Exports	Imports
Mexico								
Vehicles	0.2	3.7	3.9	3.8	30.7	34.5	1800%	730%
Parts	7.3	7.4	14.7	21.1	33.7	54.8	189%	355%
Total	7.5	11.1	18.6	24.9	64.4	89.3	232%	480%
Canada								
Vehicles	8.2	26.7	34.9	23.9	39.7	63.6	191%	49%
Parts	18.2	10.3	28.5	28.2	15.3	43.5	55%	49%
Total	26.4	37.0	63.4	52.1	55.0	107.1	97%	49%
World								
Vehicles	18.9	63.0	81.9	60.9	139.8	200.7	222%	122%
Parts	33.4	38.3	71.7	67.2	107.7	174.9	101%	181%
Total	52.3	101.3	153.6	128.1	247.5	375.6	145%	144%

Source: Compiled by CRS using data from the U.S. International Trade Commission and the U.S. Bureau of the Census. Data for 2011 is from the Office of Transportation and Machinery, U.S. Department of Commerce, available at http:// http://www.trade.

After NAFTA's entry into force, U.S. trade in vehicles and auto parts increased more rapidly than in other sectors. Mexico became a more significant trading partner in the U.S. motor vehicle market as U.S. total auto exports to Mexico increased 232% while imports increased 480% (see **Table 1**). Mexico's share in U.S. total trade in motor vehicles increased from 4% to 17% between 1993 and 2011, while the share from Canada and other countries decreased. In auto parts, Mexico's share increased from 21% to 31% over the same period. In 2011, Mexico was the leading supplier of automotive goods for the United States, accounting for 26% ($64.4 billion) of total U.S. motor vehicle and auto parts imports. Canada ranked second with 22% ($55.0 billion) of the U.S. market share in 2011.[62]

Effect on Mexico

A number of studies have found that NAFTA has brought economic and social benefits to the Mexican economy as a whole, but that the benefits have not been evenly distributed throughout the country.[63] The agreement also had a positive impact on Mexican productivity. A 2011 World Bank study found that the increase in trade integration after NAFTA had a positive effect on stimulating the productivity of Mexican plants.[64] Most post-NAFTA studies on economic effects have found that the net overall effects on the Mexican economy tended to be positive but modest. While there have been periods of positive and negative economic growth in Mexico after the agreement was implemented, it is difficult to measure precisely how much of these economic changes were attributed to NAFTA. A World Bank study assessing some of the economic impacts from NAFTA on Mexico concluded that NAFTA helped Mexico get closer to the levels of development in the United States and Canada. The study states that NAFTA helped Mexican manufacturers adapt to U.S. technological innovations more quickly; likely had positive impacts on the number and quality of jobs; reduced macroeconomic volatility, or wide variations in the GDP growth rate, in Mexico; increased the levels of synchronicity in business cycles in Mexico, the United States, and Canada; and reinforced the high sensitivity of Mexican economic sectors to economic developments in the United States.[65]

Other studies suggest that NAFTA has been disappointing in that it failed to significantly improve the Mexican economy or lower income disparities between Mexico and its northern neighbors.[66] Some argue that the success of NAFTA in Mexico was probably limited by the fact that NAFTA was not supplemented by complementary policies that could have promoted a deeper regional integration effort. These policies could have included improvements in education, industrial policies, and/or investment in infrastructure.[67]

One of the more controversial aspects of NAFTA is related to the agricultural sector in Mexico and the perception that NAFTA has caused a higher amount of worker displacement in this sector than in other economic sectors. Many critics of NAFTA say that the agreement led to severe job displacement in agriculture, especially in the corn sector. One study estimates these losses to have been over a million lost jobs in corn production between 1991 and 2000.[68] However, while some of the changes in the agricultural sector are a direct result of NAFTA as Mexico began to import more lower-priced products from the United States, many of the changes can be attributed to Mexico's unilateral agricultural reform measures in the 1980s and early 1990s. Most domestic reform measures consisted of privatization efforts and resulted in increased competition.

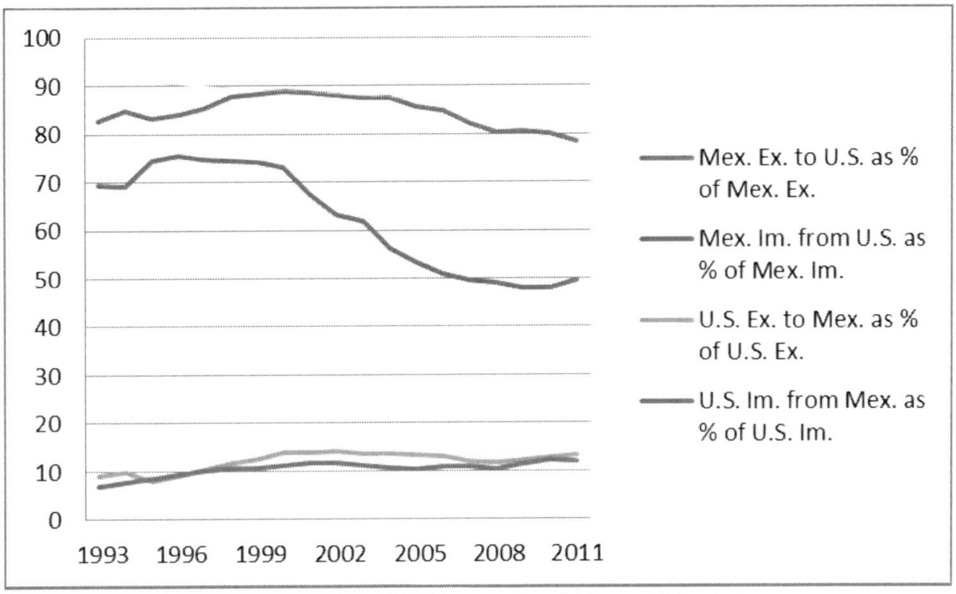

Source: Economist Intelligence Unit, from IMF International Financial Statistics.

Notes: Represents exports to and imports from other country as percentage of country's total trade. Statistics prior to 1993 are not available.

Figure 2. Market Share as Percentage of Total Trade: Mexico and the United States (1993-2011).

Measures included eliminating state enterprises related to agriculture and removing staple price supports and subsidies.[69] These reforms coincided with NAFTA negotiations and continued beyond the implementation of NAFTA in 1994. The unilateral reforms in the agricultural sector make it difficult to separate those effects from the effects of NAFTA.

U.S.-Mexico Trade Market Shares

Mexico relies heavily on the United States as an export market; this reliance has diminished very slightly over the years. The percentage of Mexico's total exports going to the United States decreased from 83% in 1993 to 79% in 2011 (see **Figure 2**). Mexico's share of the U.S. market has lost ground since 2002. In 2003, China surpassed Mexico as the second-leading supplier of U.S. imports. The United States is losing market share of Mexico's import market. Between 1993 and 2011, the U.S. share of Mexico's total imports decreased from 69% to 50%. China is Mexico's second-leading source of imports.

U.S. and Mexican Foreign Direct Investment

Foreign direct investment (FDI) has been an integral part of the economic relationship between the United States and Mexico for many years, especially after NAFTA. Two-way investment increased rapidly after the agreement went into effect. The United States is the largest source of FDI in Mexico. The stock of U.S. FDI in Mexico increased from $15.2 billion in 1993 to $91.4 billion in 2011, a 501% increase (see **Table A-4** in **Appendix A**). The flows of FDI have been affected by other factors over the years, with higher growth during the period of economic expansion during the late 1990s, and slower growth in recent years, possibly due to the economic downturn caused by the 2008 global financial crisis and/or the increased violence in Mexico. Mexican FDI in the United States, while substantially lower than U.S. investment in Mexico, has also increased rapidly, from $1.2 billion in 1993 to $13.8 billion in 2011, an increase of over 1000% (See **Table A-4**).[70]

While Mexico's unilateral trade and investment liberalization measures in the 1980s and early 1990s contributed to the increase of U.S. FDI in Mexico, NAFTA provisions on foreign investment may have helped to lock in Mexico's reforms and increase investor confidence. NAFTA helped give U.S. and Canadian investors nondiscriminatory treatment of their investments as well as investor protection in Mexico. Nearly half of total FDI investment in Mexico is in the manufacturing industry.

Income Disparity

One of the main arguments in favor of NAFTA at the time it was being proposed by policymakers was that the agreement would improve economic conditions in Mexico and narrow the income disparity between Mexico and the United States and Canada. Studies that have addressed the issue of economic convergence[71] have noted that economic convergence in North America has failed to materialize. One study states that NAFTA failed to fulfill the promise of closing the Mexico-U.S. development gap and that this was partially due to the lack of deeper forms of regional integration or cooperation between Mexico and the United States.[72] The study contends that domestic policies in both countries, along with underlying geographic and demographic realities, contribute to the continuing disparities in income. The authors argue that neither Mexico nor the United States adopted complementary policies after NAFTA that could have promoted a more successful regional integration effort. These policies could include education, industrial policies, and more investment in border and transportation infrastructure. The authors also note that other developments, such as increased security along the U.S.-Mexico border after the September 11 terrorist attacks, have made it much more difficult for the movement of goods and services across the border and for improving regional integration. They argue that the two countries could cooperate on policies that foster convergence and economic development in Mexico instead of increasing security and "building walls."[73]

A World Bank study states that NAFTA brought economic and social benefits to the Mexican economy, but that it is not enough to help narrow the disparities in economic conditions between Mexico and the United States.[74] It contends that Mexico needs to invest more in education, innovation and infrastructure, and in the quality of national institutions. The study also states that income convergence between a Latin American country and the United States is limited by the wide differences in the quality of domestic institutions, in the innovation dynamics of domestic firms, and in the skills of the labor force. While NAFTA had a positive effect on wages and employment in some Mexican states, the wage differential within the country increased as a result of trade liberalization.[75] Another study also notes that the ability of Mexico to improve economic conditions depends on its capacity to improve its national institutions, adding that Mexican institutions did not improve significantly more than those of other Latin American countries since NAFTA went into effect.[76]

Effect on Canada

As noted earlier, the U.S.-Canada FTA came into effect on January 1, 1989. Thus, trade liberalization between the two countries was well underway—or already completed—by the time of the implementation of NAFTA. This section summarizes the effect of trade liberalization from both agreements on Canada.

From the Canadian perspective, the important consequence of the FTA may have been what did not happen, i.e., that many of the fears of opening up trade with the United States did not come to pass. Canada did not become an economic appendage or "51st state" as many had feared. It did not lose control over its water or energy resources; its manufacturing sector was not gutted. Rather, as one Canadian commentator remarked, "free trade helped Canada to grow up, to turn its face out to the world, to embrace its future as a trading nation, [and] to get over its chronic sense of inferiority."[77] However, some hopes for the FTA, for example, that it would be a catalyst for greater productivity in Canadian industry, also have not come to pass.

U.S.-Canada Trade Market Shares

The United States is the number one purchaser of Canadian goods and supplier of imports to Canada. Canada's share of its exports going to the United States steadily increased during the 1980s, from 60.6% in 1980 to 70.7% in 1989, the first year of the FTA. Canada's percentage of total exports to the United States continued to increase, reaching 87.7% in 2002. The relative importance of the value of U.S. and Canadian trade with each other, however, has been falling in recent years. Since 2002, this percentage has steadily fallen back to 73.7%. The U.S. share of Canada's total imports, which reached a peak of 70.0% in 1983, topped out at 68.7% during the free trade era and has been steadily dropping ever since to a low of 49.5% in 2011 (see **Figure 3**).

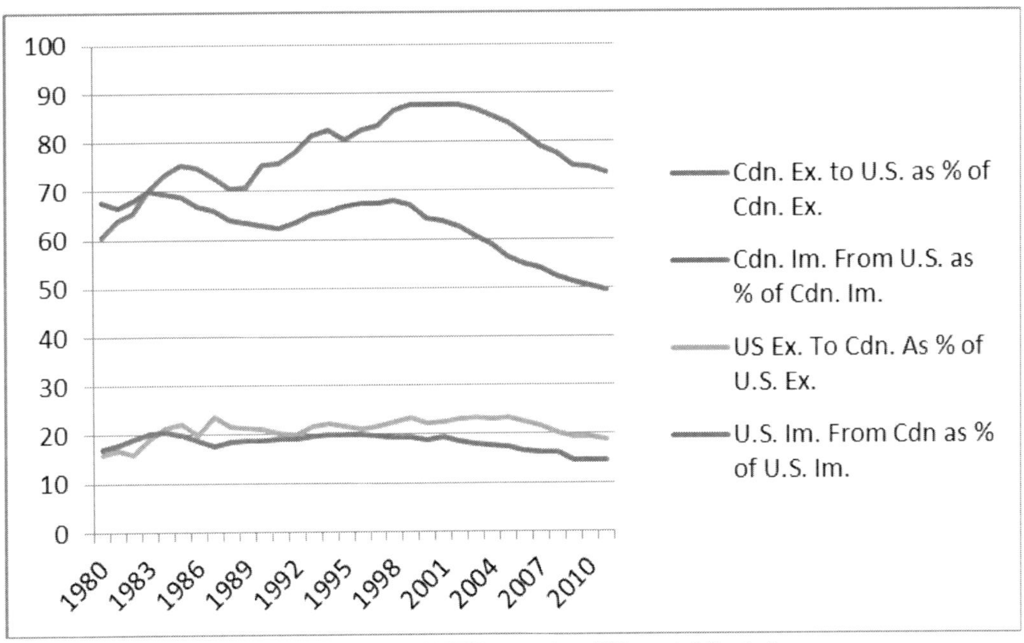

Source: Economic Intelligence Unit, from IMF International Financial Statistics.

Notes: Represents exports to and imports from other country as percentage of country's total trade.

Figure 3. Market Share as Percentage of Total Trade: Canada and the United States (1980-2011).

Traditionally, Canada was the largest purchaser of U.S. exports and supplier of U.S. imports; however, shares of both peaked before the free trade era. Canada purchased 23.5% of U.S. exports in 1987 and equaled that figure in 2005, but it has since fallen off to 18.9% in 2011. Canada traditionally was the largest supplier of U.S. imports, peaking at 20.6% in 1984, reaching a NAFTA high of 20.1% in 1996, but has declined thereafter to 14.5% in 2011. China has displaced Canada as the largest supplier of U.S. imports since 2007.

The composition of trade has also changed. Canada initially entered a manufacturing recession after the conclusion of the FTA as branch plants of U.S. companies set up behind the Canadian tariff wall were abandoned. However, more internationally competitive manufacturing sectors thrived as long as the Canadian dollar (nicknamed the loonie for the soaring loon pictured on its reverse) was relatively cheap. From a low point of a Canadian dollar worth US$0.65 in 2002, the loonie reached parity in 2007, and has hovered around the parity point ever since. The appreciation has been attributed to the boom in Canada's natural resources—oil and gas displaced motor vehicles as Canada's largest export to the United States in 2005. The "great recession" and the woes of the integrated North American auto sector also took a toll on Canadian manufacturing.

For some advocates in Canada, free trade was meant to alleviate the long-term labor productivity gap between the United States and Canada. Open competition was seen as forcing Canadian industry to be more productive. In much of the free trade era, this gap could be accounted for by the low value of the Canadian dollar. As adding capital equipment (often purchased from the United States) was relatively more expensive than hiring extra workers, the latter was often employed. The appreciation of the Canadian dollar has made additional capitalization more attractive, but labor productivity recently remained only at 72% of U.S. levels.[78] The relatively low productivity levels of Canadian industry, as well as its relatively low investments in research and development (R&D), and relatively lower expenditures on information technology, are seen as threatening to Canadian long-term competitiveness, and remain of concern to Canadian policymakers, despite leading the organization of Economic Cooperation and Development's ranking of the population with post-secondary education.[79]

U.S. and Canadian Foreign Direct Investment

Two-way investment has also increased markedly during the free trade era, both in terms of stock and flow of investment. The United States is the largest single investor in Canada with a stock of FDI into Canada reaching $318.9 billion in 2011, up from a stock of $69.9 billion in 1993 (see **Table A-4**). The average annual growth rate of 17.3% since 1988 is well above nominal GDP growth during the period. It also represents nearly 54% of the total stock of FDI in Canada from global investors. U.S. FDI flows into Canada averaged $3.28 billion in the five years prior to the FTA, and actually fell to an average of $1.7 billion in the first six years of the FTA, mainly attributed to divestments of U.S.-owned branch plants in Canada. However, flows increased markedly to an average of $13.9 billion during the years 1995 to 2011.[80] The stock of U.S. FDI is now equivalent to 19% of the value of Canadian GDP, in contrast to 1% at the beginning of the FTA.

While Canada is not the largest investor in the United States, the United States was the largest destination for Canadian FDI in 2011, with a stock of $211 billion, an increase from $26.6 billion in 1988.[81] Approximately 40.3% of Canadian FDI is invested in the United States. Canadian FDI flows into the United States annually averaged $2.3 billion in 5 years prior to the FTA, and an annual average of $1.8 billion during the FTA years, but increased to an annual average of $9.7 billion from 1995 to 2011.[82] These trends highlight the changing view of FDI among Canadians, from one that could be considered fearful or hostile to FDI as vehicles of foreign control over the Canadian economy, to one that is more welcoming of new jobs and techniques that result from FDI.

Issues for Congress

Many economists and business representatives generally look at NAFTA as a success and credit it for fueling unprecedented North American trade and creating job growth in the United States. They look to build on NAFTA's momentum to improve trade relations and economic integration within the region. However, labor groups and some consumer-advocacy groups argue that the agreement has had negative effects. They maintain that the agreement resulted in outsourcing and lower wages that have had a negative effect on the U.S. economy and that it has caused job dislocations in Mexico, especially in agriculture.[83]

Given the increasing number of regional trade agreements throughout the world and the ongoing Trans-Pacific Partnership (TPP) free trade negotiations, one general question that policymakers may consider in forming future trade policy is whether or not NAFTA has lost its relevance. The numerous FTAs that the United States, Mexico, and Canada have put into effect have given other countries the same preferences to the U.S. market that Canada and Mexico benefit from under NAFTA. Similarly, these FTAs have lessened the preferences the United States has in other markets.

Both proponents and critics of NAFTA agree that the three countries should look at what the agreement has failed to do as they look to the future of North American trade and economic relations. Policies could include strengthening institutions to protect the environment and worker rights; considering the establishment of a border infrastructure plan; increasing regulatory cooperation; promoting research and development to enhance the global competiveness of North American industries; investing in more border infrastructure to make border crossings more efficient; and/or creating more efforts to lessen income differentials within the region.

Trans-Pacific Partnership (TPP)

With the start of the Auckland Round in December 2012, Canada and Mexico began participating in the ongoing negotiations for a proposed TPP free trade agreement (FTA) among eleven countries in the Asia-Pacific region.[84] The United States is an active participant in the negotiations and was among the first tranche of countries to join the original four members of the Trans-Pacific Strategic Economic Partnership (Brunei, Chile, New Zealand, and Singapore) to launch the TPP negotiations in the fall of 2008. With 26 negotiating groups and 29 chapters under discussion, the TPP partners envision the agreement to be "comprehensive and high-standard," in that they seek to eliminate tariffs and non-tariff barriers to trade in goods, services, and agriculture, and to establish rules on a wide range of issues, including intellectual property rights, foreign direct investment and other economic activities. They also strive to create a "21st century agreement" that addresses new and cross-cutting issues presented by an increasingly globalized economy.

While the United States has indicated that it is only negotiating bilateral market access in the TPP talks with countries with which it does not have FTAs—Brunei, Malaysia, New Zealand, and Vietnam—it has sought to go beyond current U.S. FTAs in its proposed rules chapters. This has become a point of contention in the talks and may become an issue for Canada and Mexico as well. The TPP may have implications for NAFTA in several areas, including intellectual property rights (IPR), investment, services, government procurement, as well as labor and environmental provisions. The related provisions in more recent free trade agreements that the United States has negotiated, such as those with Colombia, Panama, Peru, and South Korea, include commitments that go beyond NAFTA. If agreement is reached on a TPP, Canada and Mexico may have to adhere to stronger and more enforceable labor and environmental provisions, stronger IPR provisions, as well as some issues that were not addressed in detail in the NAFTA, such as disciplines on state-owned enterprises.

Regulatory Cooperation

Policymakers may consider issues on how the United States can improve cooperation with its North American neighbors in the areas of trade, transportation, competitiveness, economic growth, and security enhancement. The United States, Canada, and Mexico have made efforts since 2005 to increase cooperation on these issues through various endeavors, most notably by participating in trilateral summits known as the North American Leaders Summits. The most recent Summit was hosted by President Barack Obama on April 2, 2012, in Washington, DC, at the White House where he met with Canadian Prime Minister Stephen Harper and Mexican President Felipe Calderón to discuss the economic well-being, safety, and security of the three countries. The three leaders renewed their commitment to North American cooperation in key areas of interest.[85]

After the first North American Leaders' Summit on March 23, 2005 in Waco, TX, the three countries agreed on enhancing regulatory cooperation through the former initiative known as the Security and Prosperity Partnership of North America (SPP). The main goal was to increase and enhance prosperity in the United States, Canada, and Mexico through regulatory cooperation.[86] The Obama Administration has affirmed its commitment to continue past efforts on North American cooperation but under a different approach from the SPP initiative. While these efforts have served as mechanisms to increase communications on issues of mutual interest, their role has been limited because there are no binding agreements.

The former SPP initiative evolved to other efforts pursued by the Obama Administration for regulatory cooperation, which have included separate bilateral endeavors. For example, in May 2010, the United States and Mexico released the Declaration Concerning Twenty-first Century Border Management and, in December 2011, the United States and Canada announced the Beyond the Border Action Plan: A Shared Vision for Perimeter Security and Economic Competiveness. In February 2012, the United States and Mexico announced the High-Level Regulatory Cooperation Council (HLRCC) to help align regulatory principles, an effort similar to the U.S.-Canada Regulatory Cooperation Council. In March 2012, the Defense Ministers of the three countries met in Ottawa, Canada, for the first ever "Trilateral

Meetings of North American Defense Ministers" to increase cooperation on national security issues.

Some critics of North American trilateral cooperation contend that the efforts are an attempt to create a common market or economic union in North America. Others contend that past efforts under the SPP were contributing to the creation of a so-called "NAFTA Superhighway" that would link the United States, Canada, and Mexico with a "super-corridor."[87] Proponents of North American competitiveness and security cooperation view the initiatives as constructive to addressing issues of mutual interest and benefit for all three countries. Business groups generally support increased North American cooperation and believe that it is necessary to enhance the competitiveness of U.S. businesses in the global market.

Proposals for Deeper Regional Integration

The rising number of regional trade agreements throughout the world, in addition to the rising presence of China in Latin America, could have implications for U.S. trade policy with its NAFTA partners beyond the proposed TPP. Some trade policy experts contend that a deepening of economic relations with Canada and Mexico will help promote a common trade agenda with shared values. In addition to economic effects, forming deeper trade and investment ties would have positive implications for corporate governance, labor rights, environmental protection, and democratic governance.[88]

Some policy experts emphasize the importance of North American trade in intermediate goods and supply chains. They argue that the governments of the three countries should improve cooperation in this area and invest more in improving border infrastructure. The increased security measures that began after September 11, 2001 have resulted in a disruption in production chains due to extended and unpredictable wait times along the border. This has disproportionately hurt small and medium sized businesses.[89] The United States and Mexico have recognized the need to enhance cooperation on prioritizing the economic relationship and security and have developed the Twenty-First Century Border Initiative for this purpose.[90] While the initiative has resulted in improvements along the border, some observers contend that policymakers could devote more energy to improving cooperation and enhancing efficiency in cross-border trade.

Other experts have proposed ideas to address ongoing problems in the region and make North American industries more competitive. Some proposals that have emerged include calls for rethinking the current trade relationship under NAFTA by broadening the scope of North American integration and cooperation. One idea, for example, is to develop a North American Investment Fund to help close the income gap between Mexico and its northern neighbors. The proposed fund would be administered by the World Bank and used to fund infrastructure projects to connect the south of Mexico to the United States and Canada, and also to improve post- secondary education in Mexico.[91] Other ideas are to set up a Customs Union in North America, such as that of the European Union, with a common external tariff to facilitate trade and deepen North American integration; develop a cooperative approach on immigration; and promote regulatory convergence.[92] The proponents of these ideas admit that it would be very difficult for Congress to approve these proposals in the near future, but argue that it is important to think about such options based on the increasing interdependence among NAFTA partners and common interests concerning the future of the region.

APPENDIX A. U.S. MERCHANDISE TRADE WITH NAFTA PARTNERS

Table A-1. U.S. Merchandise Trade with NAFTA Partners (billions of nominal U.S. dollars)

Year	Canada			Mexico			Total NAFTA		
	Exports	Imports	Trade Balance	Exports	Imports	Trade Balance	Exports	Imports	Trade Balance
1993	100.2	110.9	-10.7	41.6	39.9	1.7	141.8	150.8	-9.0
1994	114.3	128.9	-14.6	50.8	49.5	1.3	165.1	178.4	-13.3
1995	126.0	145.1	-19.1	46.3	61.7	-15.4	172.3	206.8	-34.5
1996	132.6	156.5	-23.9	56.8	73.0	-16.2	189.4	229.5	-40.1
1997	150.1	168.1	-18	71.4	85.9	-14.5	221.5	254.0	-32.5
1998	154.2	174.8	-20.6	79.0	94.7	-15.7	233.2	269.5	-36.3
1999	163.9	198.3	-34.4	87.0	109.7	-22.7	250.9	308.0	-57.1
2000	176.4	229.2	-52.8	111.7	135.9	-24.2	288.1	365.1	-77.0
2001	163.7	217.0	-53.3	101.5	131.4	-29.9	265.2	348.4	-83.2
2002	160.8	210.6	-49.8	97.5	134.7	-37.2	258.3	345.3	-87.0
2003	169.5	224.2	-54.7	97.5	138.1	-40.6	267.0	362.3	-95.3
2004	187.7	255.9	-68.2	110.8	155.8	-45	298.5	411.7	-113.2
2005	211.4	287.9	-76.5	120.0	170.2	-50.2	331.4	458.1	-126.7
2006	230.3	303.4	-73.1	134.2	198.3	-64.1	364.5	501.7	-137.2
2007	248.4	313.1	-64.7	136.5	210.8	-74.3	384.9	523.9	-139.0
2008	260.9	335.6	-74.7	151.5	215.9	-64.4	412.4	551.5	-139.1
2009	204.7	224.9	-20.2	129.0	176.5	-47.5	333.7	401.4	-67.7
2010	248.2	276.5	-28.3	164.3	229.7	-65.4	412.5	506.2	-93.7
2011	280.8	316.5	-35.7	197.5	263.1	-65.6	478.3	579.6	-101.3
2012	291.8	324.2	-32.4	216.3	277.7	-61.4	508.1	601.9	-93.8

Source: Compiled by CRS using trade data from the U.S. International Trade Commission's Interactive Tariff and Trade Data Web, at http://dataweb.usitc.gov.

Table A-2. U.S. Private Services Trade with NAFTA Partners (billions of nominal U.S. dollars)

Year	Canada			Mexico			Total NAFTA		
	Exports	Imports	Services Trade Balance	Exports	Imports	Services Trade Balance	Exports	Imports	Services Trade Balance
1993	17.0	9.1	7.9	10.4	7.4	3.0	27.4	16.5	10.9
1994	17.2	9.9	7.3	11.3	7.9	3.4	28.5	17.8	10.7
1995	17.9	11.0	6.9	8.7	7.9	0.8	26.6	18.9	7.7

Year	Canada			Mexico			Total NAFTA		
	Exports	Imports	Services Trade Balance	Exports	Imports	Services Trade Balance	Exports	Imports	Services Trade Balance
1996	19.5	12.4	7.1	9.4	8.9	0.5	28.9	21.3	7.6
1997	20.5	13.7	6.8	10.8	9.9	0.9	31.3	23.6	7.7
1998	19.4	15.0	4.4	11.7	9.8	1.9	31.1	24.8	6.3
1999	22.7	16.2	6.5	14.1	9.4	4.7	36.8	25.6	11.2
2000	24.6	17.9	6.7	15.5	10.8	4.7	40.1	28.7	11.4
2001	24.4	17.4	7.0	16.4	10.4	6.0	40.8	27.8	13.0
2002	25.0	18.0	7.0	17.4	11.6	5.8	42.4	29.6	12.8
2003	27.4	19.6	7.8	18.0	12.1	5.9	45.4	31.7	13.7
2004	29.6	20.7	8.9	19.1	13.6	5.5	48.7	34.3	14.4
2005	32.7	22.0	10.7	22.2	14.2	8.1	54.9	36.1	18.8
2006	37.7	23.1	14.6	23.5	14.6	8.9	61.2	37.7	23.5
2007	42.7	24.9	17.8	24.8	15.2	9.6	67.5	40.1	27.4
2008	45.1	25.0	20.1	25.9	15.5	10.4	71.0	40.5	30.5
2009	42.7	22.7	20.0	23.0	13.6	9.4	65.7	36.3	29.4
2010	50.8	26.2	24.6	24.1	13.5	10.6	74.9	39.7	35.2
2011	56.1	28.0	28.1	25.2	13.7	11.5	81.3	41.7	39.6

Source: Compiled by CRS using data from the Bureau of Economic Analysis online database at http://www.bea.gov.

Table A-3. U.S. Trade with NAFTA Partners by Major Product Category: 2012 (billions of U.S. dollars)

NAFTA Partner	U.S. Exports		U.S. Imports	
	Leading Items (NAIC 4-digit level)	Value	Leading Items (NAIC 4-digit level)	Value
Canada	Motor vehicle parts	26.3	Oil and gas	82.3
	Motor vehicles	24.8	Motor vehicles	46.5
	Agriculture and construction machinery	13.1	Petroleum and coal products	18.8
	Petroleum and coal products	11.9	Motor vehicle parts	13.9
	General purpose machinery	9.7	Nonferrous metal and processing	9.7
	All Other	206.0	All Other	153.1
	Total exports to Canada	280.8	Total imports from Canada	324.2
Mexico	Petroleum and coal products	20.8	Oil and gas	37.3
	Motor vehicle parts	19.6	Motor vehicles	35.3
	Computer equipment	14.5	Motor vehicle parts	33.3
	Semiconductors and other electronic components	11.4	Computer equipment	16.0
	Basic chemicals	10.1	Audio and video equipment	14.2
	All other	140.0	All other	141.4
	Total Exports to Mexico	216.3	Total Imports from Mexico	277.7

Source: Compiled by CRS using trade data from the U.S. International Trade Commission's Interactive Tariff and Trade Data Web, at http://dataweb.usitc.gov.

Table A-4. U.S. Foreign Direct Investment Positions with Canada and Mexico (1993-2011 historical cost basis [millions of U.S. dollars])

Year	Canadian FDI in the U.S.	U.S. FDI in Canada	Mexican FDI in the U.S.	U.S. FDI in Mexico
1993	40,373	69,922	1,244	15,221
1994	41,219	74,221	2,069	16,968
1995	45,618	83,498	1,850	16,873
1996	54,836	89,592	1,641	19,351
1997	65,175	96,626	3,100	24,050
1998	72,696	98,200	2,055	26,657
1999	90,559	119,590	1,999	37,151
2000	114,309	132,472	7,462	39,352
2001	92,420	152,601	6,645	52,544
2002	92,529	166,473	7,829	56,303
2003	95,707	187,953	9,022	56,851
2004	125,276	214,931	7,592	63,384
2005	165,667	231,836	3,595	73,687
2006	165,281	205,134	5,310	82,965
2007	201,924	250,642	8,478	91,046
2008	168,746	246,483	8,420	87,443
2009	188,943	265,326	11,111	82,286
2010	188,943	289,535	11,267	84,288
2011	210,864	318,964	13,763	91,402

Source: Compiled by CRS using data from the Bureau of Economic Analysis online database at http://www.bea.gov.

APPENDIX B. MEXICO'S PROTECTIONIST TRADE POLICIES PRIOR TO NAFTA

SUMMARY OF MEXICO'S PROTECTIONIST POLICIES PRIOR TO NAFTA

For decades prior to NAFTA Mexico relied on import substitution policies, restrictions on foreign investment, and a controlled exchange rate to help foster domestic growth and to protect itself from a perceived risk of foreign domination.

State-Owned Enterprises (SOEs). Mexico had a strong state presence prior to NAFTA. During the late 1950s and 1960s, the number of state-owned enterprises in Mexico almost doubled from 144 to 272. By 1982, the number of SOES had increased to 1,155. Mexico's economic reforms and divestiture of the state owned sector that occurred during the period of 1983 to 1993 decreased the number of SOEs to 258. By the end of 2003, the number of SOEs dropped to 210.

Import Licenses. Mexico had import license requirements on most, if not all, Mexican imports. The government began to phase these out in the mid-1980s. By the time NAFTA negotiations started, import licenses were required on only 230 products of the nearly 12,000 items in the Mexican tariff schedule. In agricultural goods, 60% of U.S. exports to Mexico required import licenses or faced other nontariff barriers. There was also a lack of transparency of procedures through which exporters to Mexico could apply for the proper license, certificate, or test.

Foreign Investment Restrictions. Mexico's restrictive Law to Promote Mexican Investment and Regulate Foreign Investment was in effect at the time of NAFTA negotiations, though Mexico had started liberalizing some restrictions in the mid-1980s. In 1991, 37% of Mexican economic activity was not open to 100% foreign investment ownership.

Auto Industry Import Substitution Policy (Auto Decrees). Mexico had a restrictive import substitution policy that began in the 1960s through a series of Mexican Auto Decrees in which the government sought to supply the entire Mexican market through domestically-produced automotive goods. The decrees established import tariffs as high as 25% on automotive goods and had high restrictions on foreign auto production in Mexico. The decrees prohibited imports of finished vehicles; imposed high domestic-content requirements on foreign manufacturers producing cars in Mexico; issued export requirements in which a certain amount of exports was required for every dollar of imports. The government issued the final decree in 1989, after joining the GATT, liberalizing rules on the industry but not entirely eliminating them. Auto manufacturers were still required to have a certain percentage of domestic content in their products and meet export requirements, both of which were considered huge impediments to the industry. Even after joining the GATT, Mexico had tariffs of 20% or more on imports of automobiles and auto parts.

Restrictions in Agriculture. In the period after the 1910 revolution and until the 1980s, Mexico had a land distribution system in which land was redistributed from wealthy land owners and managed by the government. This ejido system, formed under Mexico's Agrarian Law, changed in the 1980s when the government began to implement agricultural and trade policy reform measures. Changes included the privatization of the ejido system in order to stimulate competition. Mexico's unilateral reform measures included eliminating state enterprises related to agriculture and removing staple price supports and subsidies. Mexico also had a government agency known as CONASUPO which intervened in the agriculture sector. The agency bought staples from farmers at guaranteed prices and processed the products or sold them at low prices to processors and consumers. Many of Mexico's domestic reforms in agriculture coincided with NAFTA negotiations, beginning in 1991, and continued beyond the implementation of NAFTA in 1994. The unilateral reforms in the agricultural sector make it difficult to separate those effects from the effects of NAFTA. By 1999, CONASUPO had been abolished.

Sources: United States International Trade Commission (USITC), *The Likely Impact on the United States of a Free Trade Agreement with Mexico*, Publication 2353, February 1991. Gary Clyde Hufbauer and Jeffrey J. Schott, Institute for International Economics, *NAFTA Revisited*, October 2005. Alberto Chong and Florencio López-de-Silanes, *Privatization in Mexico*, Inter-American Development Bank, Working Paper #513, August 2004.

End Notes

[1] See CRS Report R42694, *The Trans-Pacific Partnership Negotiations and Issues for Congress*, coordinated by Ian F. Fergusson.

[2] Trade Promotion Authority, formerly called "fast-track authority" is the authority Congress grants to the President to enter into certain reciprocal trade agreements, and to have their implementing bills considered under expedited legislative procedures, provided the President observes certain statutory obligations. For more information, see CRS Report RL33743, *Trade Promotion Authority (TPA) and the Role of Congress in Trade Policy*, by J. F. Hornbeck and William H. Cooper.

[3] Gary Clyde Hufbauer and Jeffrey J. Schott, *NAFTA Revisited: Achievements and Challenges*, Institute for International Economics, October 2005, Chapter 1.

[4] Pardee Center Task Force Report, *The Future of North American Trade Policy: Lessons from NAFTA*, Boston University, November 2009.

[5] The Canada-United States Automotive Products Agreement removed tariffs on cars, trucks, buses, tires, and automotive parts between the two countries. NAFTA effectively superseded this agreement.

[6] Prior to the U.S.-Canada FTA, the only bilateral U.S. FTA was with Israel.

[7] United States-Canada Free-Trade Agreement Implementation Act of 1988 (P.L. 100-449).

[8] See CRS Report R40784, *Mexico's Free Trade Agreements*, by M. Angeles Villarreal.

[9] United States International Trade Commission (USITC), *The Likely Impact on the United States of a Free Trade Agreement with Mexico*, Publication 2353, February 1991.

[10] Ibid., p. 1-2.

[11] Gary Clyde Hufbauer and Jeffrey J. Schott, *NAFTA Revisited: Achievements and Challenges*, Institute for International Economics, October 2005.

[12] Ibid.

[13] Mexico has a total of 12 free trade agreements involving 44 countries. These include agreements with most countries in the Western Hemisphere including the United States, Canada, Chile, Colombia, Costa Rica, Nicaragua, Peru, Guatemala, El Salvador, and Honduras. In addition, Mexico has negotiated FTAs outside of the Western Hemisphere and entered into agreements with Israel, Japan, and the European Union.

[14] Hufbauer and Schott, *NAFTA Revisited: Achievements and Challenges*, pp. 2-3.

[15] Ibid.

[16] Woodrow Wilson International Center for Scholars, *NAFTA at 10: Progress, Potential, and Precedents*, p. 20.

[17] Governments of Canada, the United Mexican States, and the United States of America, *Description of the Proposed North American Free Trade Agreement*, August 12, 1992.

[18] Congressional Quarterly Almanac 1993, pp. 171-175, 180-181.

[19] A duty drawback is the refund or waiver in whole or in part of customs duties assessed or collected upon importation of an article or materials which are subsequently exported.

[20] Marketing orders were designed to set national guidelines for product quality, market promotion, and supply levels. The most significant Mexican products that were affected by U.S. marketing orders included tomatoes, onions, avocados, grapefruit, oranges, olives, and table grapes.

[21] NAFTA rules of origin for textiles and apparel define when imported textile or apparel goods qualify for preferential treatments. For most products, the rule of origin is "yarn forward", which means that goods must be produced from yarn made in a NAFTA country to benefit from preferential treatment.

[22] Business Roundtable, *NAFTA: A Decade of Growth*, Prepared by The Trade Partnership, Washington, DC, February 2004, p. 33.

[23] Ibid., p. 30.

[24] Governments of Canada, the United Mexican States, and the United States of America, *Description of the Proposed North American Free Trade Agreement*, August 12, 1992, p. 12.

[25] Tariff-rate quotas (TRQs) allowed NAFTA partners to export specified quantities of a product to other NAFTA countries at a relatively low tariff, but subjected all imports of the product above a pre-determined threshold to a higher tariff.

[26] Business Roundtable, *NAFTA: A Decade of Growth*, p. 35.

[27] The Governments of Canada, the United Mexican States, and the United States of America, *Description of the Proposed North American Free Trade Agreement*, August 12, 1992, p. 23-24.

[28] United States General Accounting Office (GAO), "North American Free Trade Agreement: Assessment of Major Issues, Volume 2," *Report to the Congress*, September 1993, pp. 35-36.

[29] Hufbauer and Schott, *NAFTA Revisited*, pp. 25-29.

[30] GAO, *Report to Congress*, September 1993, pp. 38-39.

[31] *Description of the Proposed North American Free Trade Agreement*, August 12, 1992, p. 29.

[32] For more information on issues regarding on U.S. investment agreements and negotiations, see CRS Report RL33978, *The U.S. Bilateral Investment Treaty Program: An Overview*, by Martin A. Weiss and Shayerah Ilias.

[33] *Description of the Proposed North American Free Trade Agreement*, August 12, 1992, pp. 30-31.

[34] Ibid., pp. 31-32.

[35] If the parties are unable to resolve the issue through consultations, they may take the dispute to the NAFTA Trade Commission, which is comprised of Ministers or cabinet-level officers designated by each country. A party may also request the establishment of an arbitral panel, which may make recommendations for the resolution of the dispute.

[36] GAO, *Report to Congress*, September 1993, pp. 69-71.

[37] The USCAIP, administered by the North American Development Bank, provides financial assistance to communities with significant job losses due to changes in trade patterns with Mexico or Canada as a result of NAFTA.

[38] For more information, see CRS Report RS22823, *Overview of Labor Enforcement Issues in Free Trade Agreements*, by Mary Jane Bolle; and CRS Report 97-291, *NAFTA: Related Environmental Issues and Initiatives*, by Mary Tiemann.

[39] Woodrow Wilson International Center for Scholars, *NAFTA at 10: Progress, Potential, and Precedents*, pp. 20-30.

[40] *The Agreement Between the Government of the United States of America and the Government of the United Mexican States Concerning the Establishment of a Border Environment Cooperation Commission and a North American Development Bank*, November 1993.

[41] Border Environment Cooperation Commission, *2011 Annual Report*, p. 7.

[42] Ibid.

[43] See Ross Perot with Pat Choate, *Save Your Job, Save Our Country: Why NAFTA Must be Stopped-Now!*, New York, 1993.

[44] For more information, see CRS Report R41660, *U.S.-South Korea Free Trade Agreement and Potential Employment Effects: Analysis of Studies*, by Mary Jane Bolle and James K. Jackson.

[45] See for example, Gary Clyde Hufbauer and Jeffrey J. Schott, *NAFTA Revisited: Achievements and Challenges, Institute for International Economics*, October 2005; Center for Strategic and International Studies, *NAFTA's Impact on North America: The First Decade*, Edited by Sidney Weintraub, 2004; and U.S. Chamber of Commerce, *Opening Markets, Creating Jobs: Estimated U.S. Employment Effects of Trade with FTA Partners*, 2010.

[46] See for example, Robert E. Scott, Heading South: *U.S.-Mexico Trade and Job Displacement under NAFTA*, Economic Policy Institute, May 3, 2011; and The Frederick S. Pardee Center, *The Future of North American Trade Policy: Lessons from NAFTA*, Boston University, November 2009.

[47] Mexico's Ministry of the Economy, *NAFTA Works, A Monthly Newsletter on NAFTA and Related Issues*, April 2012.

[48] Trade statistics in this paragraph are derived from data from the U.S. International Trade Commission's Interactive Tariff and Trade Data Web, at http://dataweb.usitc.gov.

[49] Merchandise trade statistics in this paragraph are derived from data from the U.S. International Trade Commission's Interactive Tariff and Trade Data Web, at http://dataweb.usitc.gov.

[50] Services trade statistics in this paragraph are derived from the Bureau of Economic Analysis online database at http://www.bea.gov.

[51] Trade statistics in this paragraph are derived from data from the U.S. International Trade Commission's Interactive Tariff and Trade Data Web, at http://dataweb.usitc.gov.

[52] Congressional Budget Office of the United States, "The Effects of NAFTA on U.S.-Mexican Trade and GDP," A *CBO Paper*, May 2003, p. xiv.

[53] USITC, "The Impact of Trade Agreements: Effect of the Tokyo Round, U.S.-Israel FTA, U.S.-Canada FTA, NAFTA, and the Uruguay Round on the U.S. Economy," Publication 3621, August 2003.

[54] USITC, "The Impact of the North American Free Trade Agreement on the U.S. Economy and Industries: A Three- Year Review," Publication 3045, June 1997.

[55] Ibid.

[56] Hufbauer and Schott, *NAFTA Revisited*, pp. 20-21.

[57] Ibid., p. 21.

[58] Lorenzo Caliendo and Fernando Parro, *Estimates of the Trade and Welfare Effects of NAFTA*, National Bureau of Economic Research, November 2012, pp. 1-5.

[59] Gordon H. Hanson, *North American Economic Integration and Industry Location*, National Bureau of Economic Research, June 1998.

[60] Christopher E. Wilson, *Working Together: Economic Ties Between the United States and Mexico*, Woodrow Wilson International Center for Scholars, November 2011, pp. 1-5.

[61] Business Roundtable, *NAFTA: A Decade of Growth*, p. 8.

[62] Merchandise trade statistics in this paragraph are derived from data from the U.S. International Trade Commission's Interactive Tariff and Trade Data Web, at http://dataweb.usitc.gov.

[63] See for example, Robert A. Blecker and Gerardo Esquivel, *NAFTA, Trade, and Development*, Center for U.S.-Mexican Studies (San Diego), El Colegio de la Frontera Norte, Woodrow Wilson International Center for Scholars, and El Colegio de Mexico, WP 10-03, 2010; and Daniel Lederman, William F. Maloney, and Luis Servén, *Lessons from NAFTA for Latin America and the Caribbean*, The World Bank, 2005.

[64] Rafael E. de Hoyos and Leonardo Iacovone, *Economic Performance under NAFTA*, The World Bank Development Research Group, May 2011, pp. 25-27.

[65] Daniel Lederman, William F. Maloney, and Luis Servén, *Lessons from NAFTA for Latin America and the Caribbean*, The World Bank, 2005.

[66] Robert A. Blecker and Gerardo Esquivel, NAFTA, *Trade, and Development*, Center for U.S.-Mexican Studies, the Mexico Institute of the Woodrow Wilson Center, El Colegio de la Frontera Norte, and El Colegio de México, USMEX WP 10-03, 2010.

[67] Ibid., p. 22.

[68] Robert E. Scott, Carlos Salas, Bruce Campbell and Jeff Faux, *Revisiting NAFTA: Still Not Working for North America's Workers*, Economic Policy Institute, Briefing Paper #173, p. 43.

[69] Mexico's unilateral agricultural reform measures removed government subsidies and price controls in the agricultural sector that resulted in rising prices for tortillas. Tortillas are the basic staple for the Mexican diet and a necessity of the poor. For this reason, higher prices had a greater effect on the poor than on middle- and higher-income Mexicans. Mexico also reformed its Agrarian Law. Lands that had been distributed to *ejidos* or community rural groups following the 1910 revolution gained the right to privatize. This led to more efficient production processes, especially in Northern states.

[70] Foreign direct investment data in this section is derived from data from the Bureau of Economic Analysis online database at http://www.bea.gov.

[71] Economic convergence can be broadly defined as a narrowing of the disparities in the economic levels and the manufacturing performances of particular countries or their regions. The goal of the theory of economic convergence is to research and analyze the factors influencing the rates of economic growth and real per capita income in countries.

[72] Robert A. Blecker and Gerardo Esquivel, *NAFTA, Trade, and Development*, Working Paper 10-03, Center for U.S.- Mexican Studies (San Diego), the Mexico Institute of the Woodrow Wilson Center (Washington DC), El Colegio de la Frontera Norte (Tijuana), and El Colegio de México (Mexico City), 2010, p. 2.

[73] Ibid., pp. 19-23.

[74] Lederman, Maloney, and Servén, *Lessons from NAFTA for Latin America and the Caribbean*, The World Bank, 2005.

[75] Ibid.

[76] William Easterly, Norbert Fiess, and Daniel Lederman, "NAFTA and Convergence in North America: High Expectations, Big Events, Little Time," *Economía*, Fall 2003.

[77] John Ibbitson, "After 25 Years, Free-Trade Deal with U.S. Has Helped Canada Grow Up," *The Globe and Mail*, September 29, 2012.

[78] Kevin Lynch, "Canada's Challenge—From Good to Great," *Inside Policy*, October 2012.

[79] Glen Hodgson, "Canada U.S. Competitiveness, Addressing the Canadian Economic Contradiction," Woodrow Wilson Center, Canada Institute, June 2007; Lynch, *ibid*.

[80] Investment statistics are from the U.S. Department of Commerce, Bureau of Economic Analysis, and Statistics Canada.

[81] Ibid.

[82] Douglas Porter, "Free Trade at 25: How the FTA Positioned Canada for the 21st Century," *Inside Policy*, October 2012.

[83] Julián Aguilar, "Twenty Years Later, NAFTA Remains a Source of Tension," *The New York Times*, December 7, 2012.

[84] The eleven countries involved in the Trans-Pacific Partnership (TPP) negotiations include the United States, Australia, Brunei, Canada, Chile, Malaysia, Mexico, New Zealand, Peru, Singapore, and Vietnam. For more information on the TPP, see CRS Report R42694, *The Trans-Pacific Partnership Negotiations and Issues for Congress*, coordinated by Ian F. Fergusson.

[85] The White House, Office of the Press Secretary, *Joint Statement by North American Leaders*, April 2, 2012.

[86] The SPP was endorsed by all three countries, but it was not a signed agreement or treaty and contained no legally binding commitments or obligations. Although the SPP built upon the existing trade and economic relationship of the three countries, it was distinct and separate from NAFTA.

[87] See for example, *Society for American Sovereignty*, at http://www.americansov.org.

[88] Testimony of Eric Farnsworth, Vice President, Council of the Americas, in U.S. Congress, Senate Committee on Foreign Relations, *Doing Business in Latin America: Positive Trends but Serious Challenges*, 112th Cong., 2nd sess., July 31, 2012, S.Hrg. 112-607 (Washington, DC: GPO, 2012), pp. 30-32.

[89] Christopher E. Wilson, *Working Together: Economic Ties Between the United States and Mexico*, Woodrow Wilson International Center for Scholars, November 2011, pp. 37-38.

[90] For more information, see CRS Report R41349, *U.S.-Mexican Security Cooperation: The Mérida Initiative and Beyond*, by Clare Ribando Seelke and Kristin M. Finklea.

[91] Robert A. Pastor, *The North American Idea: A Vision of a Continental Future*, Oxford University Press, 2011, pp. 169-172.

[92] Ibid., pp. 167-200.

In: Free Trade Agreements
Editor: Jenell Gallo
ISBN: 978-1-63117-366-0

Chapter 2

THE U.S.-SOUTH KOREA FREE TRADE AGREEMENT (KORUS FTA): PROVISIONS AND IMPLICATIONS*

William H. Cooper, Mark E. Manyin, Remy Jurenas and Michaela D. Platzer

SUMMARY

On October 3, 2011, President Obama submitted draft legislation (H.R. 3080/S. 1642) to implement the U.S.-South Korea Free Trade Agreement (KORUS FTA) to both houses of Congress. On October 6, the House Ways and Means Committee reported out H.R. 3080 (H.Rept. 112-239). The Senate Finance Committee reported out S. 1642 (without written report). On October 12, the House passed H.R. 3080 (278-151) and sent it to the Senate which passed it (83- 15). The President signed the legislation on October 21, 2011 (P.L. 112-41). In South Korea, after a contentious battle, the Korean National Assembly passed the agreement on November 22. On March 15, 2012, the KORUS FTA entered into force.

The KORUS FTA is the second-largest U.S. FTA (next to NAFTA). South Korea is the seventh-largest trading partner of the United States, and the United States is South Korea's third-largest trading partner. The KORUS FTA covers a wide range of trade and investment issues and, therefore, could have substantial economic implications for both the United States and South Korea.

Congress approved the KORUS FTA implementing legislation using expedited procedures authorized by the Trade Promotion Authority (TPA). Under TPA, the President had the discretion on when to submit the implementing legislation to Congress. The KORUS FTA was negotiated and signed on June 30, 2007, by President George W. Bush. However, President Bush did not submit the legislation because of differences with the Democratic leadership over treatment of autos and beef, among other issues. On December 3, 2010, after

---

* This is an edited, reformatted and augmented version of Congressional Research Service, Publication No. RL34330, dated March 7, 2013.

a series of arduous negotiations, President Obama and President Lee announced that they had reached an agreement on addressing the outstanding issues related to the KORUS FTA. As a result, U.S. and South Korean negotiators agreed, in the form of an exchange of letters and agreed minutes, to modifications to the commitments made in the 2007 agreement. These modifications included changes in phase-out periods for tariffs on autos and pork, a new safeguard provision on autos, and concessions by South Korea on allowing a larger number of U.S. cars into South Korea under U.S. safety standards than was the case under the original KORUS FTA provisions. The modifications were included in the implementing legislation.

A broad swath of the U.S. business community supported the KORUS FTA. With the modifications in the commitments reached in December 2010, this group also included the three Detroit-based auto manufacturers and the United Auto Workers (UAW) union. It still faced opposition from some labor unions and other groups, including Public Citizen. Many U.S. supporters view the KORUS FTA as important to secure new opportunities in the South Korean market, while opponents claimed that the KORUS FTA does not go far enough to break down South Korean trade barriers or that the agreement will encourage U.S. companies to move their production offshore at the expense of U.S. workers. Other observers suggested the KORUS FTA could have implications for the U.S.-South Korean alliance as a whole, as well as on U.S. Asia policy and U.S. trade policy.

INTRODUCTION

On October 3, 2011, President Obama submitted draft legislation (H.R. 3080/S. 1642) to implement the U.S.-South Korea Free Trade Agreement (KORUS FTA) to both houses of Congress. On October 6, the House Ways and Means Committee reported out H.R. 3080 (H.Rept. 112-239). The Senate Finance Committee reported out S. 1642 (without written report). On October 12, the House passed H.R. 3080 (278-151) and sent it to the Senate which passed it (83-15). The President signed the legislation on October 21, 2011 (P.L. 112-41). In South Korea, after a contentious battle, the Korean National Assembly passed the agreement on November 22. The KORUS FTA entered into force on March 15, 2012.

The KORUS FTA covers a wide range of bilateral economic activities: trade in manufactured goods, agricultural products, and services; foreign investment; government procurement; intellectual property rights; and worker rights and environment protection, among other issues.

The negotiations were conducted under the trade promotion authority (TPA), also called fast-track trade authority, that Congress granted the President under the Bipartisan Trade Promotion Act of 2002 (P.L. 107-210). Under TPA the President had the discretion on when to submit the implementing legislation to Congress. President Bush did not submit the legislation because of differences with the Democratic leadership over treatment of autos and beef, among other issues.

On December 3, 2010, U.S. and South Korean leaders announced that they had reached agreement on addressing the outstanding issues related to the KORUS FTA. As a result, U.S.- and South Korean negotiators agreed to modifications to some of the commitments made in the 2007 agreement. These modifications which were signed on February 10, 2011, are in the form of an "exchange of letters" and two "agreed minutes." They pertain mostly to the auto provisions and include changes in phase-out periods for tariffs on autos and pork, a new safeguard provision on autos, and concessions by South Korea on allowing a larger number of U.S. cars into South Korea under U.S. safety standards than was the case under the original KORUS FTA provisions.

The United States and South Korea entered into the KORUS FTA as a means to further solidify an already strong economic relationship by reducing barriers to trade and investment between them and to resolve long-standing troublesome economic issues. The United States specifically sought increased access to South Korean markets for agricultural products, services, and foreign investment. For South Korean leaders, the KORUS FTA is a mechanism to promote reform in its own economy and also to gain a competitive advantage in the U.S. market for autos and other manufactured goods.

Supporters of the FTA in the United States argued that failure to approve the KORUS FTA would have allowed those opportunities to slip away, particularly if Seoul's strategy of negotiating a web of FTAs, with South Korea at the center, is successful. On July 1, 2011, South Korea's FTA with the European Union (EU) went into effect. However, some opponents of the KORUS FTA argued that the agreement as originally concluded in June 2007 failed to go far enough in addressing South Korean trade barriers and would have been a lost opportunity if approved in its current form.

Presidents Obama's Statements on the KORUS FTA

President Obama and South Korean President Lee Myung-bak met for the first time on April 2, 2009, in London on the sidelines of the G-20 summit. Afterward, an Obama Administration official said that President Obama told Lee he wants to "make progress" on the agreement, and that the two leaders agreed that the two countries' staffs should "discuss how to move forward."[1]

The two presidents met again on June 16, 2009, in Washington, DC. In a joint statement released at the summit, they said: "We will continue to deepen our strong bilateral economic, trade and investment relations. We recognize that the Korea-U.S. (KORUS) Free Trade Agreement could further strengthen these ties and we are committed to working together to chart a way forward." In answering a question at a joint press conference, President Obama stated, "What I have done is to affirm to [South Korean] President Lee that we want to work constructively with the Republic of Korea in a systematic way to clear some of these barriers that are preventing free trade from occurring between our two countries."[2] However, President Obama did not indicate a timeframe for consideration of legislation to implement the KORUS FTA.

At a joint press conference with President Lee in Seoul in November 2009, President Obama said the agreement "holds out the promise of serving our mutual interests. And together, we're committed to working together to move the agreement forward." President Lee said the two leaders agreed to "redouble" their efforts toward this end.[3] Prior to his meeting with President Lee, President Obama said in a Fox News interview that "I want to get the deal done.... Overall, I think it's a potential good deal for US exporters. But there's certain sectors of the economy that aren't dealt with as effectively and that's something that I'm going to be talking to President Lee about."[4]

During his January 27, 2010, State of the Union address, President Obama, without mentioning the KORUS FTA per se, expressed the need for the United States to strengthen its trade ties in Asia "with partners like South Korea." During a question-and-answer session at the January 29, 2010, House Republican issues conference, the President referred to the need to seize trade opportunities, mentioning South Korea in particular.

On June 26, 2010, President Obama announced that he would direct U.S. Trade Representative Ron Kirk to work with the South Korean trade minister to resolve outstanding issues on the KORUS FTA by the time President Obama and South Korean President Lee meet again in Seoul in November 2010 for the G-20 summit. The President said that he intends "in the few months" after the November meeting to present Congress with the implementing legislation for the agreement. The President made the announcement at a joint press conference following his meeting with President Lee prior to the G-20 summit in Toronto.

On November 11, 2010, in Seoul, after the two presidents announced that the two sides had not resolved the outstanding issues, President Obama said that the U.S. and South Korean negotiating teams would be working "in the coming days and weeks ahead" to reach agreement. He said that an FTA "done right" would be a "win-win" for both countries.

On December 4, 2010, President Obama announced that U.S. and South Korean negotiators had reached agreement on modifications to the KORUS FTA making the agreement a win for the United States and for "our ally and friend" South Korea.

On July 8, 2011, the President made the following remarks as part of his statement on the latest U.S. employment report: "There are bills and trade agreements before Congress right now that could get all these ideas moving. All of them have bipartisan support. All of them could pass immediately. And I urge Congress not to wait. The American people need us to do everything we can to help strengthen this economy and make sure that we are producing more jobs."

On October 13, 2011, at a joint news conference with President Lee Myung-bak on the occasion of the latter's state visit to Washington, President Obama said: "... just as Americans buy Hyundais and Kias, I hope that South Koreans will buy more Fords, Chryslers and Chevys.... The KORUS FTA] will boost American exports by up to $11 billion and support some 70,000 American jobs. It has groundbreaking protections for labor rights, the environment and intellectual property—so that trade is free and fair. It will promote green jobs and clean energy, another area where we're deepening our cooperation. And it keeps us on track to achieve my goals of doubling American exports."

A congressionally mandated study by the United States International Trade Commission (USITC) concluded that investment and trade between the United States and South Korea would increase modestly as a result of the KORUS FTA.[5] This result was in line with other similar studies. In general and in the short-to-medium term, the KORUS FTA's largest commercial effects are expected to be microeconomic in nature. The U.S. services and agriculture industries, for instance, are expected to reap significant benefits from the agreement.

Many observers have argued that in addition to its economic implications, the KORUS FTA will have diplomatic and security implications. For example, they have suggested that it will deepen the U.S.-South Korean alliance. The United States and South Korea have been allies since the United States intervened on the Korean Peninsula in 1950 and fought to repel a North Korean takeover of South Korea. Over 33,000 U.S. troops were killed and over 100,000 were wounded during the three-year conflict.[6] South Korea subsequently has assisted U.S. deployments in other conflicts, most recently by deploying over 3,000 troops to play a non-combat role in Iraq. However, some counter this by positing that the KORUS FTA need not be seen as a necessary, let alone sufficient, condition for enhancing the U.S.-ROK alliance. Mutual interests on critical issues pertaining to North Korea and the rest of the region will continue to require close cooperation between the two countries in the national security sphere.

This report examines the provisions of the KORUS FTA in the context of the overall U.S.-South Korean economic relationship, U.S. objectives, and South Korean objectives. It also examines some of the issues that have arisen during its implementation.

THE KORUS FTA IN A NUTSHELL

Some highlights of the results of the agreement are provided below. Background information and a more detailed examination of the agreement's provisions are provided in the main sections of this report.

Agriculture

Under the KORUS FTA's agricultural provisions, South Korea immediately granted duty-free status to almost two-thirds of current U.S. agricultural exports. Tariffs and import quotas on most other agricultural goods will be phased out within 10 years, with a few commodities and food products subject to provisions that phase out such protection by year 23. However, because of their sensitivity, access for several U.S. products will slowly expand in perpetuity but remain subject to South Korean import quotas.

Much effort went into negotiating provisions covering three agricultural commodities of export interest to the United States. Under the KORUS FTA, South Korea agreed to eliminate its 40% tariff on beef muscle meats imported from the United States over a 15-year period. However, negotiators did not reach a breakthrough by the end of the talks on the separate but parallel issue of how to resolve differences on the terms of access for all U.S. beef in a way that would address Korea's human health concerns arising from the 2003 discovery of mad cow disease in the U.S. cattle herd. Though sales of U.S. boneless beef from cattle aged less than 30 months did resume in April 2007 under a separate agreement reached in early 2006, sales of bone-in beef (e.g., ribs) only began in July 2008 after the conclusion of a difficult series of negotiations—accompanied by widespread public protests in Korea—on a more comprehensive agreement. Under the terms of a commercial understanding sanctioned by both governments, exports are limited to all cuts of beef (boneless and bone-in) from cattle less than 30 months old when slaughtered. Both countries view this "voluntary private-sector" arrangement as a transitional step intended to improve Korean consumer confidence in U.S. beef.

Negotiations on access for U.S. rice and oranges into the South Korean market also were contentious. Rice was a "make-or-break" issue for Seoul, and excluded at South Korea's insistence out of U.S. recognition that if pushed, the talks would likely have collapsed. Special treatment for U.S. oranges was struck at the last moment, when negotiators compromised on a multi-part solution expected to increase U.S. navel orange exports over time. In the December 2010 changes to the initial agreement, Korea secured an extension in the tariff phase-out for one commercially important line of U.S. frozen pork product in return for changes the United States sought in its commitments under the auto and other provisions. In June 2011, South Korea's trade minister clarified that the use of generic names by U.S. cheese exporters selling to that market will not be restricted by provisions in the EU-Korea (KOREU) FTA.

Automobiles

Trade in autos and auto parts proved to be among the most difficult issues tackled by U.S. and South Korean negotiators. In recent years, South Korean auto manufacturers have increased their market share through imports and expanded car production in the United States and other major automotive markets like the European Union. U.S. industry argued that South Korea should eliminate policies and practices that seemingly discriminate against U.S. auto imports. In December 2010, the United States and South Korea reached a joint understanding on automotive trade.[7] Due to these modifications, all three U.S. automakers ultimately supported the KORUS FTA. A detailed discussion of the auto-specific provisions is provided later in this report. A few of the most important provisions are discussed below.

- The United States will eliminate its tariff of 2.5% on passenger cars, including electric and hybrid vehicles, as of 2016. South Korea cut its passenger car tariff to 4% upon implementation of the KORUS FTA and will remove the remaining tariff in 2016.[8] For trucks, South Korea dropped its 10% duty upon implementation, while the U.S. tariff of 25% will remain in place for seven years and then be phased out entirely by 2021. The KORUS FTA also includes a "snapback provision" that allows the United States to reinstate its 2.5% passenger car tariff, once the duties are completely eliminated, if U.S. automakers claim and the dispute settlement panel finds that South Korea is in violation of the agreement. The snapback could also be imposed due to violations regarding imports of trucks. South Korean commitments regarding a specified group of new and already proposed regulations on automobile fuel economy and greenhouse gas emissions do not seem to be enforceable under the dispute settlement provisions of the KORUS FTA; presumably the snapback will not apply to these commitments.[9]

- A special motor vehicle safeguard allows the United States to take action if there are "any harmful surges in South Korean auto imports due to the agreement." As a remedy under the auto-specific safeguard, the United States will be able to reimpose the 2.5% passenger vehicle tariff. However, a surge in automobile imports from South Korea seems unlikely as South Korean auto manufacturers have substantially increased their assembly production in the United States to about 720,000 cars and light trucks in 2012.[10] If U.S.-based producers–including foreign-owned automakers such as BMW or Toyota–meet U.S. federal safety standards, each manufacturer can export as many as 25,000 cars directly to South Korea from the United States without complying with South Korean safety standards. Additionally, they must satisfy KORUS FTA domestic content provisions. U.S. automakers also have some flexibility to be considered in compliance with new South Korean fuel economy and greenhouse gas emissions standards.

Other Key Provisions

The KORUS FTA covers a broad range of other areas. According to the Office of the United States Trade Representative (USTR), 95% of U.S.-South Korean trade in *consumer and industrial products* will become duty-free by 2016 and virtually all remaining tariffs will be lifted by 2021. The two countries agreed to liberalize trade in *services* by opening up their markets beyond what they have committed to do in the World Trade Organization (WTO). About 60% of U.S.-South Korea trade in *textiles and apparel* became duty-free immediately, and the KORUS FTA will provide a special safeguard mechanism to reduce the impact of textile and apparel import surges.

Trade remedies were a critical issue for South Korea and a sensitive issue for the United States. The FTA allows for the United States to exempt imports from South Korea from a "global" escape clause (§201) measure if they are not a major cause of serious injury or a threat of serious injury to the U.S. domestic industry. The FTA also provided for a binational consultative committee for information sharing on trade remedy matters.[11]

In addition, South Korea and the United States agreed to establish an independent body, a Medicines and Medical Devices Committee, to review recommendations and determinations regarding South Korean pricing and government reimbursement for *pharmaceuticals and medical devices* and to improve transparency in the process for making those determinations.

Furthermore, one year after the KORUS FTA enters into force, a binational committee was to be formed to study the possibility of eventually expanding the agreement's coverage to products from "Outward Processing Zones," including the Kaesong Industrial Complex and/or other future zones located in North Korea. (That committee has not yet been formed.)

Estimates of the Overall Economic Effects of a KORUS FTA

Economists have released several studies estimating the potential effects of the KORUS FTA. As required by the TPA statute, the USITC conducted a study in 2007 of the KORUS FTA at the request of the President.[12] The USITC study concluded that U.S. GDP will be higher by $10.1 billion to $11.9 billion (approximately 0.1%) when the KORUS FTA is fully implemented, a negligible amount given the size of the U.S. economy. The USITC based this estimate primarily on the removal of tariffs and tariff-rate-quotas, that is, barriers that can be relatively easily quantified. The study concluded that U.S. exports of goods will likely be higher by $9.7 billion to $10.9 billion, primarily in agricultural products, machinery, electronics, transportation equipment, including passenger vehicles and parts. U.S. imports will increase $6.4 billion to $6.9 billion, primarily in textiles, apparel, leather products, footwear, machinery, electronics, and passenger vehicles and parts.[13]

The range did not take into account the impact of the reduction of barriers to trade in services and to foreign investment flows and the impact of changes in regulations as a result of the KORUS FTA. The study noted that U.S. exports in services will increase as a result of South Korean commitments under the KORUS FTA, and that changes in the regulatory environment in both countries will also help to increase bilateral trade and investment flows.

The study estimated that changes in aggregate U.S. employment will be negligible given the much larger size of the U.S. economy compared to the South Korean economy. However, while some sectors, such as livestock producers, will experience increases in employment, others such as textile, wearing apparel, and electronic equipment manufacturers are expected to experience declines in employment.[14]

Other studies draw the same basic conclusions, although the magnitudes differ because they employ different models from the USITC study. For example, a University of Michigan analysis commissioned by the Korea Economic Institute estimated that U.S. GDP will increase by $25.12 billion (0.14% of U.S. GDP). This is larger than the USITC estimate, but in part this is because its authors quantified the effects of liberalization in services trade.[15] The authors also analyzed the impact of a KORUS FTA before the final text had been released and assumed, among other things, that rice trade would be liberalized, which, in the end, was not the case. In December 2005, the Korea Institute for International Economic Policy (KIEP) published a study measuring the potential economic impact of a U.S.-South Korean FTA on South Korea alone. The study estimated some of the dynamic, or long-run, economic effects in addition to the static, or one-time, effects of the FTA on South Korea. The KIEP study estimated that the FTA will eventually lead to a 0.42% to 0.59% increase in South Korea's GDP according to a static analysis, and 1.99% to 2.27% according to a dynamic analysis.[16]

An Overview of the U.S.-South Korean Economic Relationship

South Korea is a major economic partner for the United States. In 2012, two-way trade between the two countries totaled $101.1 billion, making South Korea the United States' seventh-largest trading partner. (See Table 1.) Major U.S. exports to South Korea include semiconductors, machinery (particularly semiconductor production machinery), aircraft, and agricultural products.

Table 1. Annual U.S.-South Korea Merchandise Trade, Selected Years (billions of U.S. dollars)

Year	U.S. Exports	U.S. Imports	Trade balance	Total trade
1990	14.4	18.5	-4.1	32.9
1995	25.4	24.2	1.2	49.6
2000	26.3	39.8	-13.5	66.1
2003	22.5	36.9	-14.4	59.5
2004	25.0	45.1	-20.1	70.1
2005	26.2	43.2	-17.0	69.4
2006	30.8	44.7	-13.9	75.5
2007	33.0	45.4	-12.4	78.4
2008	33.1	46.7	-13.6	79.8
2009	27.0	38.7	-11.7	65.7
2010	38.0	48.9	-10.9	86.9
2011	43.5	56.6	-13.1	100.
2012	42.3	58.9	-16.6	101.
Major U.S. Export Items	Industrial machinery; chemicals; semiconductor circuits; corn & wheat; specialized instruments.			
Major U.S. Import Items	Cell phones; semiconductor circuits; cars & car parts; iron & steel.			

Sources: 1990 and 1995 data from Global Trade Information Services. 2000-2008 data from U.S. International Trade Commission. The 2000-2012 U.S. export data are for U.S. domestic exports and the data for U.S. imports are for imports on a consumption basis.

South Korea is far more dependent economically on the United States than the United States is on South Korea. In 2012, the United States was South Korea's third-largest trading partner, second-largest export market, and the third-largest source of imports. In 2003, China for the first time displaced the United States from its perennial place as South Korea's number one trading partner. In 2005 Japan overtook the United States to become South Korea's second-largest trade partner.

Table 2. Asymmetrical Economic Interdependence (2012)

	Total Trade	**Export Market**	**Source of Imports**
For the U.S., South Korea ranks	# 7	# 8	# 6
For South Korea, U.S. ranks	# 3	# 2	# 3

Sources: U.S. Department of Commerce, U.S. Census Bureau and Bureau of Economic Analysis; Bank of Korea.

Increased economic interaction between the United States and South Korea has been accompanied by numerous disagreements over trade policies. In general, U.S. exporters and trade negotiators identify the lack of transparency of South Korea's trading and regulatory systems as the most significant barriers to trade with South Korea in almost every major product sector. Many U.S. government officials also complain that Seoul continues to use government regulations and standard-setting powers to discriminate against foreign firms in politically sensitive industries, such as automobiles and telecommunications. Another major cross-sectoral complaint is that rigidities in the South Korean labor market, such as mandatory severance pay, raise the cost of investing and doing business. Finally, the United States and other countries have pressed South Korea to open further its agricultural market, which is considered one of the most closed among members of the Organization for Economic Co-operation and Development (OECD).[17] Many of these issues arose during the KORUS FTA negotiations.

The intensity of these disputes has diminished considerably since the late 1980s and early 1990s, in part because South Korea enacted a set of sweeping market-oriented reforms as a *quid pro quo* for receiving a U.S.-led $58 billion package from the International Monetary Fund (IMF) following the near collapse of the South Korean economy in 1997. In particular, as a result of the reforms, South Korea opened its doors to foreign investors, ushering in billions of dollars of foreign portfolio and foreign direct investment (FDI). The result is that foreign companies, including U.S. firms, now are significant shareholders in many prominent industrial conglomerates (*chaebol*); at one point earlier in the decade, foreign firms owned about one-third of the South Korean banking industry and an estimated 40% of the value of the shares traded on South Korea's stock exchange. Since the 1997 crisis, FDI commitments by U.S. companies have totaled over $25 billion.[18]

Additionally, the United States and South Korea appear to have become more adept at managing their trade disputes. This may be partly due to the quarterly, working-level "trade action agenda" trade meetings that were initiated in early 2001. Both sides credit the meetings, which appear to be unique to the U.S.-South Korean trade relationship, with creating a more constructive dialogue that helped pave the way for the two sides to feel sufficiently confident to launch FTA negotiations.

U.S. and South Korean Objectives in an FTA

U.S. and South Korean policymakers shared certain goals in launching and completing the negotiations on the KORUS FTA. Both governments saw in the FTA a logical extension of an already important economic relationship that would provide a means by which the two trading partners could address and resolve fundamental issues and, thereby, raise the relationship to a higher level. For the United States these issues have included the high tariffs and other restrictions on agricultural imports. For South Korea, these difficult issues have included perceived U.S. discrimination toward South Korean imports in the application of trade remedies and treatment of products made at the Kaesong Industrial Complex in North Korea.

While sharing some broad objectives, U.S. and South Korean leaders also approached the KORUS FTA from different perspectives that were reflected in the conduct and outcome of the negotiations. A primary objective of the United States was to gain access to South Korean markets in agricultural products, pharmaceuticals and medical equipment, some other high-technology manufactured goods, and services, particularly financial and professional services— areas in which U.S. producers are internationally competitive but for which South Korean barriers seemed to be high.

For South Korea, gaining a large increase in market access was not as critical a priority since South Korean exporters already have a significant presence in areas in which they have proved to be competitive—consumer electronics and autos, for example, and in which they already face only low or zero U.S. tariffs. However, South Korea sought to preserve its share of the U.S. market in the face of growing competition from emerging East Asian producers from Thailand, Malaysia, Vietnam, and possibly China. South Korea also aimed to improve its competitive position in the U.S. market vis-à-vis Japan where the elimination of even low tariffs might give South Korean exporters some price advantage.

Launching the FTA negotiations was largely at the initiative of South Korea. Its main objective in securing an FTA with the United States was much broader than gaining reciprocal access to the U.S. market. Entering an FTA with the United States meshed with a number of former South Korean President Roh Moo-hyun's long-term economic and strategic goals. Roh made an FTA the top economic priority for the remainder of his tenure, which ended in February 2008.[19] Soon after his election in 2002, Roh committed himself to raising South Korea's per capita gross domestic product (GDP) to $20,000 by the end of the decade and to transforming South Korea into a major "economic hub" in Northeast Asia by expanding the economic reforms begun by his predecessor following the 1997 Asian financial crisis. Ongoing competitive pressure from Japanese firms, increased competition from Chinese enterprises, and the rapid ageing of the South Korean workforce has heightened the sense of urgency about boosting national competitiveness. Continuing along this line of argument, ex-Prime Minister Han Duk-soo has said that a failure to adopt significant economic changes will mean that "Korea's long term growth potential is likely to deteriorate."[20] Former President Lee Myung-bak, who succeeded Roh in December 2007, made the economy the centerpiece of his campaign and supported the KORUS FTA as part of a larger program to promote South Korean economic growth.

During the negotiations, South Korean officials and other South Korean proponents of the KORUS FTA tended not to focus on the increased access to the U.S. market. Rather, they emphasized the medium and long-term gains that would stem from increased allocative efficiency of the South Korean economy, particularly in the services industries. This would presumably be brought about by an influx of U.S. investment and technology into South Korea and by the spur of increased competition with U.S. firms.[21] Senior officials in particular emphasized the need to boost the competitiveness of South Korean service industries. An FTA with the United States, they argued, will help address South Korea's increased economic polarization by spurring job creation in fields such as medical, legal, education, and accounting services.[22] Some, however, say an FTA will worsen South Korea's income gap.[23] Also, during the talks, there were continuous and often large scale anti-FTA protests, generally led by South Korean farmers and trade unionists.

The absence of mirror-image or reciprocal U.S. and South Korean objectives in the negotiations is reflected in the structure of the KORUS FTA. Except for some provisions dealing with issues specific to U.S.-South Korea economic relations, for example, South Korea taxation of autos and the Kaesong industrial complex, the structure of the KORUS FTA largely resembles the structure of other U.S. FTAs, such as Dominican Republic-Central American FTA (DR-CAFTA). This conclusion does not suggest that South Korea did not bring to the table its own specific demands, which it did (such as the exclusion of rice) and held to them firmly.

Sector-Specific Issues and the KORUS FTA

Under the KORUS FTA, the United States and South Korea agreed to eliminate tariffs on most manufactured goods immediately upon implementation and the others no later than year-end 2021. [24] The agreement also included provisions on sensitive sectors such as agricultural products and auto trade.

Agriculture and Sanitary and Phytosanitary Issues

Overview

Attaining comprehensive market access for U.S. agricultural products to South Korea's large market and finding a way to resolve South Korea's continued restrictions on U.S. beef purchases (imposed to protect human health following the late 2003 discovery of mad cow disease in the U.S. cattle herd) were the two primary objectives pursued by U.S. agricultural negotiators. Though South Korea ranks among the leading agricultural importing countries in the world, its farm sector is highly protected with high tariffs and quotas.[25] This reflects its farmers' longstanding political influence (particularly that of rice producers) and its urban population's deep ties to its rural roots.

In concluding the KORUS FTA on April 1, 2007, the United States secured nearly complete access for all U.S. agricultural commodities and food products into South Korea's market. However, a breakthrough on the beef issue (technically not part of the FTA talks but nevertheless the subject of high-level discussions) did not occur until June 2008. This reflected the then newly elected Korean President Lee's view that an agreement spelling out the rules that apply to beef imports from the United States had to be in place before President Bush would consider sending this agreement to Capitol Hill. Several Members of Congress had for months stated that South Korea must agree to fully reopen its market to U.S. beef under scientifically based international rules and in commercially significant quantities before Congress considers or approves the agreement. U.S. agricultural groups, well aware of this deal's potential benefits for producers, had then also conditioned their support on the resumption of U.S. beef exports.

Negotiations in late 2010 to address outstanding FTA issues did not result in the full opening of South Korea's market to U.S. beef as sought by the Obama Administration and some Members of Congress. The only change made to the agreement's agricultural provisions is a concession (among others) requested by South Korea in return for changes sought by USTR in the auto provisions. The United States accepted a two-year extension in the phasing out of South Korea's tariff on the largest category of pork imports from the United States. Responding to the conclusion of these talks, the U.S. beef and pork sectors expressed their support for the KORUS FTA, emphasizing that its approval as soon as possible is vital to realizing the gains negotiated before other countries' FTAs with South Korea take effect.

In 2012, South Korea was the fifth-largest market for U.S. agriculture, as export sales totaled \$6.0 billion. Under the KORUS FTA's agricultural provisions, South Korea immediately granted duty-free status to almost two-thirds of current U.S. agricultural exports. Tariffs and tariff-rate quotas (TRQs)[26] on most other agricultural goods will be phased out within 10 years (i.e., 2021), with a few commodities and food products subject to provisions that phase out such protection in year 23 (i.e., 2034). Seven U.S. products (skim and whole milk powders, evaporated milk, in-season oranges, potatoes for table use, honey, and identity-preserved soybeans for food use) will be subject to Korean import quotas that slowly expand in perpetuity. However, the agreement does not give U.S. rice and rice products additional access to South Korea's market (see below).[27]

With the immediate elimination or phase-out of most of South Korea's relatively high agricultural trade barriers under the KORUS FTA, the U.S. agricultural and food processing sectors will noticeably benefit from additional exports. The USITC estimates that the increase in U.S. exports of agricultural commodities and processed foods will account for up to one-third of the entire projected increase in total U.S. exports to South Korea's market once the KORUS FTA's provisions are fully implemented. Sale of agricultural products will increase by $1.9 billion to $3.8 billion (44% to 89%) over exports under a no-agreement scenario. Almost half of this export increase will accrue to the U.S. beef sector, based on the USITC's assumption that U.S. beef exports recover to the level before South Korea imposed its import restrictions in late 2003. About 20% of the export increase will benefit U.S. producers and exporters of pork, poultry and other meat products.[28] In another analysis, the American Farm Bureau Federation (AFBF) projects that U.S. agricultural exports by the end of the transition period will be more than $1.5 billion (45%) higher under the KORUS FTA than would be the case otherwise. Sales of beef, poultry, and pork will account for $644 million (or 42%) of this increase.[29]

Because South Korean agricultural exports to the United States are small ($333 million in2011) and largely complementary, there was no controversy in negotiating access to the U.S. market. The United States agreed to phase out tariffs and quotas on all agricultural imports from South Korea under seven phase-out periods ranging up to 15 years (i.e., 2026). One 10-year TRQ will apply to imports of fluid milk and cream, among other specified dairy products. The USITC projects that imports of agricultural products (primarily processed food products) from South Korea under the KORUS FTA will be from $52 million to $78 million (12% to 18%) higher than such imports under a no-agreement scenario.

Beef

Market Access

Under the KORUS FTA, South Korea agreed to eliminate its 40% tariff on beef muscle meats imported from the United States over a 15-year period. Also, South Korea will have the right to impose safeguard tariffs on a temporary basis in response to any potential surge in imports of U.S. beef meats above specified levels. The trigger for this additional tariff will be 270,000 metric tons (MT) in year 1, which will increase 2% annually; in year 15, the trigger will be 354,000 MT.[30] In year 16, this protective mechanism will no longer apply. The 18% tariff on imports of beef offals (tongues, livers, tails, and feet), and tariffs ranging from 22.5% to 72% on other beef products, will also be eliminated in 15 years.

Assuming that South Korea fully lifts its restrictions on U.S. beef and bilateral beef trade returns to normal, the USITC estimates that the phase-out of South Korea's beef tariff and safeguard could increase U.S. beef exports from about $600 million to almost $1.8 billion (58% to 165%) above what would be the case otherwise. Under the KORUS FTA, the AFBF projects that U.S. beef sales would be $265 million higher as the United States recaptures its historic share of the South Korean market. However, its analysis notes that the market share of U.S. beef likely will not increase over time. That is because South Korean tastes have developed a preference for grass-fed Australian beef, according to the AFBF, and will continue to be competitive in price against U.S. beef even with the current 40% tariff removed.

Sanitary Rules

On April 18, 2008, U.S. and South Korean negotiators agreed to a protocol on the sanitary rules that South Korea will apply to beef imports from the United States. It allows for imports of all cuts of U.S. boneless and bone-in beef and other beef products from cattle, irrespective of age, as long as specified risk materials known to transmit mad cow disease are removed and other conditions are met. However, to address subsequent Korean concerns, both sides revised this agreement on June 21, 2008, to limit sales of U.S. beef from cattle less than 30 months old.

South Korea quickly published rules to put this agreement into effect, and began to inspect U.S. beef shipments. The U.S. Department of Agriculture similarly began to implement a new program to verify that the beef sold is processed from cattle under 30 months old. U.S. beef exporters have since worked to recapture a key overseas market.

In 2003, South Korea was the third-largest market for U.S. beef exports, prior to the ban imposed after the first U.S. cow infected with mad cow disease, or BSE (*bovine spongiform encephalopathy*), was discovered. Korea's commercial significance is reflected in the position taken by some Members of Congress, who had stated that congressional consideration of, and support for, the KORUS FTA depended upon South Korea fully opening its market to U.S. beef.

While the U.S. beef industry and U.S. policymakers welcomed the initial April 2008 deal, Korean TV coverage of the issue and Internet-spread rumors that questioned the safety of U.S. beef resulted in escalating protests and calls for the beef agreement to be renegotiated or scrapped. U.S. officials countered that measures already in place to prevent the introduction of BSE in U.S. cattle herds meet international scientific standards. To address mounting public pressure, the South Korean government twice pursued talks with the United States to find ways to defuse public concerns without "renegotiating" the beef agreement. In late June 2008, both governments confirmed a "voluntary private sector" arrangement that allows South Korean firms to import U.S. beef produced only from cattle less than 30 months old. Both viewed this as a transitional step until Korean consumers regain confidence in the safety of U.S. beef.

Under this arrangement, exports of U.S. beef (including bone-in cuts) to South Korea resumed in mid-2008, and by year-end reached almost $300 million, more than one-third of the record 2003 sales level. In 2009, with the drop off in beef sales worldwide due to the economic recession, U.S. beef sales to South Korea fell to $216 million. For 2010, sales more than doubled to reach $518 million, and then rose further in 2011 to $686 million. Though Australia is the main competitor, U.S. beef exporters have gained noticeable market share since the South Korean market reopened. The U.S. share (in quantity terms) rose from 15% in 2008, 26% in 2009, 32% in 2010, and 37% in 2011 (compared to 69% in 2003). Promotional efforts to rebuild consumer confidence in U.S. beef, aggressive marketing efforts by large store chains, and much lower retail prices for foreign than for Korean beef, account for the continued growth in U.S. beef sales in Korea.[31]

Obama Administration officials, following the President's June 26, 2010, announcement of his decision to present the KORUS FTA to Congress, stated their intent was to resolve the beef and auto issues with South Korea by November 2010 once consultations with Congress and stakeholders were complete. In the negotiations concluded on December 3, 2010, the beef issue reportedly received little discussion as both sides focused on revising the auto provisions. President Obama, in discussing the supplemental agreement, indicated that the United States will continue to work toward "ensuring full access for U.S. beef to the Korean market."[32]

Congressional reaction on the outcome of the beef issue was mixed. Senator Baucus (chairman of the Senate Finance Committee), who had advocated for full access for U.S. beef irrespective of the age of cattle in accordance with international scientific standards, expressed "deep disappointment" that the supplemental deal "fails to address Korea's significant barriers to American beef exports." He stated his commitment to right "this wrong" and to work with the Administration to ensure that ranchers "are not left behind." At that time, Senator Baucus said he will not support the KORUS FTA until South Korea opens up its beef market. A few other Senators, though concerned with the lack of progress on beef, viewed the deal positively and welcomed the prospect for considering the KORUS FTA in 2011.[33] Meat industry groups expressed support for this trade agreement that they expect over time will significantly increase their exports to South Korea, and urged Congress to move quickly to ratify it. Beef interests, also supportive, called for continued efforts to secure full market access.[34]

Memories of the size and intensity of the 2008 anti-beef agreement protests in South Korea appeared to have directly influenced the position then taken on the beef issue by Korean negotiators. Reflecting this political sensitivity, they reportedly rejected any discussion on this matter in the negotiations held in early November 2010 leading up to the summit between Presidents Obama and Lee and in the final talks leading to the supplemental agreement. Their position was that this issue "did not fall under" the FTA concluded in 2007. Subsequently, South Korea's trade minister confirmed that there will be no more discussions on ending the age limits of U.S. cattle slaughtered for beef—a stance that was affirmed by its ambassador to Washington in late January 2011.[35] The outcome appeared to have been successful in that it did not alter the political debate expected to occur in South Korea on the KORUS FTA. However, if changes had been made to the terms of current U.S. beef access, opponents would have been given another opening to shift the debate on the agreement.

Seeking to move closer toward submitting the KORUS FTA to Congress for consideration, the USTR on May 4, 2011, announced two measures to be taken on the U.S. beef access issue. In a letter to Senator Baucus, the Administration committed to request consultations with South Korea on the "full implementation" (e.g., opening Korea's market "to all ages and all cuts of U.S. beef") of the protocol as soon as this trade agreement takes effect. The letter referenced one specific provision that stipulates bilateral consultations on the interpretation or application of the protocol's terms "shall be held within seven days" of a request. On the same day, the U.S. Department of Agriculture (USDA) announced a $1 million award to the U.S. Meat Export Federation (USMEF) to be used in FY2011 to promote U.S. beef sales in South Korea, and its intent to consider future funding requests from the USMEF to implement its planned five-year market beef promotion strategy in this key market. Senator Baucus welcomed both steps, stating he will support the KORUS FTA and work with the Administration on a package of trade measures that includes all three FTAs and renewing trade adjustment assistance and trade preference programs.[36] The KORUS FTA entered into force, but the USTR has not yet had formal consultations with South Korea on the beef issue.

Rice

South Korean negotiators succeeded in excluding the entry of U.S. rice on preferential terms—its prime objective in negotiating agriculture in the KORUS FTA. This reflects Korea's efforts to maintain its stated policy of self-sufficiency in rice production, the national sentiment that preserving rice production is inseparable from the country's identity, and the political reality that rice farming preserves the basis for economic activity in the countryside. That rice was a makeor-break issue for Seoul is seen in the comment made by then-Deputy United States Trade Representative Karan Bhatia, the day after the talks concluded: "Ultimately, the question that confronted us was whether to accept a very, very good albeit less perfect agreement or to lose the entire agreement because South Korea refused to move on rice."[37] On rice, the KORUS FTA only requires South Korea to continue to abide by its multilateral trade commitments to increase rice imports.

At present, U.S. rice exporters have access to the South Korean market under (1) a 24% share (50,076 MT) of the rice import quota established under that country's multilateral World Trade Organization (WTO) commitments in 1995, and (2) a separate "global" quota available to all countries.[38] Rice entering under both quotas faces a 5% tariff. Entries above each quota are prohibited—a unique concession that South Korea received in the 1993 Uruguay Round of multilateral trade negotiations. U.S. rice exports against both quotas have fluctuated much from year to year, and in2011 peaked at $125 million (162,291MT). Future U.S. sales are expected to grow slowly in line with the expansion of the "global" rice quota.

Though the U.S. rice industry expressed disappointment with the rice exclusion, the United States will have other opportunities to negotiate access for additional U.S. rice in Korea's market. A further opening of the South Korean rice market could occur in the process of concluding a multilateral agreement to further liberalize agricultural trade in the WTO's Doha Development Round. Also, the United States and other rice exporting countries could press for additional access when Korea's current WTO minimum market access agreement expires in 2014.

Oranges

Differences on how quickly to liberalize trade in fresh oranges were not resolved until just before the negotiations concluded. The United States sought the complete elimination of South Korea's border protection on all citrus products, while South Korea wanted to retain its quotas and tariffs, primarily because of the importance of the citrus industry to the economy of Cheju Island. At present, South Korea imposes a 50% tariff on all imports of oranges, irrespective of whether they enter within or outside an existing TRQ.

In reaching a compromise, negotiators agreed to a multi-part solution. First, a small duty-free quota will be created for "in-season" U.S. navel oranges (a variety that is not produced in Korea) that would enter between September 1 and the end of February—a period that coincides with the Island's *unshu* (mandarin) orange harvest season. The initial 2,500 MT TRQ will increase at a compound 3% annual rate in perpetuity. Shipments in excess of the quota amount during this six-month period will continue to be subject to the 50% tariff. Second, in the first year, this high tariff will be reduced to 30% for "out-of-season" oranges that enter between March 1 and August 31, and then be completely phased out in stages by year 7. Third, South Korea's 144% tariff on other mandarin oranges will be phased out over 15 years.

The cost of selling to what already is a leading U.S. export market for fresh oranges will be significantly reduced as Korea's high 50% tariff is phased out. In 2012, South Korea ranked as the leading market, with U.S. orange and tangerine sales totaling $217 million (184,545 MT). The USDA estimates that the value of the in-season 2,500 MT quota and tariff reductions on all orange exports in the first year that the agreement is in effect will be almost $18 million. Over seven years, USDA estimates the cumulative value of savings associated with these orange access provisions at $208 million.[39]

Pork

According to the December 2010 modifications to the initial agreement, South Korea will phase out its 25% tariff on one tariff line of frozen pork cuts on January 1, 2016. This change will affect about 75% of all U.S. pork exports, as recorded by 2010 value. This is two years later than what both sides had agreed upon in the 2007 text (i.e., January 1, 2014). Korea's tariffs on other U.S. pork products will be phased out by January 1, 2014, or over 10 years. South Korea secured a safeguard to protect against import surges of some of these fresh pork products, which will expire at the end of 10 years.

In 2010, South Korea ranked as the fifth-largest market for U.S. pork (fresh, chilled and frozen), with sales of 148,626 MT valued at $433 million. The National Pork Producers Council acknowledged that, even with the last minute concession on pork in order to resolve the auto issue, the KORUS FTA is "a good deal." It expects the agreement to "be one of the most lucrative for the U.S. pork industry," with a substantial increase projected in exports to South Korea, live hog prices, and direct jobs.[40]

Geographical Indications for Dairy Products

The U.S. dairy sector in late 2010 expressed concern that the geographical indications (GI) provisions that apply to various EU cheeses in the KOREU FTA would undercut the potential benefits negotiated under the KORUS FTA for U.S. cheeses with identical names that sell into the Korean market. GIs (similar to a trademark) refer to marks that "identify a good as originating in the territory of a country, or a region or locality in that territory, where a given quality, reputation or other characteristic of the good is essentially attributable to its geographical origin."[41] To illustrate, "champagne" and "Idaho potatoes" are examples of GI designations. Products so designated are eligible for relief from acts of infringement and/or unfair competition under a country's trademark laws and regulations. Because GIs are commercially valuable in the international trade of agricultural products, wines, and spirits, the EU in negotiating its bilateral trade agreements has sought to secure additional protection for its GI-designated agricultural and beverage products in FTA-partner country markets beyond what multilateral trading rules currently provide.

More than 50 Members of the House requested the USTR to ensure that as South Korea develops regulations to implement the KOREU FTA's GI provisions, those rules "do not undercut the dairy market gains secured" in the KORUS FTA. They expressed concern that the U.S. dairy industry will not be able to increase cheese exports if the United States (1) does not "combat European efforts to carve out the sole right for their producers to use ... cheese names most familiar to consumers around the world (e.g., feta, gorgonzola, muenster, parmesan, provolone)," and (2) act to safeguard against possible threats to the use of such generic terms as cheddar and mozzarella "that could arise as a result of recent EU legal precedents" to protect the names of some EU wines and spirits.

A June 2011 exchange of letters between the USTR and Korea's trade ministry clarified that the use of generic terms used to identify types of cheeses (e.g., camembert, mozzarella, emmental, grana, parmesan, brie, cheddar) will not be restricted by the Korea-EU FTA. In other words, U.S. exporters will be able to sell these cheeses into the important South Korean market. A U.S. trade official stated the United States is satisfied with the clarifications provided by South Korea's trade minister. U.S. milk and dairy product groups welcomed these assurances, noting that Korea already is one of the largest export markets for U.S. cheese.[42]

Sanitary and Phytosanitary Provisions

As found in most other U.S. FTAs, the KORUS FTA establishes a bilateral standing committee to address food safety and animal/plant life or health issues that frequently emerge in agricultural trade. However, the agreement does not include any commodity-specific sanitary and phytosanitary (SPS) provisions to address outstanding issues, such as Korea's import health requirements on U.S. beef imports or Korean standards that have prevented sales of some U.S. horticultural products to that market. The Committee on SPS Matters will serve as a forum to implement the WTO's Agreement on the Application of SPS Measures, enhance mutual understanding of each country's SPS rules, resolve future bilateral SPS disputes that arise, coordinate technical assistance programs, and consult on issues and positions in the WTO and other international bodies where SPS issues are considered. The text of the SPS chapter specifically states that neither the United States nor South Korea has recourse to pursue dispute settlement to address any SPS issue that arises. Instead, any matter will be resolved using the formal process established under the WTO's SPS Agreement.

U.S. beef producers had argued until the 2008 bilateral agreement was reached that Korea's stance on U.S. beef imports must be scientifically based upon internationally recognized guidelines issued by the World Organization for Animal Health, also known as OIE by its French acronym.[43] Other agricultural groups also have raised concerns about Korea's implementation of SPS measures on food additives and those that have restricted U.S. fruit and vegetable exports. This new standing committee potentially could be used as the venue to attempt to resolve future SPS disputes, taking into account latest available scientific findings and knowledge.

Automobiles

The final KORUS FTA modified the initial commitments on trade in automobiles in December 2010 and subsequently in an exchange of legal texts on February 10, 2011.[44] The Obama Administration claimed this was a necessary step in approval of the agreement because "the [original] U.S.-Korea trade agreement did not go far enough to provide new market access to U.S. auto companies and to level the playing field for U.S. auto manufacturers and workers."[45] The main components of the KORUS FTA specifically related to automotive trade include:

- *Elimination of South Korean tariffs on U.S.-made motor vehicles.* South Korea has reduced its 8% tariff on U.S.-built passenger cars, including electric vehicles and plug-in hybrids, to 4% and likewise has removed its 10% tariff on trucks.[46] Tariffs on U.S.-made motor vehicles, including electric cars and plug-in hybrids, will be phased out entirely in 2016.[47] In addition, each country dropped its duties to zero on virtually all auto parts imported from the other in 2012.[48]
- Elimination of U.S. tariffs on South Korean-made automobiles and a "snapback" clause. The United States will keep its passenger vehicle rate of 2.5% until the end of 2015. U.S. electric and fuel cell vehicle tariffs dropped to 2% in 2012 and will be reduced annually until duty free in 2016. The 25% duty on trucks, a residual rate dating from an earlier trade dispute with Europe, will stay in place through 2018 and will be duty-free beginning in 2022.49 The FTA, in Annex 22- A, also establishes a special bilateral dispute settlement panel, designed to resolve automotive issues within six months. If the panel finds a violation of an auto-related commitment or the nullification/impairment of expected benefits, the complaining Party may suspend its tariff concessions on passenger vehicles and assess duties at the prevailing MFN rate (i.e., 'snapback' any tariff reductions provided by the FTA)."[50] The final agreement does not extend the snapback to the higher 25% U.S. truck tariff. But measures affecting trucks could lead to the snapback of the 2.5% passenger car tariff. [51]
- *Reduction of alleged discriminatory effects of engine displacement taxes.* Automotive-specific taxes play an important role in determining the final price of a vehicle. U.S. automakers have complained that South Korea's steeply ascending vehicle tax schedule, with very high rates on vehicles with larger engine capacities that might be exported by U.S. producers, makes U.S. imported cars more expensive than smaller South Korean cars. Moreover, the tax system has a "cascade" effect, so that subsequent taxation rates also incorporate the duty paid on an imported vehicle. A special consumption tax, an educational tax, a value-added tax, a registration tax, and a subway bond are currently among the taxes that apply to motor vehicles. As part of the KORUS FTA, the Korean government agreed to simplify and reduce the taxes imposed on each category of passenger vehicles. They also agreed to eliminate the discrepancy in the rates between imported and domestic vehicles by reducing the tax rate for vehicles in the largest engine-displacement-size categories. [52]
- Improved regulatory transparency for new automotive regulations. South Korea also committed to an improvement in its regulatory process. U.S. auto companies will be given one year between the time a final regulation relating to autos is issued and when U.S. automakers must comply with the new regulation. In addition, South Korea agreed to develop a new post-implementation review system within two years after the agreement takes effect to ensure that existing auto regulations are applied in the least burdensome manner possible.
- *Regulations on harmonization of automotive safety and environmental standards.* U.S. manufacturers have long complained that South Korea sets automotive safety and environmental regulations in a closed and non-transparent manner. This results in standards idiosyncratic to South Korea. As one remedy, the KORUS FTA provides for self-certification to U.S. federal safety standards for a limited number of U.S.-exported vehicles raising the ceiling to 25,000 per automaker per year.[53] Further, the agreement permits some flexibility in meeting new, higher South Korean

environmental standards.[54] U.S. automakers will be considered in compliance with new South Korean fuel economy or greenhouse gas emissions standards if "they meet a target level that is 19% more lenient than the relevant target level provided in the regulation that would otherwise be applicable to that manufacturer."[55] This provision applies to U.S. carmakers that sold fewer than 4,500 cars in South Korea in calendar year 2009.

- *Creation of an "Automotive Working Group."* The KORUS FTA established an Automotive Working Group, which should meet at least annually, and will review and resolve "issues with respect to developing, implementing, and enforcing relevant standards, technical regulations, and conformity assessment procedures."[56]
- *Inclusion of a Special Motor Vehicle Safeguard.* The KORUS FTA includes a special safeguard for motor vehicles to ensure that the U.S. auto industry is not hurt owing to any "harmful surges" in South Korea auto imports. The new auto-specific safeguard provision allows the United States to impose extra duties if there is an import surge due to the trade agreement. Any higher tariff that might be imposed could be applied for four years. In the case of truck tariffs, the auto safeguard could be in place until 2031 as it is allowed to continue for 10 years after the full elimination of tariffs. Another feature of the safeguard is that it can be applied to a particular auto product more than once in the event of a recurring surge that causes serious injury to U.S. production of that product. It appears easier to apply the safeguard if there are complaints because, as a White House fact sheet notes, "fewer procedural steps are required to speed up the application of the safeguard when workers need faster relief."[57]

The KORUS FTA will not affect the hundreds of thousands of cars assembled by South Korean automakers in the United States and their U.S. production capacity is poised to grow. Thus, a surge in automobile imports from South Korea seems unlikely in the next few years. GM Korea,[58] the South Korean arm of U.S. automaker GM, has manufactured over 100,000 cars in South Korea every year since 2005. See **Appendix** for an overview of South Korea's motor vehicle manufacturing industry.

The USITC simulation model of the KORUS FTA estimates that while U.S. automotive exports to South Korea will increase by a range of 45% to 59%, this will only amount to about $300 million-$400 million because of the low current baseline.[59] It states that tariff elimination "would likely have a positive effect on U.S. exports ... further, the overall tax burden on the South Korean consumer who purchases an imported vehicle would be reduced, more or less equalizing the total taxes paid on imported and domestic vehicles."[60] It particularly emphasizes the potential gain for U.S.-exported hybrid vehicles to South Korea. Whether this will eventually happen remains uncertain. Most hybrids in the U.S. market today are imported from Japan.[61] The Toyota Prius, accounted for more than half, or 136,500, of all hybrid electric vehicles sold in the United States in 2011. Hyundai's Sonata hybrid, the first South Korean hybrid sold in the United States, represented 7% of all such vehicles sold in 2011 to become the second best-selling gas-electric in the United States. Combined, the Detroit-based U.S. manufacturers have increased their hybrid electric vehicle sales in recent years, rising from 0 in 2003 to around 40,000 in 2011. [62]

Alongside hybrids, Hyundai and Kia seem to be considering the development of pickup trucks that could be sold in the U.S. market, although whether they will be produced, and where (in the United States or South Korea), in the near future remains unclear.[63] Hyundai and Kia do already produce small pickup-type vehicles in South Korea, but they would not appear to be suitable in design or style for the United States.[64]

Textiles and Apparel

Textiles and apparel are a small and dwindling portion of U.S. manufactured imports from South Korea. Their respective shares of the U.S. market have fallen in relative and absolute terms. South Korea provided 3% of textiles imported by the United States in 2012, compared with 10% in 1990. Purchases of garments by the United States from South Korea dropped to less than 1% of all apparel imports in 2012, from 10% in 1990. This decrease is largely the result of the surge in U.S. apparel imports from China, which accounted for nearly 40% of all U.S. apparel imports in 2012, from 14% in 1990. The United States exports small volumes of textiles and apparel to South Korea—about $260 million and less than $100 million in 2012, respectively. [65]

The KORUS FTA eliminated U.S. tariffs immediately on 52% (in terms of value) of U.S. imports of South Korean textiles and apparel, and will phase out U.S. tariffs on 19% by 2016 and on the remaining 21% by the end of 2021.[66] Currently, the average U.S. MFN tariff on textiles is 7.9% with a maximum applied tariff of 42%. The average applied U.S. MFN tariff on apparel imports is 11.7% with a maximum tariff of 32%.[67]

The KORUS FTA eliminates South Korean tariffs on 77% (by value) of U.S. exports of textiles and apparel in 2012, then will phase out tariffs on 13% over the next three years and the remaining 10% by 2016.[68] The average South Korean applied tariff on textiles is 9.1% with a maximum of 13%. South Korean tariffs on apparel range from 8% to 13% [69]

The KORUS FTA, with some exceptions, uses the yarn-forward rule of origin for apparel imports; that is, apparel made from yarn or fabric originating in either the United States or South Korea would be eligible for duty-free treatment under the FTA. Also included is a special safeguard provision whereby, if imports of textiles or garments to one KORUS FTA partner country from the other increases at such a rate as to cause or threaten to cause serious injury to the domestic industry of the importing country, the importing country can suspend further reduction of tariffs, or it can increase the duty on the imported product to (the lesser of) the MFN rate applicable at the time the action was taken or the MFN duty that was in force when the FTA went into effect. The safeguard action can be in place for two years with a possible extension of two years, but no more than a total of four years. However, the importing country will have to compensate the exporting country by making additional trade liberalizing concessions equivalent in value to the additional duties expected to result from the safeguard action. The concessions will be limited to textiles and apparel unless the two countries agree otherwise.

The USITC has estimated that the KORUS FTA will over time lead to an increase in U.S. imports of South Korean textiles of $1.7 billion to $1.8 billion and of apparel of $1 billion to $1.2 billion, with the major portion of the increase being diverted from other countries. The USITC also has estimated that the KORUS FTA will lead to an increase in U.S. exports of textiles of $130 million to $140 million and of apparel of $39 million to $45 million to South Korea.[70]

The KORUS FTA will allow some fibers, yarns, and fabrics originating outside the United States and South Korea to become eligible for preferential treatment if the product is not available domestically in commercial quantities in either country. The agreement also provides for the establishment of a Committee on Textile and Apparel Trade Matters to raise concerns under the FTA regarding mutual trade in these products. Absent is a cumulation-specific rule, which, in other trade preference programs and FTAs, allows preferential treatment for limited amounts of apparel woven from components outside the FTA area.

Other Manufactured Goods

Beyond the automotive sector and textiles and apparel, the KORUS FTA affects a wide range of other industries.

Capital Goods Machinery and Equipment

U.S. machinery exports could be the largest single sectoral gainer from the KORUS FTA. According to the USITC's simulation analysis, the sector stands to gain nearly $3 billion in exports of products such as U.S.-made computer-numerically controlled machine tools.[71] The tariffs on U.S. machinery and equipment imported into South Korea range from 3% to 13%, but U.S. products are often competitive and the United States runs an annual trade surplus in machinery products. Most machinery tariffs have been eliminated; others will be phased out between 2014 and 2021.[72] Already duty-free before the implementation of the KORUS FTA, aircraft is another major capital goods item in which the United States has a strong bilateral trade position. U.S. exports to South Korea of aircraft products and parts totaled $3.6 billion in 2012.[73] The U.S. Commercial Service reports that Korea is the 11th largest market for U.S. aerospace exports. Recently, South Korea has embarked on making its aerospace sector more competitive. It intends to raise domestic aerospace production to $20 billion by 2020 from $2 billion in 2009, to establish a strong aircraft production industry to supply Boeing, EADS-Airbus, and to support maintenance of both commercial and military aircraft.[74]

Electronic Products and Components

Because they are parties to the multilateral Information Technology Agreement eliminating tariffs among more than 70 countries, South Korean and U.S. tariffs on most electronics products including semiconductors, telecommunications equipment, and computers were duty-free before the implementation of the KORUS FTA. The few remaining tariffs on U.S. electronics exports such as radio and television parts, certain static converters, and certain telecommunications apparatus—most of which were at 8% prior to March 15, 2012—will be eliminated as of 2014. In 2012, the United States ran a trade deficit in computer and electronic products with South Korea of $6.4 billion, compared with $10.4 billion in 2011. The U.S. trade deficit with South Korea in semiconductors and other electronic components totaled $410 million in 2012, dropping from a record high of $3 billion in 2010.[75] Besides tariffs, the KORUS FTA can provide improvements for U.S. products in South Korea with respect to intellectual property protection, technical barriers, government procurement, and competition policy.[76]

Steel

Steel products represent a significant share of trade between the United States and South Korea. In 2012, South Korea was the 6th largest U.S. export partner in steel products and the 5th largest source of overseas steel imports. [77] South Korea's steel industry is a global player and includes South Korean Pohang Iron and Steel Company (POSCO), the fourth-largest steel producer in the world. The United States ran a record high steel products trade deficit with South Korea of $2.7 billion in 2012.

The American steel industry registered a strongly negative position on the KORUS FTA, raising various objections related to trade remedies, rules of origin provisions, the treatment of products being produced in the Kaesong Industrial Complex of North Korea, and concerns about currency manipulation issues. The specific details of the trade remedies chapter and Kaesong are discussed elsewhere in this report.

Pharmaceuticals and Medical Devices

While pharmaceuticals and medical devices (P&M) are a relatively small part of U.S.-South Korean trade, they are products in which U.S. producers compete well in the South Korean market and ones in which manufacturers see increasing export opportunities as the South Korean economy matures. For years, the U.S. industry and government have complained about a number of South Korea's pharmaceutical policies that allegedly are designed to protect South Korean industry, which predominately produces generic drugs.

South Korea is among the world's top 12 largest markets for pharmaceuticals, accounting for about $8 billion in sales annually.[78] The South Korean market for medical devices accounts for roughly $2.5 billion in sales annually and is expected to grow 10%-15% each year in the next several years, in part due to the rapid aging of the population.[79] While potentially lucrative, South Korea is a market in which U.S. P&M manufactures claim government regulations have limited their ability to penetrate that market.

In 2010, the United States exported $538 million in medical equipment and supplies to South Korea, accounting for 2.1% of total U.S. exports of those products and 1.7% of total U.S. manufactured exports to South Korea. In 2010, the United States exported $825 million in pharmaceuticals and medicines to South Korea accounting for 1.7% of total U.S. exports of pharmaceuticals and 2.1% of total U.S. merchandise exports to South Korea.[80] In the same year South Korea exported $197.3 million in medical equipment and supplies and $80.9 million in pharmaceuticals to the United States.

Of major concern was the South Korean government's May 2006 change in how it determined reimbursement amounts. Prior to the change, it maintained a "negative list" system, under which products would be eligible for reimbursement unless they appeared on the list. With the change, the South Korean government switched to a "positive list" requiring a product to be listed before it would be eligible making it potentially more difficult for a product to become eligible. Announcement of the policy came without prior notification to U.S. officials or affected U.S. manufacturers and occurred at an early point in the negotiations placing a cloud over them. Despite complaints from the United States, South Korea went ahead with implementing its positive list system.

P&M manufacturers also have cited the South Korean government's policies on reimbursements for pharmaceuticals and medical devices under its single-payer health insurance program. U.S. manufacturers have argued that the policies discriminate against innovative pharmaceuticals because they establish relatively low reimbursement amounts for medicines thus not taking into account the costs that producers of leading-edge pharmaceuticals incur and that are reflected in higher prices. The manufacturers wanted the KORUS FTA to establish transparency as an important principal in South Korea's development and implementation of pricing and reimbursement policies, including an appeal process for decisions going against U.S. manufacturers.

In response, South Korea agreed in the KORUS FTA to allow U.S. pharmaceutical makers to apply for increased reimbursement levels based on safety and efficacy. South Korea also agreed to publish proposed laws, regulations, and procedures that apply to the pricing, reimbursement, and regulation of pharmaceuticals and medical devices in a nationally available publication and to allow time for comment. In addition, South Korea agreed to establish a process for U.S. manufacturers to comment on proposed changes in laws and regulations and for them to obtain a review of administrative determinations that adversely affect them. However, the Pharmaceuticals Research and Manufacturers of America (PhRMA) has not fully implemented its commitments. USTR indicated that it is working with the South Korean to establish a date for the first meeting of the binational Medicines Committee to resolve outstanding issues.[81]

Intellectual property rights protection in South Korea has been a critical issue for U.S. pharmaceutical manufacturers. Specifically, the failure of the South Korean government to protect from competitors proprietary data that manufacturers must submit for market approval. In addition, the South Korean government has, in some cases, approved marketing of some pharmaceuticals before it has determined that the applicant is the rightful owner of the patent and trademark.[82]

In response, under the KORUS FTA's data exclusivity provisions, South Korea would not allow a third company, such as a generic drug manufacturer, from marketing a new pharmaceutical using the safety and efficacy data, supplied by an original U.S. manufacturer as part of the market approval process, without the permission of the original U.S. maker for five years from the date of marketing approval for the original product. In addition, if a third party submits safety or efficacy information for a product that an FTA partner government had already approved, the government is to notify the original patent holder of the identity of the third party and is to prevent the marketing of the third party's product on its territory if permission had not been granted by the original patent holder. In a side letter, the United States and South Korea originally agreed to not invoke the data exclusivity provision until the FTA has been in effect 18 months. Under the modifications to the commitments, the United States agreed to double to 36 months, or three years, the time South Korea will have to put in place a system of patent linkages for pharmaceuticals that is required under the FTA. Furthermore, South Korea agreed to a patent-linkage system; that is, neither government is to approve the marketing of a generic drug while the original patent is still in effect. Another provision, known as patent-term extension, would require each FTA government to adjust the length of the effective period for patents on pharmaceuticals to take into account delays incurred in receiving patent approval and marketing approval. The KORUS FTA states that no provision would prevent either government from taking measures to protect the public health of its residents from HIV/AID, tuberculosis, malaria, and other epidemics, by ensuring access to medicines. The FTA would reaffirm each country's commitment to the WTO TRIPS/health Declaration.

Reactions within the pharmaceutical and medical devices industries were somewhat split on the KORUS FTA. Makers of innovative products supported the provisions that are designed to preserve the rights of patent holders and provisions that are designed to make the South Korean regulatory, pricing, and reimbursement process more transparent and open to comments and procedural reviews. At the same time, industry representatives remained critical of South Korea's new reimbursement procedures and argued that the new system does not take into account the benefits of innovative drugs that cause drug prices to be higher. Generic drug manufacturers argue that the KORUS FTA does not contain provisions guaranteeing the availability of affordable drugs.[83] While pharmaceuticals and medical devices (P&M) are a relatively small part of U.S.-South Korean trade, they are products in which U.S. producers compete well in the South Korean market. U.S. manufacturers also see increasing export opportunities as the South Korean economy matures. For years, the U.S. industry and government have complained about a number of South Korea's pharmaceutical policies that allegedly are designed to protect South Korean industry, which predominately produces generic drugs.

Overseas sales are critical to the U.S. pharmaceutical industry; some U.S. multinational firms generate revenues of 40% or higher in foreign markets.[84] South Korea is the 5th largest market in Asia, with pharmaceutical sales at an estimated $15.4 billion in 2011. By 2016, its market is projected to grow to around $24 billion.[85] Although South Korea's pharmaceutical sector is the fast-growing developed country market, according to IMS Healthcare, it currently represents less than 2% of the global pharmaceutical market.[86]

South Korea is also an important market for U.S. medical equipment and device manufacturers valued at an estimated $3.7 billion in 2011[87] and could grow 10%-15% each year in the next several years, partly due to a rapidly aging population.[88] While potentially lucrative, South Korea is a market in which U.S. P&M manufactures claim government regulations have limited their ability to penetrate that market.

The United States sold $995 million in pharmaceuticals and medicines to South Korea in 2012, representing around 2% of all U.S. exports of pharmaceuticals to South Korea.[89] Exports of medical equipment and supplies to South Korea totaled $525 million in 2012, accounting for less than 2% of total U.S. exports of medical equipment to South Korea. In the same year, the United States ran trade surpluses with South Korea in both pharmaceuticals and medical equipment and supplies.

Of major concern during the KORUS FTA negotiations was the South Korean government's May 2006 change in how it determined reimbursement amounts. Prior to the change, it maintained a "negative list" system, under which products would be eligible for reimbursement unless they appeared on the list. With the change, the South Korean government switched to a "positive list" requiring a product to be listed before it would be eligible making it potentially more difficult for a product to become eligible. Announcement of the policy came without prior notification to U.S. officials or affected U.S. manufacturers and occurred at an early point in the negotiations placing a cloud over them. Despite complaints from the United States, South Korea went ahead with implementing its positive list system.

P&M manufacturers also cited the South Korean government's policies on reimbursements for pharmaceuticals and medical devices under its single-payer health insurance program. U.S. manufacturers argued that the policies discriminate against innovative pharmaceuticals because they establish relatively low reimbursement amounts for medicines thus not taking into account the costs that producers of leading-edge pharmaceuticals incur and that are reflected in higher prices. U.S. manufacturers wanted the

KORUS FTA to establish transparency as an important principal in South Korea's development and implementation of pricing and reimbursement policies, including an appeal process for decisions going against U.S. manufacturers.

In response to these concerns, South Korea agreed in the KORUS FTA to allow U.S. pharmaceutical makers to apply for increased reimbursement levels based on safety and efficacy. South Korea also agreed to publish proposed laws, regulations, and procedures that apply to the pricing, reimbursement, and regulation of pharmaceuticals and medical devices in a nationally available publication and to allow time for comment. In addition, South Korea agreed to establish a process for U.S. manufacturers to comment on proposed changes in laws and regulations and for them to obtain a review of administrative determinations that adversely affect them. Intellectual property rights protection in South Korea has been a critical issue for U.S. pharmaceutical manufacturers. Specifically, the failure of the South Korean government to protect from competitors proprietary data that manufacturers must submit for market approval. In addition, the South Korean government has, in some cases, approved marketing of some pharmaceuticals before it has determined that the applicant is the rightful owner of the patent and trademark.[90]

In response, under the KORUS FTA's data exclusivity provisions, South Korea will not allow a third company, such as a generic drug manufacturer, from marketing a new pharmaceutical using the safety and efficacy data, supplied by an original U.S. manufacturer as part of the market approval process, without the permission of the original U.S. maker for five years from the date of marketing approval for the original product. In addition, if a third party submits safety or efficacy information for a product that an FTA partner government had already approved, the government is to notify the original patent holder of the identity of the third party and is to prevent the marketing of the third party's product on its territory if permission had not been granted by the original patent holder. In a side letter, the United States and South Korea originally agreed to not invoke the data exclusivity provision until the FTA has been in effect 18 months. Under the modifications to the commitments, the United States agreed to double to 36 months, or three years, the time South Korea will have to put in place a system of patent linkages for pharmaceuticals that is required under the FTA. Furthermore, South Korea agreed to a patent-linkage system; that is, neither government is to approve the marketing of a generic drug while the original patent is still in effect. Another provision, known as patent-term extension, requires the United States and South Korea to adjust the length of the effective period for patents on pharmaceuticals to take into account delays incurred in receiving patent approval and marketing approval. The KORUS FTA states that no provision would prevent either government from taking measures to protect the public health of its residents from HIV/AID, tuberculosis, malaria, and other epidemics, by ensuring access to medicines. The FTA reaffirms each country's commitment to the WTO TRIPS/health Declaration.

Financial and Other Services

U.S. service providers exported $16.8 billion in services to South Korea in 2011. Among them were South Koreans' travel to the United States ($3.8 billion); other transportation, such as freight services ($2.1 billion); royalties and license fees ($4.5 billion); and other private services, such as professional services, business services, banking, insurance, and other financial services ($6.1 billion).[91] However, this amount probably undervalues the total volume of U.S. sales of services to South Korea as services are also sold through three other modes of delivery: by U.S. companies with a long-term presence in South Korea, by U.S. providers to South Korean residents located temporarily in the United States, and by U.S. providers temporarily located in South Korea.

In 2011, the United States imported $11.0 billion in services, including other transportation ($2.4 billion), U.S. travel to South Korea ($1.7 billion), expenditures by U.S. military ($2.6 billion), and other travel ($1.7 billion).[92] This figure does not include services sold to U.S. residents by South Korean firms through the other modes of delivery.

U.S.-South Korean trade in services cuts across several chapters of the KORUS FTA—Chapter 12 (cross-border trade in services); chapter 13 (financial services); and Chapter 15 (telecommunications); chapter 11 (foreign investment); among others. A major U.S. objective in the KORUS FTA negotiations was to obtain South Korean commitments to reduce barriers to trade and investment in its services sector, especially in professional, financial, and telecommunications services.

In general the two countries committed to:

- provide national treatment and most-favored-nation treatment to the services imports from each other;
- promote transparency in the development and implementation of regulations in services providing timely notice of decisions on government permission to sell services;
- prohibit limits on market access, such as a caps on the number of service providers, on the total value of services provided, on the total quantity of services provided, and on the total number of persons that can be employed by services providers;
- prohibit foreign direct investment requirements, such as export and local content requirements and employment mandates; and
- prohibit restrictions on the type of business entity through which a service provider could provide a service.

U.S. and South Korean negotiators agreed to several concepts under the KORUS FTA that could apply the agreements' provisions to a broad scope of services. The two countries agreed to the "negative list" approach in making commitments in services. That is, the KORUS FTA is to apply to all types of services unless identified as an exception in the relevant annexes. In addition, the commitments are ratcheted—when new services emerge in the U.S. or South Korean economies, those services are automatically covered by the FTA unless identified as an exception; if either country unilaterally liberalizes a measure that it had listed as an exemption, it is automatically covered under the FTA. Furthermore, if one KORUS FTA partner extends preferential treatment to service providers from a third country under another FTA, it is to extend the preferential treatment to its KORUS FTA partner.

The United States sought greater reciprocity in the treatment of *professional services* and thereby gain increased access to the South Korean market for U.S. providers. The United States and South Korea agreed to form a professional services working group to develop methods to recognize mutual standards and criteria for the licensing of professional service providers. Under the KORUS FTA, South Korea will allow U.S. law firms and U.S. licensed attorneys to provide advisory services on U.S. and international law on entry into force of the

KORUS FTA. South Korea will also permit U.S. legal representative offices to establish cooperative operations with a South Korean firm to handle matters pertaining to domestic and foreign legal matters, and, no later than five years after the agreement's entry into force, will allow U.S. law firms to form joint ventures with South Korean firms. However, South Korea will still reserve the right to restrict the activities of foreign lawyers.

Regarding *financial services*, under the KORUS FTA, if a domestic provider in one partner country develops and sells a new financial service in its home market, providers from the FTA partner country will be able to sell a like service in that market. The agreement will allow an FTA partner government to impose restrictions on the sale of financial services by providers from the other partner country for prudential reasons, for example, to protect investors, depositors, policy holders, or persons to whom a fiduciary duty is owed. The FTA will also permit either partner government to restrict monetary transfers in order to ensure the soundness of financial institutions.

The South Korean *insurance* market is the seventh-largest in the world. The USITC estimates, therefore, that U.S. insurers will be poised to obtain sizeable gains in a liberalized South Korean services market.[93] U.S. insurance companies have been concerned that the state-owned Korea Post and the cooperative insurance providers—the National Agricultural Cooperative Federation and the National Federation of Fisheries Cooperative—are not regulated by the Korean Financial Supervisory Commission or by the Financial Supervisory Service, while both private-sector foreign and domestic providers are so regulated.[94] Under the KORUS FTA, South Korea agreed that those entities will be subject to an independent state regulator as opposed to being selfregulated.[95] In addition, Korea Post will not be allowed to offer new insurance products. The two countries will allow a partner country financial services provider to transfer electronically information from its territory as necessary in the course of doing business.[96] This is a provision that the U.S. industry highlighted as being particularly important.

In *telecommunications services*, South Korea will reduce government restrictions on foreign ownership of South Korean telecommunications companies. Two years after the KORUS FTA enters into force, U.S. companies will be able to own up to 100% of voting shares in domestic South Korean telecommunications companies, and those companies will be able to own up to 100% of a facilities-based licensee.[97] These provisions do not apply to KT Corporation nor to SK Telecom Co for which a 49% foreign ownership limit will remain. In addition, each KORUS FTA partner will ensure that telecommunications providers from the other would have access to and use of its public telecommunications network for purposes of interconnection under nondiscriminatory conditions and will guarantee dialing portability among other conditions.[98]

Those who represent U.S. services providers were enthusiastic about the KORUS FTA and urged its approval. In a statement, Robert Vastine, then-president of the Coalition of Services Industries claimed:

> We commend Ambassador Schwab and the team of negotiators who secured significant benefits for U.S. services providers in this agreement.... Korea is a key market for U.S. service companies, and this is a very high-quality agreement that merits swift passage by the Congress because it creates new commercial opportunities that will support new jobs.[99]

Visas

For years, a priority for South Korea has been to convince the United States to ease restrictions on the issuance of visas for South Korean business representatives. The visa issue—along with South Korea's request to be added to the Visa Waiver program (VWP), which allows visa free travel for short-term visitors—was addressed in discussions outside of the KORUS FTA negotiations. On October 17, 2008, President Bush announced that South Korea was one of seven countries that would be admitted into the program in 4-6 weeks.[100] With this step, the VWP is likely to no longer be an issue in bilateral relations. South Korea is one of the United States' largest sources of foreign visitors. In FY2007 there were 811,251 short-term visitors for business or pleasure from South Korea.[101]

On a separate track, as part of the package of modifications agreed to on December 3, 2010, the United States agreed to extend the initial validity period of L-1A visas for South Korean nationals. These visas are used by foreigners entering the United States to work at U.S.-subsidiary of a foreign company. One group of these visas are used for foreigners coming to establish a U.S. subsidiary and the initial validity period was extended from one to five years. A second group is used for foreigners coming to work at an already established subsidiary and the initial validity period was extended from three to five years.[102]

General Provisions

The KORUS FTA text contains a number of provisions that cut across in many sectors in bilateral trade. Many of these provisions have become standard fare and have become part of the template for FTAs in which the United States participates.

Trade Remedies[103]

Trade remedies, laws, and actions designed to provide relief to domestic industries that have been injured or threatened with injury by imports, are regarded by many in Congress as an important trade policy tool to mitigate the adverse effects of lower priced imports on U.S. industries and workers.

The three most commonly used trade remedies are *antidumping* (AD), *countervailing duty* (CVD), and *safeguard* actions. Antidumping (19 U.S.C. §1673 *et seq.*) actions provide relief from the adverse impact of imports sold at prices shown to be less than fair market value, and countervailing duty (19 U.S.C. §1671 *et seq.*) actions provide similar relief from goods that have been subsidized by a foreign government or other public entity. Safeguard actions (19 U.S.C. §2251 *et seq.*) are designed to give domestic industries an opportunity to adjust to new competition and are triggered by import surges of fairly traded goods. The relief provided in a safeguard case is a temporary import duty, temporary import quota, or a combination of both, while the relief in an antidumping or countervailing duty action is an additional duty placed on the dumped or subsidized imports. These actions are authorized by the WTO as long as they are consistent with the rights and obligations of Article XIX of the General Agreement on Tariffs and Trade (GATT) 1994, the WTO Agreement on Safeguards and Countervailing Measures (Subsidies Agreement), and the WTO Agreement on Implementation of Article VI of the GATT 1994 (Antidumping Agreement).[104]

Many Members of Congress have expressed support for maintaining and strengthening U.S. trade remedy laws in the face of growing import competition. As a result, the preservation of U.S. authority to "enforce rigorously its trade laws" was a principal negotiating objective included in presidential Trade Promotion Authority (TPA) in the 107th Congress.[105]

According to news reports, the "single most important South Korean demand" in the bilateral talks was changes to U.S. antidumping rules.[106] This may be due, in part, to the significant number of U.S. trade remedy cases brought by U.S. industries on South Korean goods. As of February 12, 2010, antidumping duties were being collected on 12 South Korean imports (mostly on stainless steel specialty products such wire rod and pipe fittings), and countervailing duties were being assessed on 3 South Korean products, while South Korea had no trade remedy measures in place against U.S. products.[107] The U.S. global safeguard cases imposed on steel in February 2000 (line pipe) and March 2002 (many steel products) also significantly reduced South Korean steel imports to the United States.[108] Of the 14 WTO dispute resolution complainant cases South Korea has brought to date, 8 have been disputes against U.S. trade remedy actions.[109] South Korea is also a member "Friends of Antidumping" group in the WTO Doha Round that insists on implementing changes to the Antidumping and Subsidies Agreements in any new multilateral agreement.

In the bilateral negotiations between the United States and South Korea, talks broke down in early December 2006 when South Korea presented the United States with a list of specific changes to U.S. antidumping laws on a "basically" take-it-or-leave-it basis,[110] but in mid-January 2007, South Korean officials softened their stance after accepting the assurances of U.S. negotiators that Trade Promotion Authority had granted the Bush Administration only limited flexibility to make concessions on trade remedy issues.[111]

The KORUS FTA, just as in earlier FTAs the United States has entered into, indicates that each party to the agreement will retain all rights and obligations under the WTO agreements—meaning that the trading partners will be permitted to include each other in global safeguard actions (although, as in other FTAs, it does extend a possible exemption from global safeguard measures to either party if its imports are not a substantial cause of serious injury) and to implement AD and CVD actions against each other. Additionally, as in earlier FTAs, the trade remedies article also authorizes either party to the agreement to apply a transitional safeguard measure against imports of the other party if, as the result of the reduction or elimination of a duty mandated by the agreement, a product is being imported in increased quantities as to be a substantial cause of serious injury to a domestic industry that produces a like or directly competitive good.[112]

In the case of a safeguard, the party imposing it must provide a mutually agreed-upon amount of compensation. If the parties do not agree, the other party may suspend concessions on imports of the other party in an amount that has trade effects substantially equivalent to the safeguard measure.[113]

As such, the agreement does not require any changes to U.S. AD or CVD laws, or regulations. However, in an apparent departure from previous FTAs, the KORUS FTA seems to require a few additional administrative steps prior to initiation of a trade remedy investigation involving goods from the other party. First, each party will have to notify the other if an antidumping petition is received regarding the other party's imports, as well as provide an opportunity for a meeting between the parties before an investigation is initiated.[114] Additionally, the party initiating an AD or CVD investigation will be required to provide written information regarding its procedures for negotiating a price or quantity undertaking (known in U.S. law as a suspension agreement),[115] and, after a preliminary affirmative determination is reached, "provide due consideration and adequate opportunity for consultations regarding proposed price undertakings" which could result in suspension of the investigation without imposition of duties provided a mutually agreeable undertaking is reached.[116]

The KORUS FTA will also establish a Committee on Trade Remedies (which is to meet at least once a year) made up of representatives from each party who has responsibility for trade remedies matters. Committee functions include enhancing knowledge of the parties' trade remedy laws and practices, overseeing the implementation of the trade remedies chapter of the agreement, improving cooperation between the parties, developing educational programs on trade remedy laws, and providing a forum for exchange of information on trade remedies and other topics of mutual interest.[117]

As discussed earlier, the Industry Trade Advisory Committee on Steel (ITAC 12) believes that the procedural concessions made on trade remedies could politicize trade remedy actions, thus possibly weakening U.S. trade laws. In particular, the ITAC 12 stated that the U.S. AD-CVD investigative process is already transparent and that the pre-initiation notification and consultation requirements will delay and politicize the process.[118] It also objected to the "undertakings" provisions, saying that these provisions will encourage the use of suspension agreements and introduce actions of foreign governments into trade remedy procedures.[119] (For more information on the steel industry's reaction, see discussion in section on "Other Manufactured Goods.)

The ITAC 12 also opposed the establishment of a Committee on Trade Remedies, saying that it such a forum will give South Korea an opportunity to attempt to further try to weaken U.S. trade remedy laws.[120] Speaking in April 2007, Assistant U.S. Trade Representative for Korea, Japan, and APEC Wendy Cutler, the chief U.S. negotiator, implied that the consultative committee will focus on information sharing and "will not provide a forum to discuss specific cases."[121] She also mentioned that the committee could be a benefit to the United States by providing a platform for discussing certain industrial subsidies that the South Korean government may be supplying to manufacturing firms, and that negotiators worked out an "accommodation" that was beneficial to both sides' needs on a very contentious part of the negotiations.[122]

Kaesong Industrial Complex[123]

A consistent and significant goal for South Korea in the FTA talks was securing preferential treatment for products made in the Kaesong Industrial Complex (KIC) in North Korea, a position the United States adamantly opposed throughout most of the negotiations. Located near the North Korean city of Kaesong (also spelled "Gaesong"), 40 miles north of Seoul, the KIC is designed for South Korean companies to employ North Korean workers. As of the end of 2010, over 120 medium-sized South Korean companies were employing over 47,000 North Korean workers to manufacture products in Kaesong. The facility, which in 2010 produced $323 million in output, has the land and infrastructure to house two to three times as many firms and workers. Products vary widely, and include clothing and textiles (71 firms), kitchen utensils (4 firms), auto parts (4 firms), semiconductor parts (2 firms), and toner cartridges (1 firm).

The KIC has generated controversy because it provides an ongoing revenue stream to the Kim Jong-il regime in Pyongyang, by virtue of the share the government takes from the salaries paid to North Korean workers. South Korean and U.S. officials estimate this revenue stream to be around $20 million per year. On the other hand, the KIC arguably helps maintain stability on the Peninsula and provides a possible beachhead for market reforms in the DPRK that could eventually spill over to areas outside the park and expose tens of thousands of North Koreans to outside influences, market-oriented businesses, and incentives.

In the final KORUS FTA agreement, the two sides reached a compromise on the KIC. On the one hand, the agreement does not include any reference to the complex, and KIC products are not eligible for the agreement's special treatment provisions.[124] On the other hand, a binational committee will be formed to study the possibility of eventually incorporating products from "Outward Processing Zones" (OPZs), including those—like the KIC—that are located in North Korea.[125] The agreement identifies three general categories for which the committee is to develop more detailed criteria: progress in the denuclearization of North Korea, developments in intraKorean relations; and wages, business management practices, the environment, and labor standards. For the third category of issues, the committee is to consider relevant international norms as well as the "situation prevailing elsewhere on the Peninsula." After the committee has developed criteria, the OPZ provisions in the FTA lay out a three- step process by which products made in the KIC could be incorporated into the FTA. First, the committee must deem that an outward processing zone meets the criteria it has established. Second, the two governments must agree that the FTA should be amended accordingly. Third, both governments must seek "legislative approval for any amendments to the Agreement with respect to outward processing zones." The agreement does not lay out the size or composition of the committee, or how committee members will be chosen, or the procedures by which the committee is to arrive at decisions, except that decisions would have to be reached by unified consent.[126]

For years, neither the Bush nor Obama Administrations specified what form "legislative approval" for OPZ-related amendments to the KORUS FTA would take. In March 2011, the office of the United States Trade Representative (USTR) issued a statement that Congress "would need to pass, and the President would need to sign, a law to extend any KORUS FTA tariff benefits to products made in Kaesong or any OPZ."[127]

Some observers, particularly many opponents of the KORUS FTA, argued that the agreement could lead to increased U.S. imports of goods or components made in North Korea. The scenario they suggest involves South Korean firms obtaining low-cost Kaesong-made goods or components, incorporating the latter into finished products such as electronics or automobiles, and then reshipping the goods to the United States with "Made in [South] Korea" labels. If the KORUS FTA were in effect, the argument runs, these goods might receive preferential treatment. However, a close analysis of the agreement and the nature of trade flows reveals that unless the KIC is brought into the KORUS FTA, the FTA would likely have only a marginal impact on whether the United States imports North Korean finished products or goods that contain North Korean components. Instead, the extent of the problem of North Korea imports will be largely determined by the degree to which North Korean producers become integrated into the global economy. In addition, imports from

North Korea require U.S. government approval. This restriction includes finished goods originating in North Korea as well as goods that contain North Korea-made components.

Another criticism of the KORUS FTA was that it could constrain the United States' ability to restrict imports of North Korean goods or components, for instance, by invoking the agreement's dispute settlement procedures to challenge a U.S. decision to prohibit the entry of a South Korean product that contains North Korean components. However, provisions in the KORUS-FTA will appear to allow either the United States or South Korea to impose or maintain trade restrictions against the goods of a third country (such as North Korea); thus the agreement will accord each Party the right to restrict trade with the other Party in implementing any such embargo.

In the KORUS FTA negotiations, the United States backed away from the principle of its initial position of not ever expanding the KORUS FTA to North Korea-made products, a significant achievement for South Korea. At the same time, the United States appeared to give up little in substance in the near-to-middle term. The United States apparently would be able to control the decision to and pace of any move to grant preferential treatment to North Korea-made products. Any perceptions of foot-dragging by the United States, however, may come at a diplomatic price if future South Korean governments push for more rapid integration of North Korean industrial zones into the FTA.

Foreign Investment

Foreign investment is becoming an increasingly significant element in the U.S.-South Korean bilateral economic relationship. Over the past decade, the stock of U.S.-South Korean foreign direct investment (FDI), valued on an historical cost basis, has increased substantially, due in no small part to the market-oriented reforms South Korea undertook after its 1997 financial crisis. In 1997, the value of stock of U.S. FDI in South Korea was $6.5 billion and had increased to $31.8 billion by the end of 2011 (latest data available). South Korean FDI in the United States has also increased substantially, albeit from a much lower base. In 1997, the stock of South Korean FDI in the United States was valued at $0.6 billion and had increased to $18.4 billion by the end of 2011 (latest data available).[128]

Foreign investment has been a sensitive issue in U.S.-South Korean relations for many years as U.S. investors have tried to make inroads into the South Korean economy. U.S. investors' criticisms have included restrictions on foreign investment in key sectors, such as communications, and the lack of adequate protection for intellectual property. (See section on "Intellectual Property Rights.") Efforts to establish bilateral rules have failed in the past. In the 1990s, the two countries tried to negotiate a bilateral investment treaty (BIT), that would commit each party to provide national treatment to the investments from the other party and abstain from performance requirements for foreign investments from the other party. But the negotiations collapsed largely over U.S opposition to South Korea's so-called screen quota on domestic films and the latter's resistance to lifting or reducing it. (The South Korean government reduced the screen quotas by half just before the KORUS FTA negotiations were launched in February 2006.) The KORUS FTA chapter on investment essentially contains the commitments that would otherwise have been in a BIT.

The FTA sets down general principles for the treatment by South Korea and the United States of investors and investments from one partner in the territory of the other.[129] The principle of national treatment—that one party to the agreement will treat covered investments and investors from the other party no-less favorably than it treats domestic investors and investments—is paramount. The FTA allows each party to make exceptions to the national treatment principle, but those exceptions must be specified in the relevant annexes to the agreement.[130] A second fundamental principal is most-favored-nation treatment (MFN)—the two parties agree to treat investors and investments from the other no less favorably than it treats investors and investments from third, non-party countries. A third principle is minimum standard of treatment, that is, each party shall accord to all covered investments treatment in accordance with customary international law, including fair and equitable treatment and full protection and security.

The KORUS FTA sets limits on government expropriation of covered investments—that they be only for public purpose and carried out in a non-discriminatory manner, and affected investors will be provided with prompt and adequate compensation (fair market value). It also requires each KORUS FTA partner-country government allow for the free transfer of financial capital pertaining to covered investments both into and out of the country with exceptions, such as cases related to criminal offenses. The KORUS FTA prohibits the U.S. and South Korean governments from imposing performance requirements (domestic content requirements, export-ratios, import limits, etc.) on the investments from the other. It will allow exceptions for measures intended to accomplish social objectives, such as to increase employment in certain regions of the country, promote training of workforce, and protect the environment. The agreement also prohibits a requirement that senior managers be of a particular nationality but will allow a requirement that the majority of board of directors be of a particular nationality.

Similar to other U.S. FTAs, the KORUS FTA establishes procedures for the settlement of investor-state disputes involving investments covered under the agreement where the investor from one partner-country alleges that the government of the other partner-country is violating his rights under the FTA. The FTA stipulates that the two parties should try to first resolve the dispute through consultations and negotiations. But, if that does not work, the agreement provides for arbitration procedures and the establishment of tribunals as provided under the "Convention on the Settlement of Investment Disputes Between States and Nationals of Other States."

The USITC concluded that U.S. investors, especially investors in financial services, would likely gain from the KORUS FTA.[131] (See section on "Financial and Other Services.") The United States has been the predominate partner in terms of foreign investment and stands to gain the most from the protections provided by the KORUS FTA. However, South Korean investments in the United States are increasing, and therefore, South Korea could benefit as well.

Intellectual Property Rights

In addition to those sections addressing pharmaceutical manufacturing (see discussion above), the KORUS FTA contains other provisions on intellectual property rights (IPR) protection in U.S.- South Korean trade. Under the FTA the United States and South Korea reaffirm their commitments under the WTO Trade-Related Aspects of Intellectual Property Rights (TRIPS) agreement and other international agreements and conventions on intellectual property. But the two countries made IPR commitments beyond those agreements with provisions that

- require each government to extend national treatment to IPR holders from the other country;[132]
- require transparency through the publication of regulations and laws regarding intellectual property rights;
- facilitate the registration of and protection of trademarks and established limitations on the use of geographical indications;
- ensure the right of authors, performers, producers of recordings to determine use of copyrighted products;
- require copyright protection for no less than 70 years; thus, South Korea agrees to extend its copyright protection term, an objective of U.S. copyright holders;
- protect copyrighted material against piracy and provide penalties for those who abet piracy including the seizure and destruction of pirated and counterfeit products;
- protect copyrighted performances on the internet; and
- protect encrypted programming over satellites and cable signals.

Labor Rights and Conditions

On May 10, 2007, a bipartisan group of congressional leaders and the Bush Administration released a statement that provided language to be included in pending FTAs, including KORUS FTA. Among other things, the statement, or framework, called "The New Trade Policy for America," requires U.S. FTA partners to commit to enforcing the five basic international labor standards and would require that the commitment be enforceable under the FTA.[133] Neither country is to waive or otherwise derogate from its labor statutes that reflect the five labor rights in a manner that affects trade or investment between the two FTA countries. Each country is to ensure that those affected by their respective labor laws have access to tribunals that enforce their rights under those laws. During his nomination process, USTR Ron Kirk stated the Obama Administration's position that the KORUS FTA appropriately incorporates the May 10th understanding.[134]

Under the KORUS FTA the two countries are to form a Labor Affairs Council made up of officials from the respective labor ministries and agencies, that is to meet within the first year after the agreement enters into force. At least one session of the council will be devoted to meeting with the public in each country to discuss matters related to the enforcement of the labor provisions of the FTA. Disputes regarding labor matters under the FTA are to be resolved first by consultations, but if those fail, the parties in dispute may take the matter to the Labor Council and eventually to a dispute settlement panel if these mechanisms fail to resolve the dispute. The KORUS FTA also calls for the establishment of a Labor Cooperation Mechanism whereby the two countries would develop and work in areas pertaining to labor rights in each country.

To many outside observers, South Korea's labor rights regime is generally considered to be strong for regular workers. South Korea ranks in the top third of the OECD's thirty members in terms of employment protection for regular workers.[135] Indeed, for years, a major complaint of U.S. multinationals is that restrictions in the South Korean labor market, such as mandatory severance pay, significantly raise the cost of investing and doing business in Korea. In contrast, U.S. union representatives argue that recent changes to make South Korean labor markets more flexible are reducing the rights of South Korean workers.[136] Korea's unions have earned a reputation for activism; the number of working days lost to strikes is regularly among the highest in the OECD. Hyundai Motors, for instance, has experienced a strike every year since 1994. Moreover, strikes in South Korea are notable in that they are sometimes accompanied by violence and the occupation of workplaces and public spaces (such as highways), to which the government often responds with police action. In its comments on the KORUS FTA, the Labor Advisory Committee for Trade Negotiations and Trade Policy (LAC), criticized South Korea for the imprisonment of around 200 unionists who were "exercising basic labor rights" and for mobilizing riot police against union activity.[137]

Korea's labor pool is divided into two segments: (1) South Korean "salarymen" (salaried workers, overwhelmingly men, in large corporations) comprise less than one-third of the workforce. Over half of this segment of the workforce is represented by powerful unions. (2) The remainder of the workforce is comprised of employees in small-scale firms plus the country's temporary and day laborers. Few of these workers are unionized. The proportion of temporary workers has grown markedly, to nearly one-third of the workforce, one of the highest rates in the industrialized world.[138] These workers tend to receive low wages and receive limited coverage by the social safety net, points highlighted by the LAC. Labor markets are notoriously rigid.

Government Procurement

A great deal of business is conducted by governments through the purchase of goods and services for their own use. Most governments, including the United States have laws (The Buy American Act) which require such goods and services to be of domestic origin. However, the General Agreement on Tariffs and Trade (GATT) and now the WTO have some provisions, the WTO Government Procurement Agreement (GPA), under which the countries agree to open up some of their government procurement business, to foreign companies as a way to promote trade. This agreement is plurilateral, that is it only applies to those WTO members that have signed it. The United States and South Korea are among the 41 signatories to the GPA. The GPA established rules for governments to publish information about contract tenders, including technical specification, about qualification for suppliers, the awarding of contracts, with a specific emphasis on nondiscrimination and transparency in the conduct of government procurement.

The KORUS FTA reaffirms the GPA as a baseline for government procurement but would expand the criteria to include more contracts. The GPA applies to contracts valued at around $203,000 and above. The KORUS FTA applies to contracts valued at $100,000 and above, potentially increasing the value of bilateral government-procurement trade. The GPA applies only to contracts tendered by 79 U.S. federal government agencies and by 42 South Korean central and subcentral agencies listed in the annex. Under the KORUS FTA, South Korea add ed nine more agencies to be covered.

Environment Protection

In keeping with the May 10, 2007, understanding on labor and the environment between the Bush Administration and congressional leaders, under the KORUS FTA, the United States and South Korea commit to enforce a list of seven multilateral environmental agreements to which both are parties and to add to the list when other agreements enter into force. (See the "Labor Rights and Conditions" section above.)[139] In addition, the FTA will prevent the two countries from easing environmental standards in order to allow firms on their territory from gaining a competitive trade advantage. Furthermore, violations of the environmental provisions are to be handled in the same manner as commercial provisions through the dispute settlement mechanism of the KORUS FTA and subject to trade sanctions, unprecedented for U.S. FTAs. As mentioned earlier, the Obama Administration has indicated that the May 10, 2007 agreement is incorporated into the KORUS FTA.[140]

Transparency

Making information publically available is a fundamental principle imbedded in international trade rules and in each of the FTAs that the United States has entered into. For years U.S. exporters and trade negotiators identified the lack of transparency of South Korea's trading and regulatory systems as one of the most significant barriers to trade with South Korea, in almost every major product sector. Under KORUS FTA, the United States and South Korea commit: to publish relevant regulations and administrative decisions as well as proposed regulations; to allow persons from the other party to make comments and to ask questions regarding proposed regulations; to notify such persons of administrative proceedings and to allow them make presentations before final administrative action is taken; and to allow such persons to request review and appeal of administrative decisions.

Institutional Provisions and Dispute Settlement

The KORUS FTA provides several options for the United States and South Korea to resolve disputes arising under the agreement, in addition to the special dispute settlement provisions under the foreign investment chapter and other chapters. KORUS FTA requires the two countries to establish a joint committee chaired by the USTR and the Minister of Foreign Trade or their designees to supervise the implementation of the agreement. The trade agreement provides for the establishment of a panel to adjudicate disputes between the two countries under the agreement, if consultations do not lead to a resolution of the dispute. Annex 22A of the KORUS FTA contains provisions for the settlement of disputes regarding motor vehicles, specifically the snap-back provision. (See discussion in section on "Automobiles") Annex 22-B provides for eventual discussion of the inclusion of products made in outward processing zones in North Korea. (For more information, see discussion in "Kaesong Industrial Complex" section.)

Other Technical Provisions

The KORUS FTA includes other sets of provisions intended to facilitate market access. *Technical barriers to trade* are standards and regulations that are intended ostensibly to protect the health and safety of consumers and for other legitimate non-trade purposes but may through design and implementation discriminate against imports. The KORUS FTA commits both countries to uphold their obligations under the WTO Agreement on Technical Barriers to Trade (TBT). In addition, South Korea and the United States will promote transparency, by allowing persons from the other party to participate in the development of standards, technical regulations, and conformity assessment procedures.

Regarding *customs administration and trade facilitation,* the KORUS FTA will promote joint cooperation to ensure compliance with each other's customs laws and regulations. For example, it requires the two countries to adopt procedures and regulations to facilitate express delivery shipments.

Rules of origin define what are goods that originate in the FTA region and therefore are eligible for preferential treatment. (Textiles and apparel have separate rules of origin.) The KORUS FTA will require that goods must be wholly obtained or produced in the territory of both countries or country. The FTA sets a regional value threshold to be met to be considered originating in the FTA territory and provides formulas for determining the regional values.

National *competition laws and regulations* are intended to ensure that one firm does not so dominate a sector of the economy as to inhibit market entry and stifle competition. Among other things, the KORUS FTA requires that the United States and South Korea inform persons, who are subject to administrative actions, of hearings and provide them the opportunity to make their case. The two countries will cooperate in enforcing competition laws through the exchange of information and consultation. In addition, designated monopolies and state-enterprises will have to operate in conformance with the agreement and in accordance with commercial considerations.

The KORUS FTA includes provisions to facilitate trade via electronic commerce (*e-commerce*). They prohibit discrimination against digital products and imposing customs duties on these products. They also require the recognition of electronic authentication and electronic signatures and would promote consumer access to the Internet.

Legislative Action

On October 3, 2011, President Obama submitted draft legislation (H.R. 3080/S. 1642) to implement the U.S.-South Korea Free Trade Agreement (KORUS FTA) to both houses of Congress. On October 6, the House Ways and Means Committee reported out H.R. 3080 (H.Rept. 112-239). On October 11, the Senate Finance Committee reported out S. 1642 (S.Rept. 112-223). On October 12, the House passed H.R. 3080 (278-151) and sent it to the Senate which passed it (83-15) later the same day. The President signed the legislation on October 21, 2011 (P.L. 112- 41). The votes on the KORUS FTA implementing legislation took place after the White House and congressional leaders agreed to procedures under which legislation to implement the KORUS FTA and legislation to implement the other two pending FTAs with Colombia and Panama would be considered in tandem with legislation to renew certain aspects of the Trade Adjustment Assistance (TAA) program. An action-forcing event was the October 13, 2011, state visit of South Korean President Lee Myung-bak to Washington.

IMPLICATIONS FOR SOUTH KOREA AND THE U.S.-ROK ALLIANCE

The Ratification Debate

In South Korea, on November 22, 2011, the National Assembly ratified the KORUS FTA and over a dozen implementing bills. The debate over the agreement's ratification was contentious and divisive, despite the fact that President Lee's party, the conservative New Frontier Party (NFP), controls the National Assembly. Korea's largest opposition party, the left-of-center Democratic Party (DP), opposed the agreement. For weeks, it and its allies physically blocked the Assembly's Committee on Foreign Affairs, Trade, and Unification from considering the FTA. Additionally, many NFP leaders were reluctant ram the agreement through the Assembly for fear of repercussions in parliamentary elections scheduled for April 2012. After repeated attempts at negotiations failed to produce a breakthrough, the GNP's leadership on November 22 surprised nearly all observers by calling the full Assembly into a special session for a snap vote on the KORUS FTA and several implementing bills.[141] The National Assembly passed the KORUS FTA by a vote of 151-7, with 12 abstentions. (The Assembly has 299 members.)

South Korea's Opposition Parties Call for Re-Negotiation or Withdrawal

In the months since the vote, politicians from the DP and other left-of-center parties have continued to speak out against the KORUS FTA. In early 2012, the DP and a like-minded group merged to form the Democratic United Party (DUP). Shortly after its formation, senior DUP officials called for renegotiating nine areas of the agreement, including the investor-state dispute settlement mechanism and the 2010 automotive safeguards provisions. The coalition also has stated it wants to change the agreement's rules of origin to allow goods manufactured in the Kaesong Industrial Complex, inside North Korea, to be granted preferential trade status. In multiple fora – including a letter to President Obama, Vice President Joseph Biden, and Speaker of the House John Boehner – the DUP chairwoman, Han Myong-sook, stated that her party would withdraw South Korea from the agreement if it was voted into power and its demands were not met. Subsequently, the DUP softened its stance by calling for a "complete renegotiation" instead of "scrapping" the agreement. The change came after Han and other DUP leaders were criticized for championing the KORUS FTA while they were officials in the previous South Korean government of Roh Moo-hyun, which was in power from 2003-2008.

Upcoming Elections

Even if the DUP takes control of the National Assembly in the April 2012 vote, as a number of observers predict, it would not have the ability to withdraw from the KORUS FTA. The more important election will occur in December 2012, when South Koreans will elect a new president, who would have the power to terminate the agreement. The true significance of the April vote for the KORUS FTA may be as a bellwether: if voters are perceived as rewarding or punishing the DUP for its stance on the agreement, it is likely to determine whether the party's nominee for the presidency makes re-negotiation of or withdrawal from the agreement a priority.

South Korea's Motives for Pursuing the KORUS FTA

Entering an FTA with the United States meshed with a number of Lee's economic and strategic goals. Ongoing competitive pressure from Japanese firms, increased competition from Chinese enterprises, and the rapid aging of the South Korean workforce has heightened the sense of urgency to boost national long-term competitiveness, particularly in the services industries, where South Korean productivity typically lags compared to other industrialized countries. Indeed, former President Roh and other South Korean officials argued that the KORUS FTA is essential for South Korea's economic survival.[142] Similarly, if less grandiosely, President Lee has argued that KORUS FTA will help boost South Korea's economy. To accelerate Korea's reform efforts— and also to avoid being left out from other FTAs being created globally and in Asia—Presidents Roh and Lee have pursued an aggressive effort to negotiate FTAs. South Korea has entered into FTAs with (in order of completion) Chile, Singapore, the European Free Trade Association (EFTA), the Association of Southeast Asian Nations (ASEAN), India, the European Union, Peru, and the United States. It is negotiating FTAs with seven other countries – including Canada, Mexico, and Australia – and officially discussing nine other FTAs, including agreements with China and Japan.[143]

The United States and South Korea negotiated the KORUS FTA in part as a means to restore the health of a critical foreign policy and national security alliance.[144] While the talks were ongoing in 2006 and 2007, the KORUS FTA sometimes was discussed as a possible counterweight to the bilateral friction that was occurring over issues such as how to manage relations with North Korea and the repositioning of U.S. troops in South Korea. These tensions decreased markedly in 2007, following the Bush Administration's decision to place greater emphasis on engagement and negotiations with North Korea. The December 2007 election of Lee, who has stressed the importance of rebuilding U.S.-South Korean ties has improved relations further. Thus, with the alliance on firmer ground, the KORUS FTA no longer appears as an exceptional area of bilateral cooperation.

Although the FTA's utility as an acute salve for the alliance has been reduced, some argue it will help to boost the alliance, over the medium and longer term, by deepening bilateral economic and political ties. Entering into an FTA, some argue, is a way to help reorient the alliance to adapt to the changes on the Korean Peninsula and in East Asia. However, in concrete terms, it is difficult to see how the KORUS FTA would make a significant difference in the strategic relationship, as it is unlikely to alter either country's fundamental interests on the Peninsula or in Northeast Asia.

In contrast, while the *passage* of the KORUS FTA was unlikely to have a major substantive impact on the strategic relationship, a *collapse* of the KORUS FTA would probably have had a profound symbolic effect, particularly upon the way South Koreans view the alliance. If the KORUS FTA had been rejected or subjected to a prolonged delay by the United States, it would have been a psychological blow to many South Korean policymakers, many of whom would likely see it as a betrayal. This would be particularly true since, in their eyes, they made politically costly concessions on autos, beef, labor, and the environment to help ensure the agreement would be more favorably received in the U.S. Congress. The KORUS FTA's failure in the United States, according to some Korean politicians and policymakers, would have lent credence to arguments in South Korea that the U.S. commitment to Korea and Northeast Asia is declining. If these perceptions had taken hold, it would increase the political costs of South Korean leaders' taking unpopular decisions on behalf of the alliance, such as increasing South Korea's share of the costs of maintaining U.S. troops on the Peninsula.

IMPLICATIONS FOR U.S. TRADE POLICY AND U.S. ASIA POLICY

Leading up to the congressional vote on the KORUS FTA, President Obama faced competing pressures. On one side were those, including business community representatives and pro-trade Members of Congress, who viewed the KORUS FTA as an important opportunity for the United States to increase trade and investment with an important East Asian market and ally. They also were concerned about U.S. manufacturers and investors losing out to their EU competitors since the EU-Korea FTA entered into force before the KORUS FTA on July 1, 2011. On another side, were those who argued that the KORUS FTA did not sufficiently address South Korean barriers to imports of manufactured goods, particularly cars and some appliances. The KORUS FTA faced even deeper opposition from those who are skeptical about the benefits of FTAs, in general, at least as pursued under current trade policy.

But the commitment modifications contained in the 2011 exchange of letters appeared to have accomplished their primary objective. They shifted the politics surrounding the KORUS FTA debate in the United States, where the original agreement was encountering strong resistance and without fundamentally altering the politics in South Korea, where the agreement had broad support. Shortly after the announcement, a number of U.S. groups and individuals who had previously opposed the agreement, including several Members of Congress, announced their support. In South Korea, the modifications appeared not to have shifted the terms of political debate over the FTA, which generally had been expected to be approved by the National Assembly. Most South Korean media commentators have observed that the balance of concessions in the December deal were in the United States' favor, a dynamic that the agreement's opponents have seized upon as another reason to criticize the FTA. In contrast, South Korean supporters of the agreement appear to accept the concessions as regrettable but tolerable.

The fate of the KORUS FTA could affect U.S. efforts to institutionalize its economic presence in East Asia. In addition to the KORUS FTA, the United States has an FTA with Singapore. The Bush Administration initiated FTA negotiations with Malaysia and Thailand, but they ultimately stalled. In November 2009, President Obama announced the United States would enter into negotiations on a Trans-Pacific Partnership (TPP) trade agreement, a trade liberalization negotiation among Australia, Brunei Darussalam, Chile, New Zealand, Peru, Singapore and Vietnam. The FTA may become even larger in the coming months. Japan, Canada, and Mexico have begun consultations with these eight countries, plus the United States, over joining the TPP negotiations. President Obama, Secretary of State Hillary Clinton, and other U.S. officials have said that the KORUS FTA, along with the TPP, are key parts of their move to "pivot" U.S. strategic orientation toward the Asia-Pacific region.

U.S. use of FTAs in Asia also has been a proposed response to the plethora of bilateral and multilateral FTAs that are being negotiated in the region. None of the actual or proposed multilateral agreements include the United States. Failure of the KORUS FTA could have been viewed as a serious blow to the U.S. "competitive liberalization" strategy. With FTAs throughout East Asia proliferating, a failure of the KORUS FTA to be implemented would also likely have meant that the United States would be shut out of regional economic groupings in East Asia. In contrast, the implementation of the KORUS FTA could spark interest of other East Asian countries, such as Japan, to negotiate FTAs with the United States in order not to lose their share of the huge U.S. market to South Korea. Thus, if the proponents of the "competitive liberalization" argument are correct, the fate of the KORUS FTA could play an important role in accelerating or decelerating the move to open market regionalism in East Asia. Indeed, in the fall of 2011, the KORUS FTA's supporters in Korea argued that ratification was necessary because of Japan's intention of joining the TPP talks, much as TPP proponents in Japan had used the KORUS FTA as a justification to promote their cause.

Similarly, the fate of the KORUS FTA is likely to be seen as a bellwether for broader U.S. trade policy, which is now in a period of reevaluation. In addition to the KORUS FTA, U.S. FTAs with Colombia and Panama are pending. The Doha Development Agenda round in the WTO is, for all intent and purposes, on life support. This raises questions in the minds of U.S. policymakers and other experts, regarding the future role of the WTO and multilateral negotiations in shaping the international trading framework. The KORUS FTA will likely play a role in this reassessment. For better or worse, its rejection or indefinite delay might call into question the viability of FTAs as a serious U.S. tool to strengthen economic ties with major trading partners.

APPENDIX. SOUTH KOREAN MOTOR VEHICLE MANUFACTURING

South Korea came late to the table of major motor vehicle manufacturing nations. Government attempts to foster a domestic automobile industry began in 1962 when the South Korean government enacted the Automobile Industry Protection Law, with assembly line production of automobiles in Korea beginning that year using complete knock down kits imported from Japan.[145] The 1980 edition of the *Automotive News Market Data Book*, an authoritative industry source, listed no South Korean company among the top 50 global producers. By 2011, according to the International Organization of Motor Vehicle Manufacturers (OICA), total South Korean production of cars and commercial vehicles was given as 4.7 million units; South Korea ranked as the global number five national producer, behind, in order, China, the United States, Japan, and Germany.[146] Yet, South Korea remains only a mid-level consumer of motor vehicles, with domestic sales of 1.4 million in recent years. Exports accounted for 70% of Korea's motor vehicle production volume in 2012, a figure that is matched by no other major motor vehicle producing country.[147]

South Korea has aggressively developed and protected its automotive manufacturing base. Motor vehicle imports were prohibited in South Korea until 1987, and imports from Japan were banned until 1999.[148] Originally the South Korean government promoted the development of a fleet of domestically owned producers, but this strategy failed. In the shakeout after South Korea's economic crisis of 1997-98, only one major South Korean-owned company was left, Hyundai, which also took control of the number-two producer by volume, Kia. Others were marginalized, out of the business altogether, or controlled by foreign companies. Korea's third producer, and their only other major manufacturer left in the business, Daewoo, is now controlled by General Motors.[149] The lone major South Korean-owned producer, the Hyundai-Kia combination, in 2011 produced 6.6 million vehicles worldwide, ranking it fourth globally.[150]

Hyundai is a world-class global competitor, with current and planned assembly operations in the United States, the European Union, and other countries. The export orientation of the South Korean motor vehicle industry, the quality of South Korean cars, and the relatively low U.S. tariff on all imported motor vehicles, except trucks, has made the United States a good market of opportunity for South Korean automobile exports. Until 2016 and 2021, respectively, the United States will impose a 2.5% duty on imported passenger vehicles and a 25% duty on trucks. South Korean auto makers export many more cars to the United States than U.S. car manufacturers export to South Korea. Total South Korean motor vehicle exports to the United States peaked at more than 860,000 units in 2004, according to U.S. Commerce Department data, and have dropped every year through 2009, but increased to more than 700,000 passenger vehicles and light trucks in 2012 (see **Figure A-1**). U.S.-based automobile exporters, which could include South Korean and other foreign-owned manufacturers, shipped more than 22,600 passenger cars and light trucks to South Korea in 2012, compared with nearly 15,000 in 2011.[151]

Another important development affecting automotive exports and imports are the investments South Korean automakers have made in the U.S. market since the mid-2000s. Hyundai and Kia have established production facilities in the United States. Thus, Hyundai's Montgomery, AL, plant and Kia's West Point, GA, facilities allow them to substitute for some imports. In 2012, Hyundai and Kia sold nearly 1.3 million light vehicles in the United States, of which nearly 60%, or about 720,000 units, were produced in the United States.[152] More than 360,000 Hyundai Sonatas and Elantras were assembled in Alabama and about 230,000 Kia Sorento's and Hyundai Santa Fe's were produced in Georgia in 2012.[153] At full capacity, the Georgia Kia plant will be able to produce 300,000 vehicles. Meanwhile, GM Korea, which is the South Korean arm of U.S. automaker GM, builds and sells cars in South Korea. In 2011, GM Korea sold 125,730 domestically built cars.[154] Since these vehicles are not exported they are not covered by the KORUS FTA.

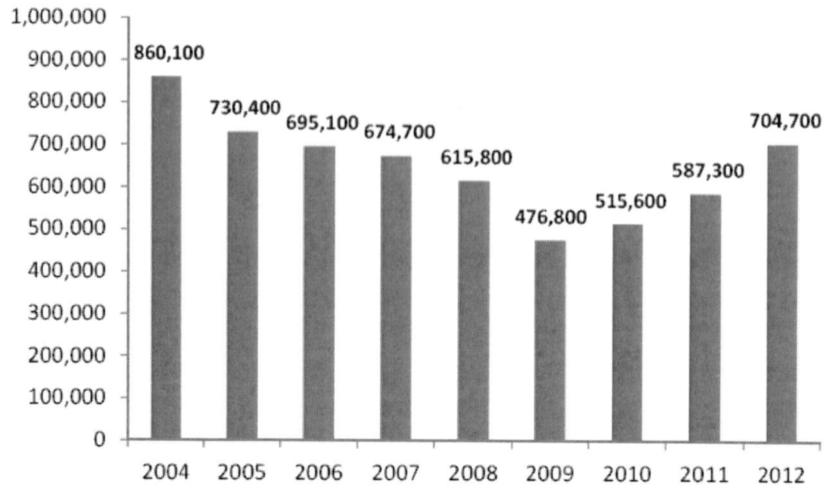

Source: U.S. Department of Commerce, Office of Transportation and Machinery and the American Automotive Policy Council.

Figure A-1. South Korean Passenger Vehicle and Light Truck Exports to the United States; (2004-2012).

The total value of South Korean automotive exports to the United States, including parts, was $18.6 billion in 2012, compared with U.S. exports of similar products to South Korea of $1.3 billion. The United States ran a bilateral trade deficit in autos of $17.3 billion in 2012, which widen from $11.3 billion five years ago.[155] One analyst who examined the effects of the FTA, found in simulation models of projected market changes, South Korea would always gain relative to the United States from bilateral liberalization, "because Korea has a comparative advantage over the United States in the automobile sector; in other words, Korea has been much more successful in accessing the U.S. market than the United States has been in accessing the Korean market."[156]

Through aggressive and successful marketing, Hyundai and Kia together have significantly increased U.S. market share from the 2000s. Both brands saw a jump in their U.S. sales (for Hyundai sales of both their domestic and imported vehicles increased by 9% from 2011 to 2012 and Kia's car and light truck sales rose by 15% during the same time period). By comparison, overall sales of U.S. light vehicles grew to 14.4 million units in 2012 from 12.7 million in 2011, or by 13%. Despite their growth in sales, South Korean automakers share of the U.S. market remained largely unchanged in 2012 over 2011 at around 8.8%, but rose from 7.1% in 2010. Sales of Chevrolet's Aveo model, which is imported from South Korea, dropped to 67 units in 2012 from 28,600 in 2011.[157]

For years, South Korean policies that allegedly restrict imports of foreign-made motor vehicles have been a major target of U.S. trade policy. In 1995 and 1998, the USTR negotiated memoranda of understanding (MOUs) with South Korea, aimed at reducing formal and informal South Korean policies that were said to discriminate against imports of U.S.-made vehicles and other foreign imports. U.S. policy primarily focused on motor vehicle taxation policies and South Korean motor vehicle standards, which supposedly did not conform to international standards, or those widely used in major markets.[158] The import share of the domestic market in South Korea has increased since the MOUs were signed.

According to data from the Korea Automobile Manufacturers Association and the Korea Automobile Importers and Dealers Association, total imports grew from a low of less than 1% of the market (4,400 units) in 2000 to 8.5% market share by 2012 (130,900 units). Together, European manufacturers accounted for three-quarters of imported cars in the South Korean market in 2012 and Japanese manufacturers combined comprised another 18%. U.S.-headquartered automakers made up the remainder with a 7.4% share of new imported cars sold in South Korea (i.e., Ford at 5,100, Chrysler at 4,100, and GM at 475).[159]

End Notes

[1] White House Office of the Press Secretary, "Background Readout by Senior Administration Officials to the Travel Pool on the President's Meeting with President Lee Of The Republic Of Korea," April 2, 2009.

[2] *International Trade Daily.* June 17, 2009.

[3] White House Press Release, "Remarks by President Barack Obama and President Lee Myung-Bak of Republic of Korea in Joint Press Conference," November 19, 2009.

[4] "TRANSCRIPT: Fox News Interviews President Obama," FOXNews.com, updated November 18, 2009.

[5] United States International Trade Commission (USITC). *U.S.-Korea Free Trade Agreement: Potential Economy-wide and Selected Sectoral Effects.* Investigation No. TA-2104-24. USITC Publication 3949. September 2007.

[6] For more on the U.S.-South Korean alliance, see CRS Report RL33567, *Korea-U.S. Relations: Issues for Congress*, by Larry A. Niksch.

[7] The December 2010 commitment modifications adjusted the tariff elimination schedule for passenger cars and trucks, a longer phase-out period was a key priority for Ford Motor Company and the United Auto Workers (UAW), added a special vehicle safeguard to protect the U.S. market from a possible surge in South Korean auto imports, and increased the exemption for U.S. car manufacturers from South Korean safety standards if they meet U.S. federal safety standards. U.S. and South Korean trade negotiators signed legal texts, which included these new commitments for the automotive sector, on February 10, 2011.

[8] In the initial 2007 agreement the United States and South Korea had agreed to phase out their respective electric and hybrid car tariffs of 2.5% and 8%, over ten years.

[9] For more information see pp. 2-4 of CRS Report R-41544, *Trade Promotion Authority and the U.S.-South Korea Free Trade Agreement*, by Emily Barbour.

[10] "*U.S. Light Vehicle Sales, December & YTD*," WardsAuto, January 4, 2013, http://www.ward sauto.com and data from the American Automotive Policy Council.

[11] Trade Remedy Piece of Korea FTA Ignores Korean ADF Demands. *Inside U.S. Trade.* April 13, 2007.

[12] §2104(f) Trade of 2002. P.L. 107-210. United States International Trade Commission (USITC). *U.S.-Korea Free Trade Agreement: Potential Economy-wide and Selected Sectoral Effects.* Investigation No. TA-2104-24. USITC Publication 3949. September 2007. (Hereafter referred to as USITC (2007).) In March 2011, the USITC released a study updating its analysis of the KORUS FTA's impact on the U.S. passenger vehicle market as a result of the December 2010 modifications, *U.S.-Korea Free Trade Agreement: Passenger Vehicle Sector Update,* Investigation No. 332-523, USITC Publication 4220, March 2011.

[13] USITC (2007). pp. xvii-xviii.

[14] USITC (2007). p. xix.

[15] Kiyota, Kozo and Robert M. Stern. *Economic Effects of a Korea-U.S. Free Trade Agreement.* Korea Economic Institute, Special Studies 4. 2007.

[16] Lee, Junyu and Hongshik Lee. *Feasibility and Economic Effects of a Korea-U.S. FTA.* Korean Institute for International Economic Policy. December 2005. p. 86.

[17] OECD, *Economic Surveys–Korea*, 2007.

[18] Korea Economic Institute, "Current Economic Info, South Korean Economic Data," at http://www.keia.org, January 2, 2008.

[19] "ROK Editorial: Roh's 'Special Lecture'," *The Korea Times*, posted on the Open Source Center, KPP20060329042002, March 29, 2006.

[20] Ministry of Finance and Economy Weekly Briefing, "Korea-US FTA Projected to Boost the Korean Economy," March 9, 2006.

[21] See, for instance, Junkyu Lee and Hongshik Lee, *Feasibility and Economic Effects of a Korea-U.S. FTA* (Seoul: Korea Institute for International Economic Policy, 2005), pp. 116-117; Inbom Choi and Jeffrey Schott, *Free Trade between Korea and the United States?* (Washington, DC: Institute for International Economics, 2001), pp. 79-82.

[22] "Roh's 'Special Lecture'," *The Korea Times*, March 26, 2006.

[23] Korea Broadcast System, March 31, 2006, Broadcast.

[24] The KORUS FTA Tariff Schedule can be found in the USITC report, *Modifications to the Harmonized Tariff Schedule of the United States to Implement the United States-Korea Free Trade Agreement*, USITC Publication 4308, February 2012, http://www.usitc.gov /publications/tariff_affairs/USITCPub4308.pdf.

[25] South Korea's average applied agricultural tariff in 2010 was 48.6%, compared to 5.0% for the United States, from WTO, "Country Profiles" for South Korea and the United States, September 2012, available at http://stat.wto.org/CountryProfiles/KR_e.htm and http://stat.wto.org/CountryProfiles/US_e.htm.

[26] A TRQ is a two-part tool used by countries to protect their more sensitive agricultural and food products, often while transitioning over time to free trade. The quota component provides for duty-free access of a specified quantity of a commodity, which in an FTA usually expands over time depending on the outcome of the negotiations. Imports above this quota are subject to a prohibitive tariff that in an FTA may or may not decline over time. At the end of a product's transition period to free trade under an FTA, both the quota and tariff usually no longer apply (unless specific exceptions are made), allowing for its unrestricted access to the partner's market.

[27] Summaries of commodity-specific market access provisions (tariff reduction schedules, transition periods, TRQ amounts and growth rates, and safeguards) are found in the USDA fact sheets "U.S. - Korea Trade Agreement," March 2011, available at http://www.fas.usda. gov/itp/KoreaTA/KORUS%20One-Page%20Fact%20Sheet%2003-11.pdf, and "U.S. Korea Trade Agreement - Benefits for Agriculture," March 2011, available at http://www.fas.usda. gov/itp/KoreaTA/KORUS%20Detailed%20Fact%20Sheet%2003-11.pdf. Detailed fact sheets on the agreement's commodity provisions and prospective impacts for agriculture in 45 states are available at http://www.fas.usda.gov/info/factsheets/Korea/us-korea tafactsheets.asp.

[28] Derived by CRS from Table 2.2 in USITC, *U.S.-Korea Free Trade Agreement: Potential Economy-wide and Selected Sectoral Effects,* Publication 3948, September 2007, pp. 2-8 and 2-9.

[29] Derived by CRS from the AFBF's *Implications of a South Korea-U.S. Free Trade Agreement on U.S. Agriculture*, July 2007, p. 17. To be consistent with the agricultural and food product categories used to derive the USITC's estimate, AFBF's exports of fish products are not included in the estimated increase in agricultural exports and agriculture's share stated above.

[30] In 2003, U.S. exports of beef muscle meats to South Korea totaled 213,083 MT. The safeguard level in year 1 would allow for duty-free access for about 20% more U.S. beef than the average 2002-2003 level of U.S. beef exports to the South Korean market. For comparison to the recent past (in 2012), U.S. beef muscle cut meat exports were 111,991 MT.

[31] For more information, see CRS Report RL34528, *U.S.-South Korea Beef Dispute: Issues and Status*, by Remy Jurenas and Mark E. Manyin.

[32] White House, Office of the Secretary, "Remarks by the President at the Announcement of a U.S.-Korea Free Trade Agreement," December 4, 2010.

[33] Senate Finance Committee, "Baucus Deeply Disappointed With Announcement on Korea Trade Deal, Commits to Keep Fighting for American Ranchers," December 3, 2010; Senate Agriculture Committee, "Sen. Chambliss Statement on U.S.-South Korea Free Trade Agreement," December 3, 2010; Senator Grassley, "Conference Call with Farm Broadcasters," December 7, 2010; *Washington Post*, "Senator's objection may slow trade pact," February 3, 2011, p. A4.

[34] Meatingplace.com, "U.S.-Korea FTA deal leaves beef unchanged, phases out tariffs," December 6, 2010;National Cattlemen's Beef Association, "Statement from NCBA Chief Economist Gregg Doud on US, Korea Trade Deal," December 3, 2010; American Meat Institute, "AMI Statement on Finalized U.S. Free Trade Agreement with South Korea," December 3, 2010.

[35] *Inside U.S. Trade*, "Korean Negotiators Refused To Engage On Beef Issue In Seoul," November 19, 2010; *Washington Trade Daily*, "The KorUS Supplemental Agreement," December 6, 2010, p. 3; Washington Post, Political Economy Blog, "Obama, Lee outlined U.S.-Korea trade deal in Seoul, official says," December 6, 2010; Bloomberg, "South Korea's Kim Rules Out Negotiations on U.S. Beef Imports," December 6, 2010; *Inside U.S. Trade*, "Baucus to Oppose Korea FTA Unless More Progress Made on Beef Issue," December 10, 2010, p. 3; International Trade Daily, "Korea Has No Plans to Discuss Beef Prior to Action on FTA, Ambassador Says," February 1, 2011.

[36] Senate Finance Committee, "Baucus Secures Administration's Commitment to Expand U.S. Beef Access in Korea," May 4, 2011, accessed at http://finance.senate.gov/newsroom /chairman/release/?id=514813d3-9192-4a38-8f5aea602675f442.

[37] *Inside U.S. Trade*, "USTR Says Beef Market Access Must Precede Signing of Korea FTA," April 6, 2007, p. 5.

[38] Following the 2004 renegotiation of South Korea's WTO agricultural commitments, the United States and most other rice exporting countries beginning in 2005 have been able to take advantage of this separate global quota. Expanding by 20,347 MT each year through 2014, market access is on a first-come, first served basis. By 2014, both rice import quotas (under country allocations made to four countries including the United States, and the quota available to any country) will total 408,700 MT. For background on Korea's market access and domestic policies for rice, see USDA, Economic Research Service, South Korea Briefing page titled "Policy," available at: http://www.ers.usda.gov/topics/international-markets-trade/countries-regions/south-korea/policy.aspx.

[39] USDA, Foreign Agricultural Service, Fact Sheet "U.S.-Korea Free Trade Agreement—What's At Stake for Fresh Citrus and Orange Juice," September 2008.

[40] NPPC, "U.S.-South Korea FTA Remains A Good Deal For U.S. Pork Producers," December 3, 2010.

[41] Uruguay Round Agreement on Trade-Related Aspects of Intellectual Property Rights (TRIPS), Article 22.1.

[42] Letter from Korea's Trade Minister Jong-Hoon Kim to USTR Ron Kirk, June 20, 2011; *Inside U.S. Trade*, South Korea Clarifies GI Provisions in EU-Korea FTA to USTR Satisfaction, June 24, 2011; U.S. Dairy Industry press release, "U.S. Rights to Export Variety of Cheeses to Korea Upheld," June 23, 2011, available at http://www.usdec.org/ files/PressReleases /NMPFUSDECIDFA-U.S.RightstoExportVarietyofCheesesto KoreaUpheld.pdf.

[43] This stance is reflected in testimony by the National Cattlemen's Beef Association before the USITC on June 20, 2007.

[44] USTR, Legal Texts Reflecting December 3, 2010 Agreement, February 10, 2011, http://www.ustr.gov/trade-agreements/free-trade-agreements/korus-fta/legal-texts-reflecting-december-3-2010-agreement.

[45] White House. "*Increasing U.S. Auto Exports and Growing U.S. Auto Jobs Through the U.S.-Korea Trade Agreement*," December 3, 2010, http://www.whitehouse.gov/sites/default/files /fact_sheet_increasing_us_auto_exports_us_korea_free_trade_agreement. pdf.

[46] Tariffs on trucks cover pickup trucks, panel vans, and commercial vehicles. Many light trucks such as SUVs and minivans are counted as cars.

[47] Tariffs for electric cars and plug-in hybrids will phase out between 2012 and 2016, whereas passenger car tariffs will remain at 4% until 2016.

[48] Office of USTR. *KORUS FTA: Opportunities for Automotive Exports* October 2008, http://www.ustr.gov/archive/assets/Document_Library/Fact_Sheets/2008/asset_upload_file500_15206.pdf.

[49] The 2007 agreement would have required the United States to begin phasing out its 25% tariff on light truck imports immediately until full elimination in year 10 following implementation of KORUS FTA.

[50] USTR, "Auto-Related Provisions," p. 1; USITC. *U.S.-Korea FTA*, p. 3-80 (Box 3-4). In the case of the United States the most-favored-nation (MFN) tariff (HTS 8703) would be 2.5% and for South Korea it would be 8%.

[51] The truck tariff applies to "motor vehicles for the transport of goods (HTS 8704)" which would include trucks like the Ford F-150.

[52] Displacement is one measurement of car engines. An engine in cubic centimeters shows the volumes displaced by the cylinders through one revolution. Typically, a higher number means a more powerful engine. Engine displacement can also be measured in liters (e.g., a 1.4 liter engine is equivalent to 1,400 cc and a 1.8 liter engine is equivalent to 1,800 cc). A small car engine is generally around 1.6 liter such as the Hyundai Elantra; examples of larger engines include the Ford Fusion at 2.5 liters and the Chevy Impala with an engine as large as 5.3 liters.

[53] The 2007 agreement allowed no more than 6,500 vehicles per year per U.S. automotive manufacturer.

[54] South Korea's new environmental regulations will become more stringent over the next five years. These new regulations, which are still being developed, took effect in 2012 and are expected to remain in place until 2015. South Korea will raise the average fuel economy of automobiles seating 10 or fewer passengers to 17 kilometers per liter and will lower the standard for carbon dioxide emissions to 140 grams per kilometer by 2015. Automobile importers would be able to choose either standard to satisfy the requirement.

[55] USTR. *Agreed Minutes*, February 10, 2011, http://www.ustr.gov/webfm_send/2555.

[56] A list of KORUS Committees and Working Groups can be found at http://www.ustr.gov /countries-regions/japan-korea-apec/korea/korus-committees-and-working-groups.

[57] White House. "*Increasing U.S. Auto Exports and Growing U.S. Auto Jobs Through the U.S.-Korea Trade Agreement*," December 3, 2010, http://www.whitehouse.gov/sites/default /files/ fact_sheet_increasing_us_ auto_exports_us_ korea_free_trade_agreement.pdf.

[58] Bryan Laviolette, *GM Daewoo Changing Name to GM Korea*, Detr oit News, January 20, 2011.

[59] Ibid. *U.S.-Korea FTA*, Table 2.2.

[60] Ibid. *U.S.-Korea FTA*, p. 3-78.

[61] Ibid. *U.S.-Korea FTA*.

[62] Energy Efficiency and Renewable Energy, U.S. Department of Energy, *Alternative Fuels & Advanced Vehicles Data Center*, HEV Sales by Model, 1999-2011, http://www.afdc.energy. gov/data/tab/vehicles/data_set/10301.

[63] Mark Williams, *"Hyundai Says No, But Kia Could Say Yes,"* PickupTrucks.com, February, 20, 2012, http://news.pickuptrucks.com/2012/02/hyundai-says-no-but-kia-could-say-yes.html.

[64] According to *WardsAuto*, Hyundai produced 113,000 "Porters," and Kia produced 87,000 "Bongos," both described as pickups in 2012.

[65] Textile and apparel statistics are compiled from the Office of Textiles and Apparel (OTEXA) U.S, textiles and apparel trade balance report. Textiles comprise yarn, fabric, and made-up articles (e.g., sheets and towels), http://otexa.ita.doc.gov/.

[66] United States International Trade Commission. *U.S.-Korea Free Trade Agreement: Potential Economy-Wide and Selected Sectoral Effects*. USITC Publication 3949. September 2007. pp. 3-52.

[67] World Trade Organization. *Tariff Profiles for South Korea and the United States*, 2012, http://www.wto.org/ english/res_e/booksp_e/tariff_profiles12_e.pdf.

[68] USITC. pp. 3-52.

[69] OTEXA, South Korea, Market Reports, Textiles, Apparel, Footwear, and Travel Goods, http://web.ita.doc.gov/tacgi/overseasnew.nsf/country/Korea-South.

[70] Ibid. *U.S.-Korea FTA*, pp. 3-53.

[71] Ibid., *U.S.-Korea FTA* , Table 2.2.

[72] Ibid., pp. 3-68 and 3-71.

[73] Aerospace products and parts are classified under North American Industry Classification System (NAICS) code 3364. Data compiled from the International Trade Commission, Interactive Tariff and Trade Dataweb, (accessed March 1, 2013).

[74] U.S. Commercial Service, *Doing Business in Korea: 2012 Country Commercial Guide for U.S. Companies*, p. 25, 2012.

[75] Computers and electronic products are classified under NAICS 334 and semiconductors and other electronic components under NAICS 3344. Data compiled from the International Trade Commission, Interactive Tariff and Trade Dataweb, (accessed March 1, 2013).

[76] Ibid., *U.S.-Korea FTA* , pp. 3-68 through 3-73.

[77] Steel products include all iron and steel items listed with the two digit Harmonized Tariff Schedule (HTS) codes 72 and 73.

[78] USITC. p. 3-64.

[79] Ibid. p. 3-91.

[80] The pharmaceuticals and medicines statistics are based on NAICS 3254 and medical equipment and supplies NAICS 3391 were compiled using the International Trade Administration's Trade Stats Express, http://tse.export.gov/TSE/ TSEhome.aspx

[81] *WorldTrade Online,* March 16, 2012.

[82] Primosch, William. *Testimony of Senior Director, International Business Policy, National Association of Manufacturers on the Proposed United States-Korea Free Trade Agreement for the Trade Policy Staff Committee, Office of the U.S. Trade Representative*. March 14, 2006. p. 6.

[83] Report of the United States Industry Trade Advisory Committee for Chemicals, Pharmaceuticals, Health/Science Products, and Service (ITAC-3) on The United States-South Korea Trade Promotion Agreement. April 24, 2007.

[84] International Trade Administration, *Pharmaceuticals Industry Profile 2010*, p. 8, July 2010.

[85] Economist Intelligence Unit, *South Korea: Healthcare and Pharmaceuticals Report*, Industry Briefing, August 23, 2012.

[86] Jeong-Seok Lee, Industrial and Regulatory Perspectives on Pharmaceuticals in Korea, p. 6, November 2011.

[87] U.S. Commercial Service, *Doing Business In Korea: 2012 Country Commercial Guide for U.S. Companies*, pp. 46-8, 2012.

[88] USITC. *U.S.-Korea FTA*, p. 3-91.

[89] Pharmaceuticals are classified under NAICS 3254 and medical equipment and supplies under NAICS 3391. Data compiled from the International Trade Commission, Interactive Tariff and Trade Dataweb, (accessed March 1, 2013).

[90] Primosch, William. *Testimony of Senior Director, International Business Policy, National Association of Manufacturers on the Proposed United States-Korea Free Trade Agreement for the Trade Policy Staff Committee, Office of the U.S. Trade Representative.* March 14, 2006. p. 6.

[91] Data obtained from U.S. Department of Commerce. Bureau of Economic Analysis.

[92] Ibid.

[93] USITC. p. 4-8.

[94] Office of the United States Trade Representative. *2007 National Trade Estimates Report—Foreign Trade Barriers.* p. 366.

[95] The United States-Korea Free Trade Agreement (KORUS FTA). Report of the Industry Trade Advisory Committee on Services and Finance Industries (ITAC 10) April 2007.

[96] The Free Trade Agreement Between South Korea and the United States (KORUS FTA). Chapter 13 (Financial Services)—Confirming Letter.

[97] Annex -I (Korea).

[98] KORUS FTA Chapter 14 Telecommunications.

[99] Coalition of Service Industries. *Coalition of Service Industries Expresses Strong Support for U.S.-Korea FTA; Urges Swift Congressional Passage.* Press release. June 30, 2007.

[100] White House Office of the Press Secretary, "President Bush Discusses the Visa Waiver Program," October 17, 2008. South Korea's path to entry into the VWP was made possible by reforms of the VWP that were embodied in H.R. 1 (P.L. 110-53), the Implementing the 9/11 Commission Recommendations Act of 2007. For more on the U.S. Visa Waiver Program, see CRS Report RL32221, *Visa Waiver Program*, by Alison Siskin.

[101] Department of Homeland Security, Temporary Admissions in *Yearbook of Immigration Statistics: 2007* Table 28.

[102] *Inside U.S. Trade*, December 10, 2010.

[103] This section on trade remedies was written by Vivian C. Jones, Specialist in International Trade and Finance, Foreign Affairs, Defense, and Trade Division, CRS.

[104] For more information, see CRS Report RL32371, *Trade Remedies: A Primer*, by Vivian C. Jones.

[105] P.L. 107-210, Trade Act of 2002, §2102(b)(14).

[106] "South Korea Retracts Key Demand in Anti-Dumping Rules: Leaked Government Report," *Yonhap* (South Korea), January 19, 2007.

[107] USITC. "Antidumping and Countervailing Duty Orders In Place As of September 10, 2008, by Country." Available at http://www.usitc.gov. Korea Trade Commission, TR Measures, available at http://www.ktc.go.kr/en/kboard_child/ list.jsp?bm=86&pg=1.

[108] Schott, Jeffrey J., Bradford, Scott C., and Moll, Thomas. *Negotiating the Korea - United States Free Trade Agreement*, Institute for International Economics, June 2006.

[109] World Trade Organization dispute settlement statistics, http://www.wto.org/english /tratop_e/dispu_e/ dispu_by_country_e.htm. South Korea was one of the complainants in the WTO dispute brought against the U.S. safeguard measures on steel, as well as that against the Continued Dumping and Subsidy Offset Act ("Byrd Amendment").

[110] "Cutler says U.S.-Korea Talks Hit Snag in Three Negotiating Groups, *FDA Week*, December 8, 2006. Although the particulars of South Korean demands were not made public, according to news reports, one of Korea's demands was to be excluded from the cumulation of imports used to determine injury in a safeguards case, if its share of imports into the U.S. are below a certain threshold.

[111] "South Korea Retracts Key Demand on Anti-dumping Rules: Leaked Government Report." *Yonhap*, January 19, 2007.

[112] See Chapter 10, §A, Article 10.1 Application of a Safeguard Measure and Article 10.5 Global Safeguard Actions.

[113] Article 10.4, Compensation.

[114] Chapter 10, §B. Antidumping and Countervailing.

[115] CVD: 19 U.S.C. 1671c; AD: 19 U.S.C. 1673c. Under these statutes, a quantitative restriction or price offset suspension agreement must completely eliminate the injurious effect of the dumping or subsidy, must be in the public interest and must be able to be effectively monitored by U.S. authorities.

[116] Chapter 10, §B. Antidumping and Countervailing Duties, Article 10.7, paragraphs 3 and 4.

[117] Chapter 10, §C. Committee on Trade Remedies, Article 10.8, paragraph 2.
[118] ITAC (12) on Steel, Advisory Committee Report, April 27, 2007, p. 7.
[119] Ibid., p. 4
[120] Ibid.
[121] "Trade Remedy Piece of Korea FTA Ignores Korean AD Demands," *Inside U.S. Trade*, April 13, 2007.
[122] Ibid.
[123] For more, see CRS Report RL34093, *The Kaesong North-South Korean Industrial Complex*, by Mark E. Manyin and Dick K. Nanto.
[124] In July 2011, South Korea's largest opposition party, the Democratic Party, called for the KORUS FTA to be re-written to recognize KIC-made products as South Korean in origin.
[125] Chapter 22, Annex B, Committee on Outward Processing Zones on the Korean Peninsula.
[126] April 2007 interviews with U.S. and Korean officials; remarks by Assistant U.S. Trade Representative for Japan, Korea and APEC Affairs Wendy Cutler at an April 5, 2007, Korea Economic Institute forum; "Behind the Korea FTA Negotiations," *Washington Trade Daily*, April 12, 2007.
[127] March 2011 document issued by the Office Of The United States Trade Representative, "Outward Processing Zones, Kaesong, and the U.S.-Korea Trade Agreement Frequently Asked Questions"; Deputy United States Trade Representative reiterated this point in April 7, 2011, testimony before the House Ways and Means Trade Subcommittee.
[128] CRS calculations based on data from U.S. Department of Commerce. Bureau of Economic Analysis, at http://www.bea.gov.
[129] A range of factors determine the climate for foreign investment—government regulations, skills of local labor, general economic conditions, intellectual property rights protection, among others. Therefore, U.S.-South Korean investment ties could be affected by not only the provisions of the investment chapter of the agreement, but other chapters as well.
[130] The USITC report on the KORUS FTA points out that South Korea's list these "nonconforming measures" in the KORUS FTA is longer than in previous FTAs that the United States has signed; however, industry representatives generally believe that the KORUS FTA would still render significant opportunities for U.S. investors. USITC. p. 6-5.
[131] USITC. p. 6-5.
[132] A national treatment exception is made with respect to the secondary uses of recordings by means of analog communications, including over-the-air broadcasts, whereby a Party can limit the rights of performers and producers of sound recordings from the other Party on its own territory. This exception was a disappointment to U.S. industry, which otherwise praise the agreement. *Korea-U.S. Free Trade Agreement: Benefits to America's Entertainment Industries.* Testimony Before the U.S. International Trade Commission by Greg Frazier, Executive Vice-President Worldwide Government Policy Motion Picture Association of America. June 6, 2007. p.7.
[133] The FTA would require each Party to adopt and maintain five internationally accepted labor rights that are contained in the ILO Declaration on Fundamental Principles and Rights at Work and Its Follow-Up (1998) (ILO Declaration) Article 19:2 specifies these rights as the freedom of association, the effective recognition of the right to collective bargaining, the elimination of all forms of compulsory or forced labor, the effective abolition of child labor and the elimination of discrimination in respect of employment and occupation. The framework also requires FTAs to adhere to seven major multilateral environmental agreements and for this commitment to be enforceable under the FTA. "The Trade Policy for America" was completed after President Bush notified Congress on April 1, 2007, of his intention to sign the KORUS FTA but prior to the signing on June 30. At first, South Korean officials balked at opening negotiations to add the language but eventually agreed to do so. After, the two sides held negotiations, they included the language in the final text that was signed on June 30, 2007.
[134] In Questions for the Record posed by members of the Senate Finance Committee, USTR Kirk was asked "Do you think that the labor and environment provisions of the U.S.-Korea FTA are appropriate?" He responded that "the U.S.- Korea FTA incorporates the May 10th Agreement, which established a strong foundation for bipartisan progress on trade." United States Senate Committee on Finance, "Finance Committee Questions For The Record. Hearing on Confirmation of Mr. Ronald Kirk to be United States Trade Representative," March 9, 2009.
[135] OECD, *Economic Survey—Korea 2007*, p. 138.
[136] Report of the Labor Advisory Committee for Trade Negotiations and Trade Policy (LAC) on the KORUS FTA, April 27, 2007, p. 9.

[137] *Ibid.*

[138] OECD, *Economic Survey—Korea 2007*, pp. 128-40.

[139] The seven agreements are: the Convention on International Trade in Endangered Species; the Montreal Protocol on Ozone Depleting Substances; the Convention on Marine Pollution; the Inter-American Tropical Tuna Convention; the Ramsar Convention on the Wetlands; the International Convention for the Regulation of Whaling; and the Convention on Conservation of Antarctic Marine Living Resources.

[140] United States Senate Committee on Finance, "Finance Committee Questions For The Record. Hearing on Confirmation of Mr. Ronald Kirk to be United States Trade Representative," March 9, 2009.

[141] Reportedly, the GNP took this step after learning that the DP and its allies were planning to occupy the National Assembly's main chamber in order to block a vote on the KORUS FTA.

[142] Korea Broadcast System, March 31, 2006, Broadcast in Korean, summarized by the Open Source Center, "ROK TV Carries Economic Minister's Comments on ROK-US FTA," April 10, 2006, FEA20060410021900. (Han was Finance Minister when he made these remarks.) South Korean Blue House, "Address to the Nation," April 2, 2007.

[143] EFTA is comprised of Iceland, Norway, Switzerland, and Liechtenstein. The 10-member ASEAN consists of Brunei, Cambodia, Indonesia, Laos, Malaysia, Myanmar, Philippines, Singapore, Thailand, and Vietnam.

[144] For more, see CRS Report R41481, *U.S.-South Korea Relations*, coordinated by Mark E. Manyin.

[145] Andrew Green, "South Korea's Automobile Industry: Development and Prospects," *Asian Survey*, vol. 32, no. 5 (May 1992), pp. 413-414.

[146] International Organization of Motor Vehicle Manufacturers (OICA), *World Motor Vehicle Production*, World Ranking of Manufacturers, 2011 Production Statistics, http://oica.net/category/production-statistics/.

[147] American Automotive Policy Council, "*Statistical Overview of the Korean Automotive Industry/Market & U.S. Trade Relationship, 1990-2012*," http://www.americanautocouncil. org/industry-facts.

[148] USITC. *Industry and Trade Summary: Motor Vehicles* (USITC Publication 3545, September 2002), p. 60.

[149] Ibid., pp. 60-61; Graeme P. Maxton and John Wormald, *Time for a Model Change*: *Re-Engineering the Global Automotive Industry*. Cambridge, U.K.: Cambridge University Press, 2004. pp. 101-2; CRS Report RL32883, *U.S. Automotive Industry: Recent History and Issues*, by Stephen Cooney and Brent D. Yacobucci, pp. 75-76.

[150] OICA, *World Motor Vehicle Production*, World Ranking of Manufacturers, Year 2011, http://oica.net/wp-content/uploads/ranking-without-china-30-nov-12.pdf.

[151] American Automotive Policy Council, "*Statistical Overview of the Korean Automotive Industry/Market & U.S. Trade Relationship, 1990-2012*," http://www.americanautocouncil. org/industry-facts

[152] "*U.S. Light Vehicle Sales, December & YTD*," WardsAuto, January 4, 2013, http://www.wardsauto.com and data from the American Automotive Policy Council.

[153] "*North American Production by Vehicle Line*," WardsAuto, January 10, 2013, http://wardsauto.com.

[154] American Automotive Policy Council, *Facts about the Korean Auto Industry and Economy*, http://www.americanautocouncil.org/.

[155] Ibid.

[156] Sang-yirl Nam, "Implications of Liberalizing Korea-U.S. Trade in the Automobile Sector: Potential Impact of the Korea-U.S. Free Trade Agreement," Korea Economic Institute *Academic Paper Series*, III:1 (February 2008), p. 10.

[157] "*U.S. Light Vehicle Sales,*" WardsAuto, January 4, 2013, http://www.wardsauto.com and data from the American Automotive Policy Council.

[158] CRS Report RL32883, *U.S. Automotive Industry: Recent History and Issues*, by Stephen Cooney and Brent D. Yacobucci, p. 60.

[159] To complete the picture, General Motors has sold over 100,000 cars annually since 2005 through its South Korean subsidiary, the GM Korea operations. The rest of its production, which totaled nearly 882,000 vehicles, were shipped abroad. General Motors Corporation and Korea's Daewoo Motor Company launched the GM Daewoo Auto & Technology Company in 2002, renamed GM Korea in 2011. GM holds a 72% stake in the Korean car maker, with the rest of the company controlled by the state run Korea Development Bank. GM Daewoo operates five manufacturing facilities in Korea and one assembly plant in Vietnam.

In: Free Trade Agreements
Editor: Jenell Gallo

ISBN: 978-1-63117-366-0

Chapter 3

THE TRANS-PACIFIC PARTNERSHIP (TPP) NEGOTIATIONS AND ISSUES FOR CONGRESS*

Ian F. Fergusson, William H. Cooper, Remy Jurenas and Brock R. Williams

SUMMARY

The Trans-Pacific Partnership (TPP) is a proposed regional free trade agreement (FTA) being negotiated among the United States, Australia, Brunei, Canada, Chile, Japan, Malaysia, Mexico, New Zealand, Peru, Singapore, and Vietnam. U.S. negotiators and others describe and envision the TPP as a "comprehensive and high-standard" FTA that aims to liberalize trade in nearly all goods and services and include commitments beyond those currently established in the World Trade Organization (WTO). The broad outline of an agreement was announced on the sidelines of the Asia-Pacific Economic Cooperation (APEC) ministerial in November 2011, in Honolulu, HI. If concluded as envisioned, the TPP potentially could eliminate tariff and non-tariff barriers to trade and investment among the parties and could serve as a template for a future trade pact among APEC members and potentially other countries. Congress has a direct interest in the negotiations, both through influencing U.S. negotiating positions with the executive branch, and by passing legislation to implement any resulting agreement.

The 19th round of negotiations was held in Bandar Seri Begawan, Brunei, on August 23-30. TPP leaders, with Vice President Biden representing the United States, met on the sidelines of the APEC meetings on October 8, reaffirming their objective to conclude the negotiations in 2013. Issue-specific intercessional meetings continue, and a ministerial meeting is reportedly scheduled for December 7-10 in Singapore. For the year-end deadline to be achieved, outstanding issues involving sensitivities for the participants will likely require political decisions to be made. The negotiating dynamic itself is complex: decisions on key

---

* This is an edited, reformatted and augmented version of a Congressional Research Service Publication, CRS Report for Congress R42694, dated December 5, 2013.

market access issues such as dairy, sugar, and textiles and apparel may depend on the outcome of rules negotiations such as intellectual property rights or state-owned enterprises.

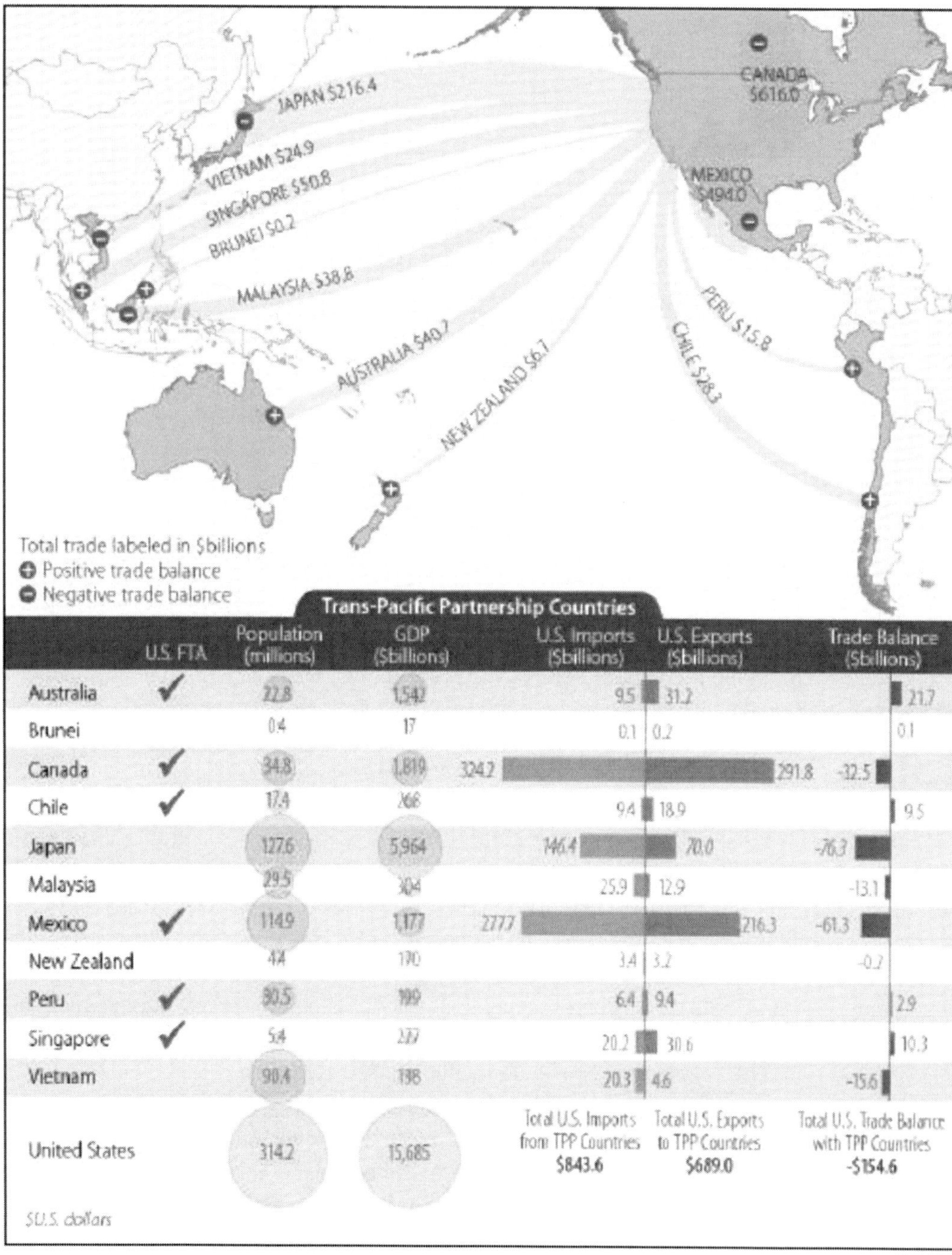

Trans-Pacific Partnership Countries

	U.S. FTA	Population (millions)	GDP ($billions)	U.S. Imports ($billions)	U.S. Exports ($billions)	Trade Balance ($billions)
Australia	✔	22.8	1,542	9.5	31.2	21.7
Brunei		0.4	17	0.1	0.2	0.1
Canada	✔	34.8	1,819	324.2	291.8	-32.5
Chile	✔	17.4	268	9.4	18.9	9.5
Japan		127.6	5,964	146.4	70.0	-76.3
Malaysia		29.5	304	25.9	12.9	-13.1
Mexico	✔	114.9	1,177	277.7	216.3	-61.3
New Zealand		4.4	170	3.4	3.2	-0.2
Peru	✔	30.5	199	6.4	9.4	2.9
Singapore	✔	5.4	277	20.2	30.6	10.3
Vietnam		90.4	138	20.3	4.6	-15.6
United States		314.2	15,685	Total U.S. Imports from TPP Countries **$843.6**	Total U.S. Exports to TPP Countries **$689.0**	Total U.S. Trade Balance with TPP Countries **-$154.6**

$U.S. dollars

Sources: Analysis by CRS. Population and GOP data from IMF, World Economic Outlook, April2013. Trade data from the U.S. International Trade Commission (ITC). Total trade includes both imports and exports, but does not include services trade.

Figure 1. Trans-Pacific Partnership Countries (2012).

Twenty-nine chapters in the agreement are under discussion. The United States is negotiating market access for goods, services, and agriculture with countries with which it does not currently have FTAs: Brunei, Japan, Malaysia, New Zealand, and Vietnam. Negotiations are also being conducted on disciplines to intellectual property rights, trade in services, government procurement, investment, rules of origin, competition, labor, and environmental standards and other issues. In many cases, the rules being negotiated are intended to be more rigorous than comparable rules found in the WTO. Some topics, such as state-owned enterprises, regulatory coherence, and supply chain competitiveness, may break new ground in FTA negotiations. As the countries that make up the TPP negotiating partners include advanced industrialized, middle income, and developing economies, the TPP, if implemented, may involve substantial restructuring of the economies of some participants.

The TPP serves several strategic goals in U.S. trade policy. First, it is the leading trade policy initiative of the Obama Administration, and is a manifestation of the Administration's "rebalance" to the Asia-Pacific. If concluded, it may serve to shape the economic architecture of the Asia- Pacific region by harmonizing existing agreements with U.S. FTA partners, attracting new participants, and establishing regional rules on new policy issues facing the global economy— possibly providing impetus to future multilateral liberalization under the WTO.

As the negotiations proceed, a number of issues important to Congress are emerging. One is whether the United States can balance its vision of creating a "comprehensive and high standard" agreement with a large and expanding group of countries, while not insisting on terms that other countries will reject. Another issue is how Congress will consider the TPP, if concluded. The present negotiations are not being conducted under the auspices of formal trade promotion authority (TPA)—the latest TPA expired on July 1, 2007—although the Administration informally is following the procedures of the former TPA. If TPP implementing legislation is brought to Congress, TPA may need to be considered if the legislation is not to be subject to potentially debilitating amendments or rejection. In addition, Members of Congress may wish to consider whether the current chapters included in the agreement appropriately address their trade policy concerns, as well as the potential agreement's impact on the multilateral trading system.

INTRODUCTION

The Trans-Pacific Partnership (TPP) is a potential free trade agreement (FTA) among 12, and perhaps more, countries. The United States and 11 other countries of the Asia-Pacific region— Australia, Brunei, Canada, Chile, Japan, Malaysia, Mexico, New Zealand, Peru, Singapore, and Vietnam—are negotiating the text of the FTA. With 29 chapters under negotiation, the TPP partners envision the agreement to be "comprehensive and high-standard," in that they seek to eliminate tariffs and non-tariff barriers to trade in goods, services, and agriculture, and to establish rules on a wide range of issues including foreign direct investment and other economic activities. They also strive to create a "21st-century agreement" that addresses new and cross- cutting issues presented by an increasingly globalized economy.

The TPP draws congressional interest on a number of fronts. Congress would have to approve implementing legislation for U.S. commitments under the agreement to enter into force. In addition, under long-established executive-legislative practice, the Administration notifies and consults with congressional leaders, before, during, and after trade agreements have been negotiated. Furthermore, the TPP will likely affect a range of sectors and regions of the U.S. economy of direct interest to Members of Congress and could influence the shape and path of U.S. trade policy for the foreseeable future.

This report examines the issues related to the proposed TPP, the state and substance of the negotiations (to the degree that the information is publically available), the specific areas under negotiation, the policy and economic contexts in which the TPP would fit, and the issues for Congress that the TPP presents.

2011 TPP Leaders Statement

At the 2011 APEC Leaders meeting in Honolulu, the leaders of the (then) nine TPP countries agreed to the broad outlines of an agreement. In their statement, they categorized the TPP as "a comprehensive, next- generation regional agreement that liberalizes trade and investment and addresses new and traditional trade issues and 21st-century challenges." TPP trade ministers also highlighted the following five key areas of the so- called historic and standard-setting agreement.

- **Comprehensive Market Access**—Removal of both tariff and non-tariff barriers is "comprehensive and ambitious in all areas."
- **Regional Agreement**—Fully regional agreement that facilitates trade and the development of production and supply chains among TPP members.
- **Cross-Cutting Trade Issues**—Holistic, agreement-wide approach to specific areas: regulatory coherence, competitiveness and business facilitation, small- and medium-sized enterprises, and development.
- **New Trade Challenges**—Addresses emerging trade issues such as those caused by new technology (e.g., cloud-computing).
- **Living Agreement**—Agreement will "evolve in response to developments in trade, technology or other emerging issues" and expand "to include other economies from across the Asia-Pacific region."

Source: TPP Leader's Statement, Honolulu, Hawaii, November 12, 2011.

The Evolution of the TPP

The Trans-Pacific Strategic Economic Partnership, as it was originally known, was conceived in 2003 by Singapore, New Zealand, and Chile as a path to trade liberalization in the Asia-Pacific region. Brunei joined negotiations in 2005, and the Trans-Pacific Strategic Economic Partnership (P-4) agreement was concluded in 2006. In March 2008, the United

States joined the negotiations to conclude the still outstanding investment and financial services provisions. President Bush notified Congress of his intention to negotiate with the existing P-4 members on September 22, 2008, and with other countries, Australia, Peru, and Vietnam, on December 30, 2008.

After a period of reflection on U.S. trade policy, the new Obama Administration decided to continue with the TPP negotiations. On November 14, 2009, President Obama committed the United States to engage with the TPP countries "with the goal of shaping a regional agreement that will have broad-based membership and the high standards worthy of a 21st -century trade agreement."[1]

President Obama formally notified Congress of his Administration's intention to enter into negotiations with the TPP countries on December 14, 2009. That notification set off a 90-day timeline under the now expired 2002 trade promotion authority (TPA) legislation, for congressional consultations prior to the beginning of negotiations.[2] In October 2010, TPP participants agreed to by consensus to the inclusion of Malaysia as a negotiating partner.

The negotiating partners announced a framework for the agreement at the sidelines of the Asia- Pacific Economic Cooperation (APEC) Ministerial in Honolulu, HI, November 8-13, 2011. At this time, Canada, Japan, and Mexico started to consult with the existing TPP partners on joining the negotiations. After several months of intense bilateral consultations with each of the current TPP countries, the TPP countries agreed by consensus to the inclusion of Mexico and Canada and they began participating as negotiating partners in the December 2012 round in Auckland, New Zealand. Japan continued to debate internally the question of joining the negotiations, but on March 15, 2013, Prime Minister Shinzo Abe announced Japan's definitive interest and the bilateral consultations intensified. On April 21, the current participants announced their support of Japan's joining the negotiations, and Japan began to fully participate in the final days of the July 2013 Malaysia round. Nineteen rounds of negotiations have taken place to date.

> The Trans-Pacific Partnership is perhaps the most ambitious trade negotiation underway in the world. It will break new ground on important issues from the challenges of state-owned enterprises, to ensuring the free flow of data across borders, to enhancing regional supply chains, to ensuring transparency in cutting red tape. We're also working to strengthen protections for labor and the environment... Our goal is for high standards for the Trans-Pacific Partnership to enter the bloodstream of the global system and improve the rules and norms.
>
> —Vice President Joseph P. Biden, April 5, 2013

THE TPP IN CONTEXT

If completed as intended, the proposed TPP agreement would strengthen and deepen trade and investment ties among its participants. However, it could also have implications in larger, strategic contexts beyond the immediate participants: for U.S. trade policy in general; for the emerging trade architecture in the Asia-Pacific region; for the multilateral trade regime within the WTO; and for U.S strategic interests in the Asia-Pacific region.

The TPP and U.S. Trade Policy

U.S. participation in TPP negotiations serves several strategic goals in U.S. trade policy. First, it continues and expands a U.S. trade policy strategy that began with the North American Free Trade Agreement (NAFTA), which entered into force in 1994, of using FTAs to promote trade liberalization and potentially to spark multilateral negotiations in the World Trade Organization (WTO). The George W. Bush Administration expanded the use of this strategy under the rubric of "competitive liberalization," negotiating 11 FTAs with 16 countries. The last three of these FTAs—with Colombia, Panama, and South Korea—were approved by Congress in 2011.[3] However, the future direction of this policy was uncertain, given the low commercial value of some of these agreements and lack of new obvious partner countries. Meanwhile, an increasing web of bilateral and regional FTAs, were being concluded among other parties in the Asia-Pacific region and worldwide. The Bush Administration's and then the Obama Administration's adoption of the TPP signaled that the United States remains engaged in regional free trade negotiations.

The TPP arguably provides the United States with the opportunity to project its trade interests by negotiating a "comprehensive and high-standard" FTA with provisions that build off those in FTAs the United States concluded throughout the 2000s, especially the most recent ones. The TPP partner countries share a reliance on world trade and have been some of the greatest advocates for trade liberalization. While they differ in economic levels of development, they have committed themselves to negotiating a high-standard FTA. That, by itself is not new; the United States has often conducted asymmetrical negotiations with countries of differing levels of development in which it has dominated. This time, however, with more players at varied levels of development, and with an economic heavyweight like Japan participating, the United States may not be able simply to impose its vision or standards on those countries, and they are likely to make demands for concessions from the United States.

TRADE PROMOTION AUTHORITY

Trade Promotion Authority (TPA)—formerly fast track—is a statutory mechanism under which Congress defines negotiating objectives and consultative procedures for trade agreements, and authorizes the President to enter into reciprocal trade agreements governing tariff and non-tariff barriers. Under TPA, implementing bills for reciprocal trade agreements are considered under expedited legislative procedures, that is, limited debate, no amendments, and an up-or-down vote. The expedited consideration is conditioned on the President observing certain statutory obligations in negotiating trade agreements, including notifying and consulting Congress. The purpose of TPA is to preserve the constitutional role of Congress to regulate foreign commerce in consideration of implementing legislation for trade agreements that require changes in domestic law, while also bolstering the negotiating credibility of the executive branch by assuring that a trade agreement, once signed, will not be changed during the legislative process. TPA expired in 2007 and, as of this writing, has not been renewed by Congress.[4]

Practically speaking, the TPP approach could eclipse the alternative model of narrower goods- based FTAs that are offered by China or somewhat more comprehensive agreements used by the European Union and Japan that, nonetheless, exclude sensitive agriculture products. Adoption of these other models, even if open to U.S. participation, could be seen as disadvantageous to U.S. businesses and workers because they exclude provisions important to U.S. commercial trade— disciplines on services, investment, and intellectual property rights, as well as enforceable provisions on labor and environment. In addition, the TPP aims to establish disciplines on new trade issues, such as state-owned enterprises or supply chain facilitation, that could serve as a model for future negotiations bilaterally, regionally, or in the WTO.

The TPP and Other Asia-Pacific Trade Agreements

The current 12 TPP countries already form part of a growing network of Asia-Pacific FTAs (**Error! Reference source not found**.).[5] The United States has FTAs in place with six of the TPP countries: Australia, Canada, Chile, Mexico, Peru, and Singapore. In addition, the proposed TPP seeks to build on the existing Trans-Pacific Strategic Economic Partnership (P-4), a free trade area among Brunei, Chile, New Zealand, and Singapore. The current TPP partners also include 4 of the 10 members of the Association of Southeast Asian Nations (ASEAN): Brunei, Malaysia, Singapore, and Vietnam.[6] ASEAN countries have negotiated a free trade area amongst each other as well as several external FTAs. All 12 TPP partners are also members of the 21-member Asia- Pacific Economic Cooperation (APEC) forum, which does not negotiate FTAs among its membership, but serves as a forum for dialogue on and establishes non-binding commitments toward the goals of open and free trade and investment within the region.[7]

To some, the United States and its TPP partners are jump-starting the consensus-based approach of APEC.[8] In the context of this forum for dialogue and non-binding commitments, APEC Leaders in 2010 agreed to push forward the creation of a Free Trade Area of the Asia-Pacific (FTAAP). They acknowledged the TPP as potentially one of a number of "ongoing regional undertakings" on which to build to eventually achieve an FTAAP.[9] Other ongoing regional undertakings include potential trade agreements between ASEAN and other Asian countries.

Most recently, officials announced the launch of negotiations for the Regional Comprehensive Economic Partnership (RCEP). This agreement would join ASEAN and its six FTA partners— Australia, China, India, Japan, New Zealand, and South Korea—in one collective FTA. It is unclear how these two regional undertakings, RCEP and TPP, may impact one another and how they will affect the potential for an FTAAP.[10] The RCEP may not aim for the same level of ambition in terms of tariff reduction and trade liberalization as the TPP. By allowing sensitive items to be left out of the negotiations, this platform could be more appealing to countries less inclined to the declared if yet unrealized high-standard ambitions of the TPP.

Yet, several countries, including Australia, Brunei, Japan, Malaysia, New Zealand, Singapore, and Vietnam, are moving forward as negotiating partners in both the TPP and

RCEP. The TPP partners, including the United States, have also expressed an interest in expanding the TPP to additional countries across the Asia-Pacific region. They maintain that new members are welcome so long as they strive for the same level of trade liberalization as the current negotiating partners.

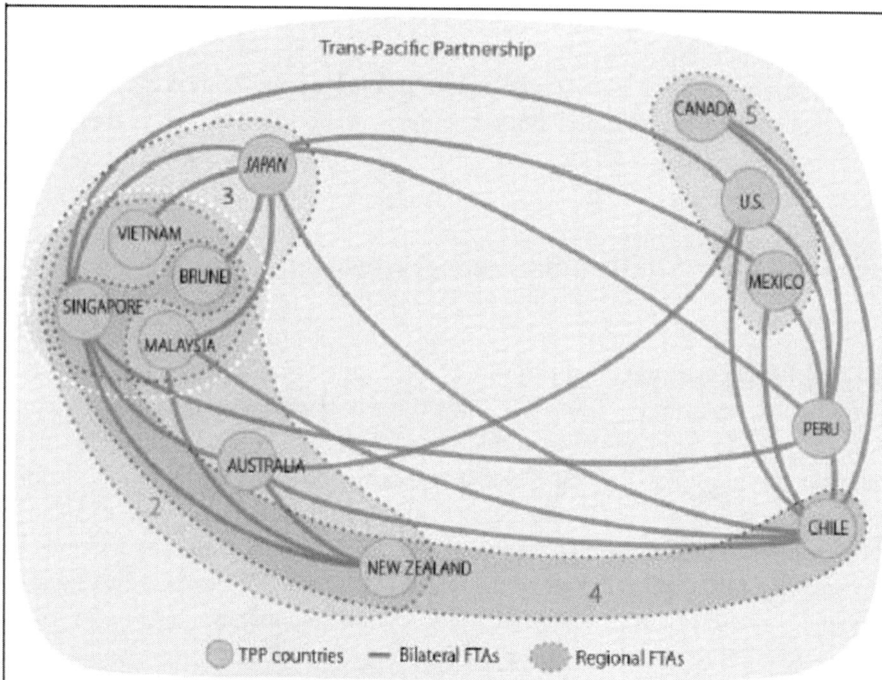

Encompassed Regional Trade Agreements	1 ASEAN	2 ASEAN-Australia-NZ	3 ASEAN-Japan	4 P-4	5 NAFTA
Australia		●			
Brunei	●	●	●	●	
Canada					●
Chile				●	
Japan			●		
Malaysia	●	●	●		
Mexico					●
New Zealand		●		●	
Peru					
Singapore	●	●	●	●	
United States					●
Vietnam	●	●	●		

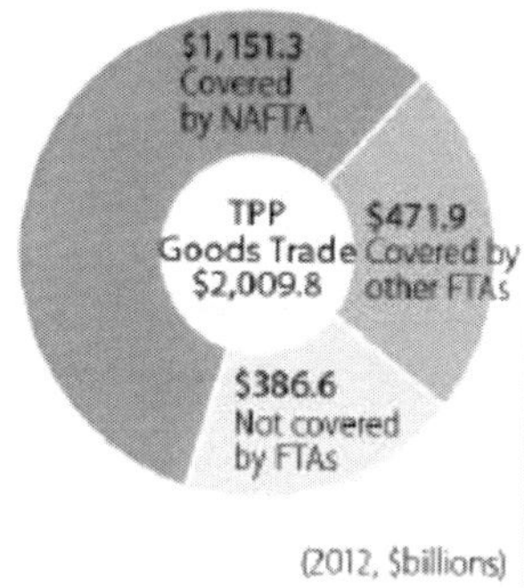

Source: WTO FTA database and websites of TPP countries' trade ministries. Trade data from IMF.

Notes: Aggregate TPP goods trade, both imports and exports, as reported above. ASEAN also includes countries outside the TPP: Burma (Myanmar), Cambodia, Indonesia, Laos, the Philippines, and Thailand. TPP goods trade covered by existing FTAs, as depicted above, reflects all goods trade between FTA partners. This measure slightly overstates trade covered under FTAs, as most FTAs exclude market access for at least some goods.

Figure 2. Existing FTAs among TPP Countries.

During the Auckland round in December 2012, Canada and Mexico participated in the negotiations for the first time, thus completing their year-long quest to join the talks. Since then, Japan's request to join the TPP was accepted by all the members and Japan participated in the negotiations beginning in July 2013. On November 29, 2013, South Korea, which previously had expressed varying degrees of interest in the TPP, announced that it would begin bilateral consultations with each of the 12 countries—the first step in seeking to join the agreement. According to USTR Froman, South Korea or any new country would be expected to join after negotiations among the current 12 are completed.[11] There is as yet no formal limit to the potential membership of the TPP, aside from excluding those countries unwilling to commit to the ambition of the proposed FTA. As mentioned, all current members of the TPP negotiations are also members of APEC, and the current TPP countries have publically stated that membership expansion will likely focus on other APEC members first, such as South Korea, though other non- APEC countries with a strong focus on trade liberalization, such as Colombia and Costa Rica, have also expressed an interest in joining TPP.

Many policy observers, however, note the absence of China, the region and world's second- largest economy, from ongoing negotiations. At a November 20, 2013, speech, National Security Advisor to the President Susan Rice reiterated U.S. policy that, "we welcome any nation that is willing to live up to the high-standards of this agreement to join and share in the benefits of the TPP, and that includes China."[12] The degree to which a potential TPP agreement and its participants are prepared to include China, as well as China's willingness or interest in participating in a comprehensive, high-standard agreement, will help determine if the TPP truly has the potential to become an FTAAP. With the agreement's focus on expansion throughout the region, the current negotiating partners may wish to establish disciplines now on certain aspects of the Chinese and other Asia-Pacific economies. This may, in part, explain the push for potential new disciplines on state-owned enterprises inside the TPP.

The TPP and the WTO

Though structured as a regional agreement, the TPP may have an impact on the multilateral process of the WTO and the Doha Development Agenda (Doha Round) of multilateral trade negotiations. While the WTO ministers continue to discuss a Doha Round agenda that critics contend is increasingly irrelevant to the present trading system, the TPP represents a way for the United States and its partners to advance discussions of a "21st-century trade agenda."

The influence of the TPP impact could be great due to its potential expansion and, hence, the fact that it could eventually affect a substantial amount of world trade—over 60% of U.S. trade alone is with other APEC members. The debate over whether FTAs have a positive or negative effect on the multilateral system continues. Proponents of bilateral and regional agreements would argue that[13]

- successful negotiation and implementation of proposed new trade rules in the TPP, on such emerging issues as State-owned enterprises and regulatory coherence, could serve as a template for future WTO negotiations;

- a successful TPP agreement among the current negotiating partners could cause other regional economies to consider joining (as seen recently with the addition of Canada, Japan, and Mexico) in order to ensure they remain competitive in TPP markets, thus furthering the WTO goal of greater global trade liberalization; and
- TPP could help promote and ensure the longevity of domestic economic policy reforms, particularly for countries such as Vietnam.

Opponents, however, would counter that

- efforts toward the TPP and other regional/bilateral FTAs may divert attention and resources from multilateral WTO efforts;
- increased trade among TPP members due to the preferential tariff structures of the agreement could simply be diverted from other regions rather than be newly created; and
- the spread of FTAs may actually make international commerce more difficult as companies must navigate varying rules and standards associated with different agreements.[14]

This last issue of overlapping trade rules may be particularly relevant for the potential TPP agreement as it will encompass countries with numerous existing FTAs. The proposed TPP agreement could add another layer of complexity or it could simplify the existing trade rules in the region by unifying them under one agreement. For example, according to the USTR, the TPP countries have committed to establishing a common set of rules of origin for determining whether a product originates inside the TPP.[15] How these and other trade rules inside the potential TPP agreement relate to those in existing FTAs will be of interest moving forward.

The TPP and the "Rebalance" in the Asia-Pacific Region

> The centerpiece of our economic rebalancing is the Trans-Pacific Partnership (TPP)- a high- standard agreement the United States is crafting with Asia-Pacific economies from Chile and Peru to New Zealand and Singapore.[...] We always envisioned the TPP as a growing platform for regional economic integration. *–Thomas Donilon, U.S. National Security Adviser, March 11, 2013*

The TPP could have implications beyond U.S. economic interests in the Asia-Pacific. The region has become increasingly viewed as of vital strategic importance to the United States. Throughout the post-World War II period, the region has served as an anchor of U.S. strategic relationships, first in the containment of communism and more recently as a counterweight to the rise of China. This trend has recently been accentuated by the Obama Administration's "pivot to Asia" along with the perception that the center of gravity of U.S. foreign, economic, and military policy is shifting to the Asia-Pacific region. The TPP is viewed as an important element in the U.S. "rebalancing" toward Asia.[16]

U.S.-TPP Economic and Trade Relations[17]

The overall economic impact of the potential TPP agreement will depend on a number of factors, including the extent of the liberalization achieved in the agreement, as well as the current level and potential growth of trade and investment with TPP members. On both measures, the TPP appears significant given that the TPP region accounts for a large share of U.S. trade and TPP negotiators have expressed their intent to achieve a "comprehensive and high-standard" FTA that will broadly liberalize regional trade and investment. From the U.S. perspective, a significant share of this liberalization has already occurred due to existing U.S. FTAs with 6 of the 11 TPP partners (**Error! Reference source not found.**), although potential disciplines in areas not covered in previous FTAs may be significant for some sectors.

Japan's entry, however, has changed this dynamic somewhat. Without Japan in the agreement, only 5% of total U.S.-TPP trade in 2012 was with countries not party to an existing U.S. FTA (and hence with greater scope for trade liberalization with the United States); with Japan in the agreement that number rises to 20% for U.S.-TPP merchandise trade, and even further to 32% for U.S.-TPP services trade. As a high-income country, U.S.-Japan trade differs considerably from U.S. trade with the other, mostly lower income negotiating partners without U.S. FTAs. Hence, Japan's participation in the agreement has drawn the interest of a wide range of U.S. industries, including sectors like agriculture, automotive, and insurance.

Malaysia and Vietnam also stand out in terms of their current trade and investment with the United States and their potential for future growth. Together these countries have a population of over 120 million and their economies have experienced rapid growth in recent years.[18] Moreover, Malaysia's and Vietnam's average applied MFN tariffs—the average tariff on imports from other members of the WTO, such as the United States—are 6.5% and 9.8%, respectively, two of the highest levels among TPP members (**Figure 6**).

Key U.S.-TPP Trade Statistics

- TPP countries collectively represent, the largest U.S. trading partner accounting for 40% of total U.S. goods trade and 25% of total U.S. services trade;
- U.S. FTAs already exist with several U.S. trading partners among TPP participants, particularly Canada and Mexico, which account for 72% of U.S. goods trade with TPP partners and 51% of U.S.-TPP services trade; and
- the agreement has the potential to expand in an economically important region and, most recently, has expanded to include Japan, a country without an existing U.S.-FTA and which accounted for 6% of all U.S. goods trade and 7% of all U.S. services trade in 2012.

U.S.-TPP Trade—Aggregate Overview

Total U.S. trade with TPP countries in 2012 was more than $1.5 trillion in merchandise and more than $260 billion in services. Even before Canada and Mexico became negotiating partners in the TPP, the agreement had the potential to become the second-largest U.S. FTA by trade flows. Now with the NAFTA countries and Japan participating, the TPP has the potential to become the largest U.S. FTA (**Figure 4** and **Figure 5**).

The current group of 12 countries is diverse in population, geographic location, and economic development, and U.S. trade relations with the countries reflect this diversity. The major U.S. merchandise exports are fairly similar to most TPP countries and include motor vehicles and parts; petroleum and coal products; computer equipment, semiconductors, and electronic components; agriculture and construction machinery; and aircraft. However, the top U.S. merchandise imports vary greatly by country. Agriculture and natural resources products are key U.S. imports from Australia, Chile, New Zealand, and Peru, while apparel products are the main U.S. imports from Vietnam. Canada and Mexico are both major suppliers of crude oil to the United States, but they also supply manufactured products like motor vehicles and motor vehicle parts. U.S. imports from Malaysia and Singapore consist primarily of manufactured products such as computers, semiconductors, and electronic components. Motor vehicles and motor vehicle parts make up over 35% of U.S. goods imports from Japan.

In terms of value, Canada and Mexico are by far the largest U.S. trading partners among TPP countries in goods, and both are significant U.S. services trade and investment partners. Both countries share a large border with the United States and are among the oldest U.S. FTA partners. Japan is the third-largest U.S.-TPP goods trade partner, and second-largest services trade and investment partner. Considering the other eight TPP partners, Singapore and Australia are the top U.S. goods export markets and top overall services trade and investment partners with the United States, while Malaysia, Vietnam, and Singapore are the top sources of U.S. goods imports.

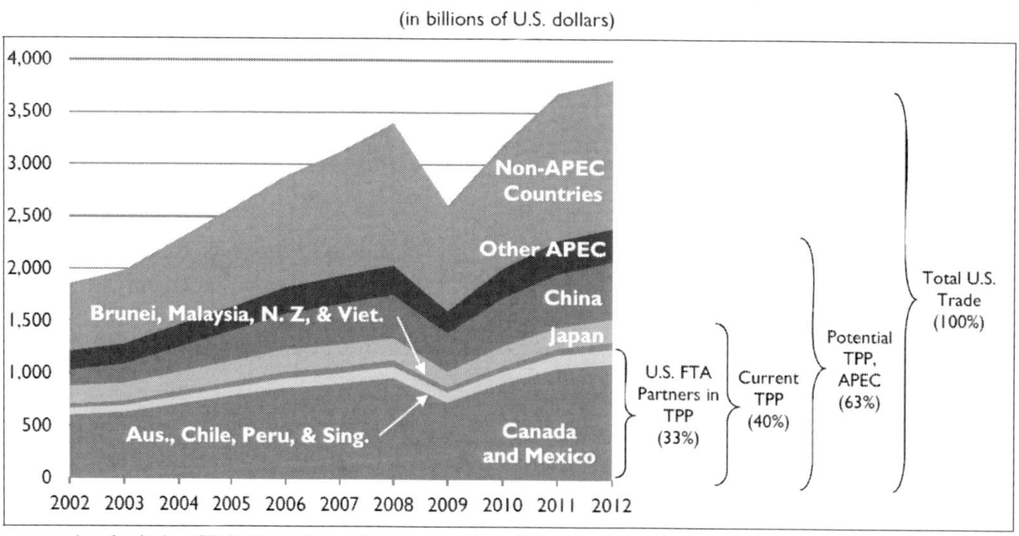

Source: Analysis by CRS. Data from the International Trade Commission.

Figure 3. U.S.-World, APEC, and TPP Goods Trade.

(in billions of U.S. dollars, 2012)

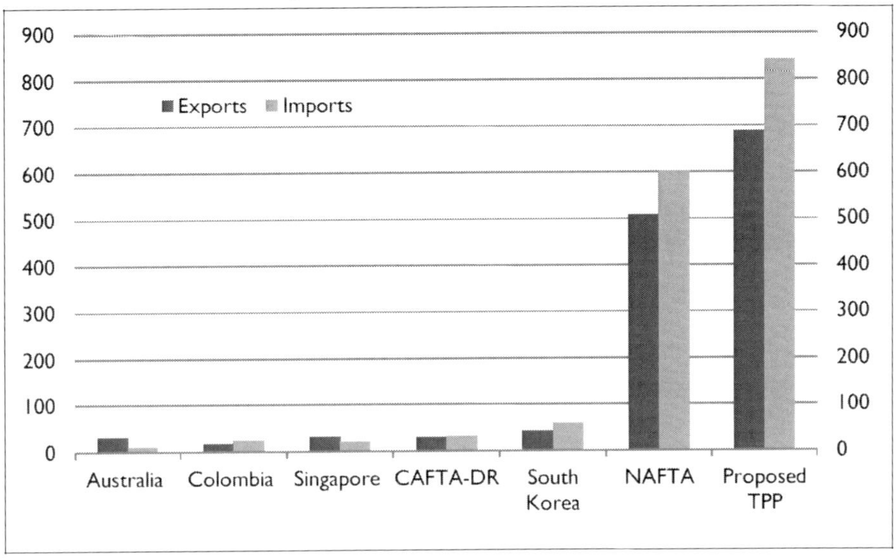

Source: Analysis by CRS. Data from ITC.

Figure 4. Largest U.S. FTAs—Goods.

(in billions of U.S. dollars, 2012)

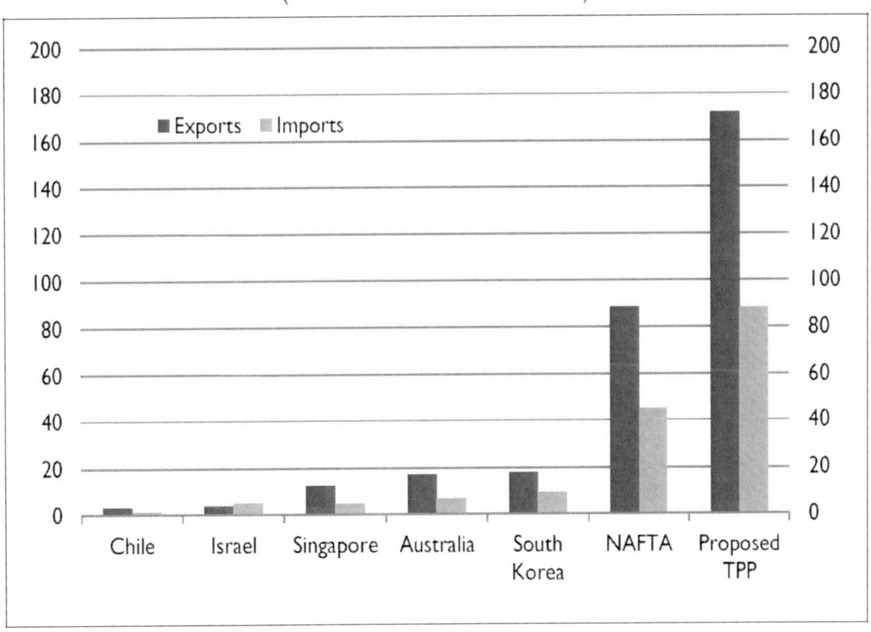

Source: Analysis by CRS. Data from BEA.
Notes: Services trade data not available for all FTA partners.

Figure 5. Largest U.S. FTAs—Services.

U.S.-TPP Trade—Bilateral Trends[19]

Twelve countries, including highly developed economies such as Australia, Canada, Japan, and New Zealand; middle income countries such as Mexico, Chile, and Malaysia; and emerging economies such as Vietnam are potential U.S. FTA partners in the TPP. This section provides a snapshot of each country's economic relationship with the United States and key bilateral negotiating topics. The appendix includes additional information on bilateral trade flows between the United States and TPP countries (**Table A-1** and **Table A-2**).

Australia

Total goods trade between the United States and Australia was $38.8 billion in 2012, while U.S.- Australia services trade totaled $24 billion in 2011. It is the third-largest U.S. trading partner in services behind Canada and Mexico. The U.S. trade surplus with Australia in 2012 was the largest of any TPP country for goods ($21.7 billion) and the fourth-largest in services ($10.4 billion). Part of this large surplus is due to quickly growing exports to Australia in both goods and services over the past decade. From January 1, 2005, when the Australian-U.S. FTA (AUSFTA) took effect, through 2011, U.S. agricultural exports to Australia more than doubled to $200 million. The primary U.S. goods exports to Australia are machinery, vehicles, and optical/medical instruments, while the top U.S. imports are meat, precious stones/metals, and optical/medical instruments. Fuels and mining products make up the bulk of Australia's exports to the rest of the world.

- The U.S.-Australian FTA (AUSFTA) took effect in 2005 and as a result most goods are or will eventually be exchanged tariff-free.[20]
- The AUSFTA does not contain an investor-state dispute (ISDS) mechanism, a prominent feature in bilateral and regional FTAs the United States has negotiated and a U.S. negotiating objective in the TPP talks. The newly elected conservative government led by Tony Abbott has reportedly stated that it will consider the issue of ISDS on a case-by-case basis.[21] The previous government reportedly insisted on an opt-out from such a provision if is included in a final TPP agreement.
- Australia may seek additional access for its sugar, which was excluded from AUSFTA. Australia may also seek to speed up the trade liberalization schedules for its beef and dairy products into the U.S. market. USTR maintains that it will not re-open the market access negotiations of AUSFTA.

Brunei

Brunei is by far the smallest U.S. trading partner among TPP countries. In 2012, total goods trade between the United States and Brunei was $243 million. U.S. imports from Brunei have declined considerably over the past decade. In 2012, they were only $86 million, a fraction of their 2005 level of $562 million. The top U.S. imports from Brunei are oil and oil products. These products are crucial to Brunei's economy, where fuel and mining products make up over 96% of total exports. The United States exports primarily machinery and aircraft to Brunei.

- The United States does not currently have an FTA with Brunei.
- Brunei remained on the USTR IPR "watch list" in 2012, due to U.S. concern over intellectual property rights enforcement.[22]

Canada

Canada is the largest trading partner of the United States, overall and among TPP participants, with total trade in 2012 of over $616 billion in goods and $90 billion in services.[23] The U.S. goods trade deficit with Canada has been falling in recent years to $32.5 billion in 2012, and the United States recorded a substantial trade surplus in services trade with Canada of $31 billion in 2012. Although rich in natural resources and energy, Canada is also part of an integrated North American supply chain and exchanges many manufactured products with the United States, especially autos, at different stages of production.

- The United States-Canada Free Trade Agreement entered into force on January 1, 1989, and was incorporated into NAFTA on January 1, 1994. As a result, nearly all trade is conducted tariff and restriction free between the two countries, and with Mexico.
- Canada's willingness to negotiate over its supply management programs for dairy and poultry was reported to be an obstacle for the United States, Australia, and New Zealand to allow Canada's participation in the TPP.
- For the past several years, the U.S. Trade Representative has placed Canada on its "priority watch list" of countries meriting bilateral attention over intellectual property rights enforcement.[24] Just prior to joining the talks in June 2012, the Canadian House of Commons passed copyright modernization legislation.

Chile

U.S. goods trade with Chile has been growing over the past decade, with U.S. exports more than quadrupling to nearly $18.9 billion in 2012 from the advent of the U.S.-Chile FTA in 2004. Total U.S. services trade with Chile was $4.6 billion in 2012. As with Australia and Brunei, Chile's major exports to the world are fuel and mining products, particularly copper. However, it also has a well-developed agriculture sector, which contributes to exports. Manufactured goods make up over 60% of its world imports. Chile-U.S. trade mirrors these world patterns. The top U.S. imports from Chile are copper, fruits/nuts, and seafood. Meanwhile, U.S. exports to Chile consist mostly of machinery, refined oil products, and vehicles. The United States is a major trading partner for the country, providing about 17% of Chile's total imports.

- The U.S.-Chile FTA entered into force on January 1, 2004, and as a result most goods are or will eventually be exchanged tariff-free.[25]
- Despite welcoming Chile's "significant commitment" to address outstanding intellectual property rights (IPR) issues under the U.S.-Chile FTA, the country remained on the United States "Special 301" 'priority watch list' of countries meriting bilateral attention.[26]

- The results of Chile's presidential election, which looks likely to bring to power a new left-leaning administration, may impact Chile's TPP negotiating positions and ratification. The new leader will take office in March 2014.[27]

Japan[28]

Japan is the third-largest U.S trading partner in the TPP negotiations, and the largest among the five TPP countries with which the United States does not have an existing FTA. U.S. trade with Japan was $216 billion in merchandise and $73 billion in services in 2012. As the second-largest economy in Asia, the third-largest economy in the world, and a key link in global supply/production chains, many view Japan's participation as pivotal to enhancing the credibility and viability of the TPP as a regional free trade arrangement, and believe it may encourage other Asian countries to join. Prior to Japan's full participation in the negotiations, the United States required Japan to undertake "confidence building measures" in three issues (beef, autos, and insurance), though further liberalization in these areas remains a key goal of U.S. negotiators.

- Japanese farmers have been vocal opponents of the TPP over concerns of increased foreign competition, as have some Japanese health providers, claiming TPP would force Japanese citizens to buy foreign-produced pharmaceuticals and medical devices. However, many Japanese business interests, including manufacturers, strongly support the TPP.
- The Detroit-based U.S. auto industry, the United Autoworkers union, and Members of Congress with a large auto-industry presence in their districts have expressed strong opposition to Japan's involvement in the TPP, raising concerns about Japan's currency policies and purported non-tariff barriers, which they blame for Japan's minimal U.S. auto imports.
- U.S. providers of insurance and express delivery services have expressed the need for disciplines that ensure a "level-playing field" with the subsidiaries of the government-run Japan Post, which compete directly in their industries.
- A large segment of the U.S. business community has expressed support for Japanese participation in the TPP, if Japan can resolve long-standing issues on access to its markets for U.S. goods, services, and agriculture.
- Japan and the United States agreed to hold negotiations in parallel to the TPP negotiations to address issues regarding non-tariff measures (NTMs) in insurance, government procurement, competition policy, express delivery, autos, and sanitary and phytosanitary (SPS) measures. The parallel negotiations are to achieve "tangible and meaningful" results by the completion of the main TPP negotiations and will be legally binding at the time a TPP agreement would enter into force.

Malaysia

Malaysia is the fifth-largest U.S. goods trading partner among TPP countries, totaling nearly $39 billion in 2012. U.S. services trade with Malaysia was just over $1 billion in 2012. The United States imports nearly twice as much as it exports to Malaysia, resulting in a large goods trade deficit of nearly $13.1 billion in 2012. Over the past decade, U.S. imports from Malaysia have been somewhat volatile, though declining considerably in the past five years.

From 2000 to 2006, imports increased from $25 billion to over $35 billion, then fell back to $25.9 billion in 2012. Electrical machinery makes up nearly half of all U.S. imports from, and exports to, Malaysia. Some of this trade comprises the same product category flowing both in and out of the United States and may represent intermediate goods crossing borders at various stages of production.

- The United States and Malaysia previously engaged in FTA negotiations. Those negotiations stalled in 2008 due to disagreements over government procurement practices among other issues.[29]
- In the TPP negotiations, Malaysia may seek additional access to the U.S. market for sugar and dairy products that now are subject to U.S. tariff-rate quotas.
- In 2012, Malaysia was dropped from the U.S. IPR watch list, signifying legislative and regulatory improvements to the country's IPR regime.[30]
- A brief on the TPP published by the Malaysian Ministry of International Trade and Industry highlighted government procurement, intellectual property rights, state-owned enterprises, and labor and environment as challenging issues for the country in the ongoing negotiations.[31]

Mexico

Mexico is the third-largest trading partner of the United States, and the second-largest among the TPP participant countries.[32] Total U.S.-Mexico goods trade was $494 billion in 2012 while services trade between the two countries was $42 billion. Although Mexico's reliance on the United States as an export market has diminished slightly, the United States remains Mexico's largest trading partner by far. Among the TPP participants, the United States had its largest goods trade deficit with Mexico ($61.3 billion) in 2012, but carried a large services surplus ($12.2 billion). As with Canada, Mexico is part of an integrated North American manufacturing supply chain and exchanges goods with the United States—and Canada—at different stages of production.

- NAFTA came into effect between Canada, Mexico, and the United States on January 1, 1994. As a result, nearly all trade between the three countries is now conducted duty and barrier free.[33]
- The TPP negotiations may provide a venue for addressing additional issues, such as reconsideration of Mexico's exclusion of foreign investment in its petroleum industry.
- The prospect of enhancing disciplines in a TPP agreement to address sanitary and phytosanitary (SPS) issues and non-tariff barriers would be welcomed by U.S. agricultural exporters. They have complained that Mexico has held up shipments without providing justification based on "sound science" and imposed burdensome prior inspection requirements.

New Zealand

U.S. trade with New Zealand was relatively small among TPP members in 2012, larger only than Brunei, with total goods trade of $6.7 billion and total services trade of $3.9 billion. U.S.-New Zealand trade is relatively balanced with a small U.S. trade deficit in goods in 2012

($216 million) and a small U.S. trade surplus in services ($149 million). With the rest of the world, New Zealand primarily exports agricultural products and imports manufactured goods. Its trade with the United States is quite similar to its world pattern with top exports to the United States in meat, dairy, and beverages, and imports from the United States in aircraft and machinery.

- The United States does not currently have an FTA with New Zealand, but New Zealand has long sought an FTA and improved access to the large U.S. market.
- The United States has expressed concern that the practices and procedures of the New Zealand Pharmaceutical Management Agency (Pharmac) put "innovative pharmaceutical products," often made in the United States, at a disadvantage to older, generic products.
- Increased dairy market access in the United States is both a top priority for New Zealand and a chief concern among U.S. dairy interests.

Peru

The U.S. trade relationship with Peru is similar to that of its Latin American neighbor, Chile, though on a smaller scale. U.S.-Peru trade totaled $15.8 billion in goods in 2012. Relative to other TPP countries, Peru is the third-smallest U.S. trade partner, in front of New Zealand and Brunei. The United States had a goods trade surplus with Peru of $2.9 billion in 2012, with U.S. exports to Peru increasing four-fold over the past decade. The major U.S. imports from Peru are oil and oil products, copper, and knitted apparel, whereas the major U.S. exports to Peru are machinery, refined oils, and electrical machinery. As with Chile, the United States is a major trading partner with Peru, providing nearly 20% of the country's total imports.

- The United States-Peru Trade Promotion Agreement (an FTA) entered into force on February 1, 2009.[34] As a result, nearly all trade between the two countries is or will soon be conducted tariff and restriction free.
- In its FTA with the United States, Peru agreed to IPR provisions—known as the May 10th agreement—that reflected certain lasting U.S. concerns regarding accessibility to medicines. The IPR chapter proposed by the United States in the TPP negotiations reportedly reflects prior U.S. FTA provisions. Peru has expressed concerns that the new provisions would require it to adopt stricter patent protections, and would negate the previous FTA provisions.[35]
- Peru remains on the U.S. IPR watch list due to concerns over the "widespread availability of counterfeit and pirated products in Peru" and its need to devote additional resources to IPR enforcement, among other issues.[36]

Singapore

Among TPP members, Singapore is a large U.S. trading partner in both goods and services. Total U.S.-Singapore trade was $50.8 billion in goods and $17.2 billion in services in 2012. The United States had a large surplus with Singapore in both goods ($10.3 billion) and services ($7.3 billion) in 2012. Singapore imports primarily business/professional/ technical services from the United States, unlike most countries whose services imports from the United States are mostly in travel/transportation. As an important trade and transshipment hub, Singapore's world goods trade is dominated by manufactured goods, comprising over 70% of exports and 65% of imports. The United States' goods trade with Singapore, as with Malaysia, is also mostly manufactured goods, primarily machinery and electrical machinery.

- The United States-Singapore Free Trade Agreement entered into force on January 1, 2004.[37] As a result, nearly all their trade is conducted tariff and restriction free.
- Due to the importance of State-owned enterprises (SOE) in Singapore's economy, its FTA with the United States contained provisions relating to SOEs. The United States is seeking further disciplines on SOEs in the TPP to ensure private actors can compete equally with state-backed entities. Temasek, Singapore's investment holding company, reportedly has concerns that the disciplines proposed by the United States may put it at a disadvantage relative to private actors.[38]

Vietnam

Vietnam's trade with the United States has increased rapidly over the past decade to $24.9 billion in goods in 2012. At least part of this increase is due to changes in the formal U.S.-Vietnamese trade relationship. In 2001, the United States granted Vietnam conditional normal trade relations, increasing that status to permanent normal trade relations in 2006 with Vietnam's accession to the World Trade Organization (WTO).[39] While U.S. trade with Vietnam has increased in both directions, imports have risen much faster than exports. Hence, the United States had a relatively large ($15.6 billion) goods trade deficit with Vietnam in 2012. Vietnam supplies the United States with mostly labor-intensive products such as knitted and woven apparel. Meanwhile, its top U.S. imports are relatively more high-tech goods, including machinery and vehicles.

- There is no FTA currently in effect between the United States and Vietnam.
- Due to the high volume of U.S. imports of Vietnamese apparel and footwear, better market access in these areas is likely a top priority for Vietnam in the negotiations. Vietnam is seeking "cut and sew" rules of origin that would allow it to source textile inputs from non-TPP countries and still receive the preferences established under the TPP. Certain segments of the U.S. textile and apparel industry, meanwhile, have expressed their opposition to making such concessions to Vietnam in the negotiations.
- As mentioned above, the United States is seeking disciplines on SOEs to address possible unfair competitive advantages. Vietnam has publically expressed concerns over the proposed U.S. negotiating text on SOEs, and with SOEs accounting for perhaps 40% of its GDP, it is the country most likely to challenge the United States on its proposal.[40]
- Additional issues regarding Vietnamese trade relations include U.S. restrictions on Vietnamese seafood and the United States' continued designation of Vietnam as a "non-market economy." While Vietnam has made large strides in liberalizing its economy and has been granted WTO membership, criticism of its standards on labor rights, intellectual property protection, and corruption has persisted in various quarters.

- Vietnam remains on the United States' IPR watch list due, in part, to the continued existence of widespread counterfeiting and piracy, including internet piracy.[41]

Negotiating Topics in TPP (Potential Chapters)

Goods Market Access	Competition/State-owned Enterprises
Agriculture Market Access	Trade Remedies
Textiles and Apparel	Transparency
Customs	Labor
Rules of Origin	Environment
Technical Barriers to Trade	Exceptions
Sanitary and Phytosanitary Standards	Definitions
Services	Dispute Settlement
Investment	Cooperation and Capacity Building
Financial Services	Regulatory Coherence
Telecommunications	Business Facilitation and Competitiveness (supply chains)
E-Commerce	Development
Temporary Entry	Small- and Medium-Sized Enterprises
Intellectual Property Rights	Living Agreement
Government Procurement	

Core Negotiating Issues: Market Access

Market access for goods, services, and agriculture often forms the crux of FTA negotiations. However, non-tariff barriers such as technical barriers to trade and sanitary and phytosanitary standards, while considered rules, also have an impact on market access. Negotiations on these latter issues are designed to ensure that, as tariff barriers are reduced, they are not replaced by other forms of protection.

Market Access for Goods and Services

A fundamental element of most FTAs is commitments among FTA partners to eliminate most, if not all, tariffs and quotas on their trade in goods. Current average MFN tariff levels for TPP countries vary from 0% to nearly 10% (**Figure 6**). The TPP will include tariff phase-out schedules that cover more than 11,000 commodity categories for each of the partner countries. At their November 2011 meeting in Honolulu, the TPP trade ministers stated that they are aiming for duty-free access for trade in goods. The tariff schedules will likely provide for phase-out of tariffs, with tariffs on many products phased-out immediately when the agreement enters into force, and tariffs on more sensitive products phased out over varying periods of time. All of the current TPP countries are in the process of some tariff elimination as each has an FTA with one or more of the other TPP partners. As mentioned above, the United States has free trade agreements with Australia, Canada, Chile, Mexico,

Peru, and Singapore, and the original P-4 countries have already negotiated FTA provisions among themselves. The TPP may build on these previous commitments and harmonize tariff elimination for all members. TPP partners are also discussing provisions that deal with export and import licensing procedures, customs issues, and trade facilitation.

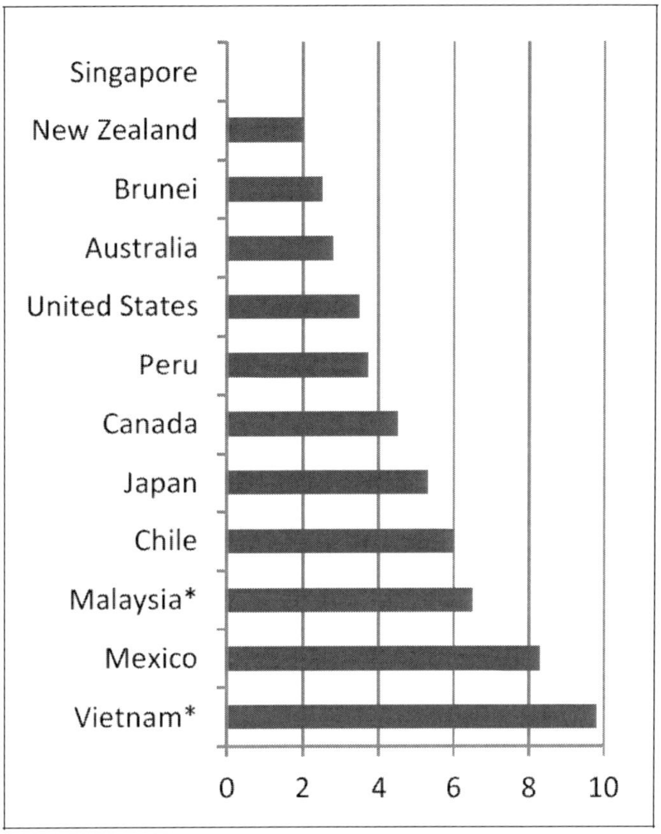

Source: WTO Tariff Profiles, 2012.

Notes: These are the WTO-wide average MFN applied tariff rates, and hence do not reflect FTA tariff rates (e.g., the average tariff applied to U.S. exports to Canada and Mexico would be much lower due to NAFTA). * Signifies data from 2010.

Figure 6. Average MFN Applied Tariffs.

Textiles, Apparel, and Footwear

Differences are likely to arise between the developed countries and some of the developing countries, including Vietnam, over elimination of tariffs on labor-intensive products, such as textiles and apparel and footwear. The United States, for example, has included in its FTAs long tariff phase-out periods, special safeguards, and restrictive rules of origin (see below) to protect U.S. domestic producers from the adverse effects of import-sensitive products. For example, certain U.S. footwear manufacturers have argued for maintaining high tariffs on imported footwear, while Vietnam is pressing for lower tariffs to gain greater access to the U.S. market.[42] Developing countries have argued that they need preferential access to the large markets in order to compete with producers from other countries, such as China.[43]

Trade in Services

A high priority for the United States in its negotiations of bilateral and regional free trade agreements has been increased market access for services providers, especially financial services, including insurance and banking; professional services, including legal services and private educational services; telecommunication services; express delivery; and e-commerce (see e- commerce section below). In doing so, the United States has sought to expand on modest commitments that trade partners have made in the World Trade Organization (WTO) under the General Agreement on Trade in Services (GATS), especially in light of the perceived failure of WTO partners to expand on those commitments in the now dormant Doha Round.

U.S. FTAs with TPP partners Australia, Canada, Chile, Mexico, Peru, and Singapore already cover trade in services. Although these countries cover more than half of U.S.-TPP services trade, Japan is also a major U.S.-services trade partner, so its entry has increased the significance of these provisions. Moreover, innovations regarding trade in services is a key part of the Obama Administration's vision of the TPP as a "21st -century model" for trade agreements, and the United States seeks TPP services provisions to be as broad as possible to cover trade with future entrants.

Cross-border Services

According to the agreed outline, the TPP will cover services trade in several separate chapters, with some overlap. The section on cross-border trade in services—in which the buyer and seller are located in different territories—will employ the "negative list approach" (as did the P-4 agreement), that is, the provisions are to apply to all types of services unless specifically excluded by a partner country in an annex to the agreement. This approach is generally considered to be more comprehensive than the "positive list approach" used in the GATS that requires each covered service to be identified. The negative approach also implies that any new type of service that is developed after the agreement enters into force is automatically covered unless it is specifically excluded.

Most trade agreements on cross-border services trade, including U.S. FTAs and the original P-4 agreement, contain basic provisions on services that will likely be part of the TPP:

- non-discriminatory treatment of services from partner-country providers, including national treatment and most-favored-nation treatment;
- market access—no limitations on the number of service suppliers, the total value or volume of services provided, the number of persons employed, or the types of legal entities or joint ventures that a foreign service supplier may employ;
- prohibition on requirements that a partner-based service provider maintain a commercial presence in the country of the buyer;
- mutual recognition of professional qualifications for certification of service providers;
- transparency in the development and application of government regulations; and
- allowance for payments and transfers of capital flows in the provision of services.

In recent FTAs, including KORUS FTA, the United States has made market access of *express delivery services* a priority, which could also be the case in its negotiations on the

TPP. Of particular concern are cases where a government-owned and operated postal system provides express delivery services competing with private sector providers. The KORUS FTA (Annex-12- B) stipulates that the postal system cannot use its monopoly power in providing postal services to give an express delivery subsidiary an unfair advantage. Nor should it divert revenues from its postal services to subsidize its express delivery services to the disadvantage of other providers.

Financial Services

The draft TPP outline indicates that financial services, including insurance and insurance-related services, banking and related services, as well as auxiliary services of a financial nature, will be addressed in a separate chapter as in previous FTAs. The original P-4 agreement did not include financial services provisions when it came into force in 2006. However, the P-4 partners committed to concluding a financial services (and investment) chapter within two years—a commitment that was overtaken by the launch of the TPP. The financial services chapter would adapt relevant provisions from the foreign investment chapter and the cross-border trade in services chapter. The KORUS FTA was the most recent U.S. FTA in which the United States negotiated provisions on financial services and which presumably will serve as a model for U.S. negotiations of the TPP in this area. The KORUS FTA distinguishes between financial services traded across borders and those sold by a provider with a commercial presence in the home country of the buyer. In the case of providers with a foreign commercial presence, the KORUS FTA applies the negative list approach; in the case of cross-border trade, the KORUS FTA limits coverage to specific banking and insurance services.[44]

The KORUS FTA and other U.S. FTAs provide that nothing in the FTA would prevent a party to the agreement from imposing prudential measures to ensure the integrity and stability of the financial system. The KORUS FTA also addresses insurance sold by Korea Post, in particular that Korea Post is not regulated as other financial institutions. U.S. providers have argued that government-owned and operated insurance providers are not regulated as stringently and therefore, have a competitive advantage over their privately owned counterparts. The KORUS FTA stipulates Korea Post insurance operations would be subject to tighter regulation. Another issue of U.S. concern regarding financial services was assurances that a U.S. financial service provider located in South Korea would be able to transfer information electronically or by other means from the host country where it is required in the ordinary course of business. Such information could include accounting information and human resources information that a company would want to transfer and process to a central location rather than having to process and keep at individual locations. The KORUS FTA indicates that South Korea would comply with this commitment two years after the agreement enters into force (2014). Host governments are cautious that such transfers of information might violate domestic privacy laws and considerations.

In addition, other chapters in the proposed agreement would affect trade in services because of the nature of services and their modes of delivery. Most services require the provider and buyer to be co-located, and the largest volume of services trade occurs when the provider has a commercial presence in the form of a direct investment in the country of the buyer and sells the service to the buyer. Therefore, provisions of the TPP that may pertain to foreign investments (discussed elsewhere) relate to trade in services. In addition, many service providers, such as sellers of entertainment programming, are intellectual property owners and argue for strong IP rights protection, the subject of another chapter in the proposed TPP (and discussed elsewhere). Furthermore, most of the barriers to trade in services are in the form of domestic regulations; therefore, the cross-cutting objective for regulatory coherence would affect trade in services.

According to the November 2011 outline, as in previous U.S. FTAs, the TPP will have a separate chapter on telecommunications trade. The TPP is to promote access to telecommunications networks for foreign services suppliers and transparency of regulations pertaining to telecommunications services. Along with these objectives, the United States sought and obtained in the KORUS FTA commitments to allow U.S. investment in foreign telecommunications companies.

Negotiations over the services provisions likely will lead to controversy between the developed countries, including the United States, Australia, Canada, Japan, New Zealand, and Singapore, and developing countries. Developed countries have pushed for greater market access for services. Developing countries have been more cautious on liberalization in services trade as they fear competition in sectors they view as a source of domestic employment and worry about the political implications of forcing open sectors that are often controlled by politically powerful interests. Also, the United States may be challenged to open its market to providers of maritime services. The United States has also been pressed to liberalize access to its market through the so- called mode-4 delivery—temporary entry of personnel to provide services. No U.S. FTA negotiated after the agreements with Chile and Singapore agreements includes provisions on the temporary movement of personnel.

Government Procurement

The United States is a member of the plurilateral WTO Government Procurement Agreement (GPA) and has sought the inclusion of government procurement provisions in its FTAs. Among TPP partner countries, only Japan and Singapore are members of the GPA, although New Zealand announced on August 15, 2012, that it will seek to join the agreement.[45] In previous FTA negotiations with Malaysia, the United States had sought concessions on government procurement, a sensitive area for Malaysia which since 1969 has maintained preferences designed to assist the ethnic Malay population. U.S. FTAs with Australia, Peru, Chile, Singapore, and NAFTA include chapters on government procurement, which provide opportunities for firms of each nation to bid on certain federal and state contracts over a set monetary threshold on a reciprocal basis. A similar chapter has been proposed by U.S. negotiators in the TPP talks.

In the 112th Congress, 68 Members of Congress wrote to President Obama to urge the Administration not to negotiate government procurement provisions that would limit the application of Buy American provisions through extension of government procurement opportunities and obligations to TPP partner countries.[46] However, Canada reportedly may seek to address remaining U.S. Buy American exclusions concerning state and municipal projects funded by the federal government through the TPP.[47] Supporters argue that the reciprocal nature of the government procurement provisions will allow U.S. firms access to major government procurement programs overseas. This market potentially could be quite large. According to the WTO, government procurement accounts for 15%-20% of a country's GDP, and the size of the government procurement market among GPA members was $1.6 trillion in 2008.[48]

At the Dallas round of negotiations, the United States reportedly proposed that TPP countries negotiate access commitments for central government procurement before addressing sub-federal or state level commitments.[49] This may be due to resistance among some U.S. states in providing access to their procurement markets. States must voluntarily opt in to government procurement commitments in FTA, but the number of states doing so has dropped substantially from the 37 states that signed up to the GPA to 8 states that have acceded to commitments under the most recent U.S. bilateral FTAs with South Korea, Panama, and Colombia. However, Canada reportedly tabled a proposal during the Singapore round that would obligate sub-federal entities to open procurement projects funded by a central government to competition from firms in TPP countries.[50]

Agriculture

Most attention in negotiating agricultural provisions in bilateral FTAs focuses on what additional market access the United States can secure for its farm commodities and food products in prospective partner countries. The outcome is usually reflected in a "National Treatment and Market Access for Goods" chapter and accompanying detailed tariff-line schedules. However, negotiators also address matters in other FTA chapters that affect commerce in agricultural products. The TPP agreement will similarly deal with a wide range of agricultural issues as described below.

Market Access

U.S. agriculture has both offensive and defensive interests in the TPP negotiations. Many in the U.S. agriculture and the agribusiness/food manufacturing sectors view positively the prospect of market openings in the three commercially significant countries with which the United States does not yet have an FTA (i.e., Japan, Malaysia, and Vietnam). Though Japan currently is the fourth-largest U.S. agricultural export market, it protects producers of its sensitive commodities with very high tariffs and restrictive quotas. Malaysia and Vietnam, due to their expanding populations and growing incomes, likely will continue to fuel demand for consumer-ready U.S. food products. U.S. cotton could also see higher demand from Vietnam for its textile sector. Of the three, Japan is viewed as the most promising market for U.S. agriculture.

The U.S. dairy sector, however, has adopted a multi-pronged posture, eyeing opportunities in certain TPP markets, but is also concerned about the competition that New Zealand's dairy exporters would pose in the U.S. market as well as other TPP country markets. The U.S. sugar production sector opposes opening the U.S. sugar market to any additional imports from the TPP region.

The U.S. agriculture and food processing sectors welcomed the decisions made to invite Canada, Mexico, and Japan to join the TPP talks. They view Canada's participation as an opportunity to reopen unfinished business from the U.S.-Canada FTA (i.e., seek improved access for U.S. dairy and poultry products in the restricted Canadian market). Both sectors also will seek to address ongoing non-tariff barriers that arise at times in shipping agricultural commodities to Mexico, and to create market openings for those commodities that are highly protected by Japan.

In negotiating market access (whether for agricultural or non-agricultural products), the TPP countries have engaged in a process where offers are exchanged with each other and then responded to with requests to improve the offer. Each country's initial offer laid out the terms under which it would open up its market to the products of a partner country. These terms detail for each tariff line (about 2,000 for agricultural products) the transition or phase-out time period over which current trade barriers (tariffs, quotas, and other forms of protection) are removed. They specify whether these barriers would be eliminated immediately or in stages—set at specific future points in time (e.g., 3, 5, 10, 15 years, etc.). In U.S.-concluded FTAs, tariffs on a large portion of all products have been eliminated immediately. Decisions on what to offer as a phase- out period for each product depend on how sensitive a country perceives imports from a partner country to be to domestic producers. For the most import-sensitive agricultural products, offers lay out the longest transition periods or call for product exclusions. Each country then responds to a negotiating partner with a request to improve the latter's market access offer on a line-by-line basis (e.g., speed up tariff reduction, increase a quota more quickly, remove a marketing barrier). This iterative process narrows outstanding differences to a small group of products, which then are left to lead negotiators and political leaders to resolve (if possible) in the last stages of the trade negotiations. The offer/request process frequently involves countries taking possible market access outcomes into account as trade-offs are negotiated on controversial issues elsewhere in a trade agreement (i.e., rules of origin, intellectual property rights, competition policy, among others).

To date, USTR has engaged in a separate offer/request process with each of the five countries that the United States does not yet have a bilateral FTA—Brunei, Japan, Malaysia, New Zealand, and Vietnam—and with Canada on products not fully liberalized under the U.S.-Canada FTA. The U.S. bilateral offers spell out different stages of tariff cuts for various TPP partners. With respect to the other countries with which the United States has an FTA, the U.S. position is that it will not engage in talks to reopen any existing market access provision. Japan and Peru reportedly have taken the same approach, tabling offers that would apply different tariff levels for the same product to different TPP countries that reflect varying levels of sensitivities. All other TPP countries have followed a plurilateral approach—making a common offer to all other participants except the United States, and then likely handling the requests received in some unified way. Japan reportedly planned to follow a hybrid approach—presenting tariff offers that would cut tariffs by the same amount for all TPP countries.[51]

Border Protection Issues for Sensitive Agricultural Products

In contrast to relatively low average tariffs levied on imports of manufactured goods, some TPP countries impose high average tariffs on imports of agricultural commodities and food products and/or rely on quotas to limit the quantity allowed to enter their domestic markets. These higher tariffs and restrictive quotas serve to protect producers and processors of commodities and foods deemed to be "sensitive." They argue that their livelihoods would be threatened if these forms of border protection are relaxed or eliminated (i.e., they would not be able to compete against cheaper imports). As a result, commodity groups and agricultural coalitions in Canada, Japan, Malaysia, and the United States have urged their trade negotiators to exclude their sensitive products from the trade liberalization envisioned in the TPP negotiations. In opposition to this stance, business groups in some of these countries argue that excluding any product will damage the possibility of securing openings for services, enhancing protection for intellectual property rights on media and medicines, and attaining other objectives. New Zealand, for example, argues that excluding any agricultural product would set a precedent and encourage other countries to seek exclusions for their own sensitive products. Observers note that if this scenario unfolds, the level of ambition and comprehensiveness that TPP country leaders agreed to in Honolulu in late 2011 would not be realized.

Facing these pressures as the TPP talks near conclusion, each country's policy makers and trade negotiators are now weighing possible tradeoffs between retaining some protection for, or excluding, sensitive agricultural products, securing trade liberalization for their other products, and adopting rules and disciplines that would apply to how firms transact business throughout the TPP region. The outcome of how TPP countries engage Japan on the exclusion issue could well set the parameters for how ambitious and comprehensive the final overall TPP agreement is. Once Japan joined the TPP negotiations, its largest agricultural lobby continued to call on its government to exclude opening up Japan's market to any additional imports of its most sensitive agricultural commodities (rice, barley, wheat, dairy products, beef, pork, and sweeteners). While Japan's initial offers reportedly incorporated these exclusions and limited tariff reductions for many other agricultural and food products, bilateral negotiations with the United States may be leading to a slight shift in Japan's position.

In mid-November 2013, Japan reportedly offered to retain special import quotas for rice and other sensitive agricultural products that would allow for additional imports from the TPP region at very low or zero tariffs. Imports above set quota amounts would continue to face existing high tariffs. The United States has continued to insist that Japan take steps to completely eliminate these high tariffs, likely over a long transition period. In high-level discussions between trade ministers held on December 1, 2013, Japan repeated its stance that concessions on these sensitive farm commodities cannot be made. This meeting concluded without any change in positions. While in Tokyo on December 3, Vice President Joe Biden highlighted these sensitivities, and called for bilateral cooperation to solve these differences in order to strike the difficult compromises needed to conclude the TPP negotiations in 2013. Other TPP countries, in turn, are carefully monitoring these U.S.-Japanese talks for signs on how their requests will be considered and to gauge the prospects for what political deals might be struck at the critical TPP Ministerial to be held in Singapore from December 7 to 10.[52]

Other countries have staked out similar positions and/or face calls from producers to have their "sensitive" commodities exempted from or adequately protected under any TPP agreement. Malaysian civil society groups seek to exclude tobacco and tobacco products, a stance possibly prompted by an effort to retain "complete leeway" in how TPP countries regulate tobacco within the tobacco control provisions that may be incorporated in the final text (see below).[53] Canadian producers of dairy products, eggs, and poultry expect their negotiators to control imports in prospective trade agreements to ensure that they receive the full benefits of domestic supply management intended to ensure their economic viability. Their objective in the TPP talks is to either exclude and/or tightly limit any additional access granted to imports of these products from New Zealand, the United States, and other TPP countries. A sign of the pressures that Canada's negotiators will face is the negative reaction expressed by its dairy producers to the access for specialty cheeses that Canada provided to the European Union (EU) in their recently concluded free trade agreement. The Dairy

Farmers of Canada stated it will not support this deal, claiming that subsidized cheese from the EU will displace domestic production of its fine artisan and local cheeses that the industry has worked hard to develop.[54]

Dairy products and sugar are two of the most significant sensitive agricultural commodities for the United States. U.S. producers of milk and some processors of dairy products initially called on U.S. negotiators to exclude dairy from the TPP, but their position shifted when it appeared Canada and Japan would join the negotiations. U.S. sugar producers and processors, though, oppose reopening the sugar market access provisions in any current FTA with a TPP country (e.g., Australia). However, manufacturers that use milk and sugar as inputs in food products argue for different reasons that these commodities should be liberalized in the TPP agreement. Their trade associations have joined broad business groups, food sector firms, and other agricultural commodity groups to argue that excluding any U.S. commodity or product from TPP coverage would prompt other countries to refuse to open up their markets to competition from U.S. exports or include disciplines and rules on other issues that FTAs have not previously addressed.[55] The following sections present the views of those with interests in how the TPP talks might affect two U.S. sensitive agricultural commodities—dairy and sugar.

Dairy

The U.S. dairy production sector, represented by the National Milk Producers Federation (NMPF) and the U.S. Dairy Export Council (USDEC),[56] has four objectives in the TPP negotiations: (1) limit New Zealand's access to the U.S. market for its dairy products; (2) secure complete free access for U.S. dairy exports into Canada, (3) gain comprehensive market access for dairy products into the Japanese market, and (4) realize the enforcement of food safety and health rules in traded agricultural products. It has signaled that its support for a final TPP deal depends on its assessment of the benefits and drawbacks of the final dairy and related provisions that U.S. negotiators reach. In a late July 2013 letter, 74 House Members called on the Obama Administration to place a high priority on achieving a positive outcome for the U.S. dairy sector in the TPP by pursuing these objectives.[57]

New Zealand is a major dairy exporter in world markets. It exports some products to the United States both under established import quotas and also outside these quotas. The U.S. dairy sector has long viewed New Zealand as a competitive threat, but that perspective may be changing as some U.S. dairy firms have increasingly begun to take advantage of export opportunities in many markets, including those in Asia. The sector's concern that dairy trade does not take place on a "level playing field" targets Fonterra, New Zealand's leading dairy cooperative, which purchases about 90% of the country's milk output. They argue that Fonterra's domination of New Zealand's market provides it with a privileged position and makes fair competition impossible. To counteract Fonterra's status, the NMPF and USDEC want the United States to negotiate tough competition disciplines in the TPP.

Under the U.S.-Canada FTA, Canada retained the use of tariff-rate quotas to limit imports of dairy products from the United States. Imports above quota levels are subject to prohibitively high tariffs (e.g., 245% for cheese, 298% for butter). These quotas and tariffs are an integral component of Canada's dairy supply management program, which supports milk prices by limiting production to meet domestic demand at a cost-determined price.[58] In addition to seeking the elimination of these quotas, the NMPF and USDEC want U.S. negotiators to tackle outstanding non-tariff measures that have limited, and could further restrict, access for U.S. fluid milk, various dairy ingredients, and cheese in the Canadian market.

Sugar

The United States excluded sugar in extending market access to Australia for all other products as negotiators concluded talks on a bilateral FTA in early 2004. However, Australia at the urging of its sugar producers may seek to reopen this issue in the final stages of the TPP talks in return for engaging with U.S. priorities in such areas as e-commerce, investor-state dispute settlement, and state-owned enterprises. Australia's Trade Minister has signaled that concluding the TPP must resolve 19th-century market access issues in order to conclude a 21st-century agreement that includes commitments in these new areas. USTR, though, has for some time held the position that the United States will not reopen market access provisions in any existing FTA, including Australia.[59]

U.S. sugar producers and processors are opposed to granting any additional access to sugar entering from any current or future TPP partner. They point out that when additional sugar supplies are needed, provisions in the 2008 farm bill allow USDA to increase existing import quotas to meet domestic demand.[60] Producers and processors argue that granting additional or new duty-free access to sugar would instead result in an oversupply of sugar in the U.S. market, depress U.S. prices below loan rate levels, cause a major decline in the incomes of U.S. sugar producers, and trigger large federal outlays.[61]

U.S. food manufacturers want to see sugar included in the TPP, in order to gain access to additional imports of sugar and get closer to attaining a more market oriented U.S. sugar policy. They list the potential benefits associated with such a step—increased competition in the U.S. market associated with diversifying the sources of imported sugar to meet U.S. sugar demand; a stemming of job losses in sugar-using food processing sectors, particularly the confectionery industry which claims to have moved operations offshore to take advantage of lower-priced sugar; the generating of foreign exchange by sugar exporting countries that can be used to buy U.S. agricultural and food products; and gains that U.S. consumers and businesses would realize with lower sugar prices.[62]

Agricultural Issues in Other TPP Chapters

In TPP's "Rules" chapter, negotiators are seeking to address how to better address disputes that can arise over differences on how to handle human health and animal/plant safety issues (i.e., sanitary and phytosanitary standards (SPS)) associated with trade in agricultural products, and the possible ramifications of regulating the sale of some tobacco products on trade in tobacco. The "Intellectual Property Rights" chapter could include provisions to prescribe how agricultural products with a "geographical indications" designation and traded in the TPP region are to be treated. The "Competition" chapter may address objectives sought by Australia and New Zealand to secure disciplines on TPP countries' use of export subsidies, export credits, and food aid to promote their agricultural sectors. How negotiators address some of these issues could involve tradeoffs on the degree to which markets are opened.

Sanitary and Phytosanitary Standards

Efforts to resolve outstanding bilateral sanitary and phytosanitary (SPS) disputes with some TPP partners, if successful, can be expected to lead to additional U.S. agricultural exports above and beyond what U.S. negotiators might secure in market access talks alone. In negotiating its bilateral FTAs, though, the United States has pursued a two track process. Each concluded FTA includes a chapter that reaffirms multilateral commitments made in the World Trade Organization's (WTO's) SPS Agreement. This Agreement lays out the rules and disciplines to be followed by all WTO members to ensure that each country's food safety and animal and plant health laws and regulations are transparent, scientifically defensible, and fair. Also, U.S. negotiators have also sought to address outstanding bilateral SPS disputes in parallel talks, using them as leverage to cut deals on sensitive matters in FTA talks or to secure political support back home for a concluded trade agreement.

As part of the effort to make the TPP a 21st-century agreement, negotiators have drafted an SPS chapter laying out more detailed commitments relating to human health and animal/plant safety issues which would go beyond those found in the WTO SPS Agreement. At the same time, USTR reportedly is working bilaterally to resolve existing SPS disputes (e.g., in parallel talks with Japan), aiming to bring home breakthroughs to garner support for an eventual TPP agreement.

At the May 2013 Lima Round, USTR tabled text to establish both a "consultative mechanism" to address SPS disputes that arise and a "rapid-response mechanism" designed to quickly resolve SPS barriers that block shipments of perishable products. This proposal does not include any enforcement mechanism, a top TPP priority sought by U.S. agriculture and food groups. Other TPP countries that are significant agricultural exporters also appear to similarly favor a dispute settlement process for SPS obligations.[63] Previously, a letter from 24 Members of Congress called for the inclusion of "effective and enforceable rules" to strengthen the role of science in resolving differences; one agricultural group leader stated efforts to deal with strengthening SPS rules are a waste of time without enforceable rules.[64] But a dairy sector representative expects that the issue of a binding SPS dispute mechanism likely will not be resolved until the TPP talks near their conclusion.[65]

Negotiators reportedly have completed all of the technical work on the SPS chapter, and have laid aside outstanding issues to be resolved by higher-level officials for when TPP talks move closer to conclusion. The major issue on which strong differences still exist is over what approach should be included in this chapter to resolve SPS issues that arise among TPP members. At the Lima Round, Peru reportedly tabled a counterproposal calling for full dispute settlement, in contrast to the "consultative" and "rapid-response" mechanisms proposed by the United States.[66]

Tobacco Regulation

In August 2013, USTR decided to take a different approach in the TPP talks on the issue of controlling tobacco use compared with the initial draft that generated considerable controversy. The original USTR proposal, made public in May 2012, would have allowed public health authorities in TPP countries to adopt regulations that "impose origin-neutral, science-based restrictions on specific tobacco products/classes in order to safeguard public health."[67] The Administration's objective was to create a "safe harbor" for the Food and Drug Administration (FDA) to regulate tobacco products under the Family Smoking Prevention and Tobacco Control Act of 2009. This law gives FDA broad new regulatory authority over the manufacture, distribution, marketing, and sale of tobacco products in order to improve public health.[68] USTR's proposal was intended to protect that authority and reduce the likelihood that the final-negotiated TPP agreement is used in a manner that would prevent

FDA from regulating tobacco products. Responding to this draft proposal, some Members of Congress expressed concerns that the proposal would prejudice the interests of tobacco producers and cigarette manufacturers seeking export openings in the other TPP countries. Business groups argued that it would undermine the long-standing claim made by USTR that provisions in previous FTAs grant governments sufficient flexibility to issue regulations to protect public health objectives.

USTR's proposal, tabled at the August 2013 Brunei Round, would clarify that TPP countries agree that exceptions allowed under two multilateral trade agreements include measures "necessary to prevent or reduce tobacco use or its harms." Article XX(b) of the General Agreement on Tariffs and Trade (GATT) states that WTO members agree that measures deemed to be "necessary to protect human, animal or plant life or health" would not violate the GATT if the measure is not a "disguised" trade barrier and meets several other criteria. Article XVI of the General Agreement on Trade in Services (GATS) includes a similar exception. Also, the proposal would require a TPP country to consult with other members before beginning a legal challenge under whatever tobacco control measures are adopted in the final TPP text.[69]

Other Members and anti-tobacco groups criticized the proposal as not going far enough to protect public health, and wanted to see USTR's proposal include tobacco control laws, as well as regulatory rules, and to exclude tobacco products from trade liberalization. Others argue that the proposal opens the door for other countries to seek similar exemptions for other agricultural products.

Reactions to USTR's reported new proposal have been critical of the change in approach and say it raises additional questions. Five anti-smoking groups expressed disappointment that USTR retreated from its earlier proposal that would have made it more difficult for tobacco companies to challenge domestic tobacco control measures under trade agreements. These groups note that USTR's latest approach is "far weaker" than originally envisioned because it does not recognize tobacco as a "uniquely harmful product" or provide a way for countries to regulate tobacco in order to reduce its use. They also point out the new language would not cover lawsuits filed by tobacco firms and would not provide countries that have strong tobacco control measures with the protection needed to fend off challenges by the tobacco industry.[70] Observers wonder how TPP members would handle the proposed interpretation of a multilaterally negotiated right laid out in the WTO agreements in the context of a regional trade agreement. Some note that the proposal does not make it easier for any tobacco control measure to meet the other requirements stated in GATT Article XX to meet its "protection" criterion. They also point out that the consultation requirement may still not stave off legal challenges, and argue that tobacco is still singled out as a unique product in the way that special rules for tobacco control measures would be applied.[71]

Geographical Indications

The WTO's intellectual property rights agreement and related provisions in the FTAs negotiated by the United States recognize the use of geographical indications (GIs) to protect the quality and reputation of a distinctive product produced in a particular region of a country. The use of GIs applies primarily to agricultural products, wines, and spirits. Examples of geographical indications are Roquefort cheese, Idaho potatoes, Champagne, or Tuscan olive oil. Products so designated are eligible for relief from acts of infringement and/or unfair competition under a country's trademark laws and regulations. The GI designation (similar to a registered trademark) protects consumers from the use of deceptive or misleading labels, and provides them with choices among products and with information on which to base their purchase decisions. Producers benefit because a GI designation recognizes the distinctiveness of their products in the marketplace.[72]

In May 2012, a group of U.S., Australian and New Zealand food and commodity organizations presented recommendations to TPP negotiators to limit the protection of products with geographic names.[73] One recommendation calls for a GI protected by a TPP country in a trade agreement with a third party (e.g., the European Union (EU)) to be limited to compound phrases that include the name of the region or sub-region where the product is produced together with the name of the product. For example, GI protection would extend to cheese marked Parmigiano Reggiano—a compound term—but not to parmesan, which would be considered a common name not eligible for special protection. The group states that limiting GI designations only to compound names would prevent confusion with the use of related common or generic terms. This proposal's intent is to challenge the EU's efforts to protect its expansive system of GIs in negotiating FTAs with other TPP countries, by creating exclusive rights for products that this group considers to have common names.

The differing perspectives on the use of GIs reportedly surfaced among TPP countries at the December 2012 Auckland Round. Canada and Singapore, which are negotiating FTAs with the EU, are seeking strong GI protections on its dairy products (e.g., cheeses), and are reported to have sensitivities on this issue. Australia, and New Zealand, and the United States, though, favor the less specific naming approach.[74]

Agricultural Competition

One of Australia's TPP negotiating objectives, supported by New Zealand, is to secure disciplines on other TPP countries' use of export subsidies, official export credits, and food aid in support of their agricultural sectors. Its negotiators have argued for years in the multilateral Doha Round that these programmatic tools distort agricultural trade and should be modified when negotiating trade agreements in order to minimize such impacts. They highlight the widely held view that the use of these tools provides a competitive edge to agricultural exporters in those countries.[75]

Australia's proposed text on agricultural export competition reportedly reflects in part the rules proposed in the 2008 Doha text on the use of export financing and international food aid.[76] In that draft, developed countries would agree to phase out export subsidies, curtail the use of export credits, and prescribe under what circumstances food aid is to be provided.[77] With the Doha Round stalled, Australia and New Zealand view the TPP as a venue to "to address these issues that can cause negative effects on agricultural exporters."[78]

In the September 2012 Leesburg talks, Australia reportedly continued to press its position. At their conclusion, USTR's lead negotiator acknowledged that this issue "is extremely sensitive" and made clear it is "not [one the United States is] inclined to address in this negotiation." U.S. negotiators in previous FTA negotiations have always maintained that export competition issues should be addressed in the multilateral context, and succeeded in keeping them out of final trade agreements. But in light of continued interest in including these issues in the TPP negotiations, she stated USTR would begin consultations with domestic stakeholders and Congress on this matter.[79] Just before the December 2012 Auckland Round, the United States signaled its opposition to any effort to include food aid disciplines in the TPP, reiterating that such rules should be developed on a multilateral basis.[80]

Observers offer various views on Australia's motivations. Some characterize its position as a tactical maneuver to advance one of its priority objectives in the Doha Round. Others view the export competition/SOE linkage as part of Australia's strategy to see the United States address its other priorities (e.g., obtaining additional sugar and dairy product access into the U.S. market, securing an exclusion for Australia from TPP's final investor-state dispute settlement mechanism).[81]

CORE NEGOTIATING ISSUES: RULES

In addition to market access, the TPP contains several provisions that build upon disciplines contained in the World Trade Organization's Uruguay Round agreements. Many of these provisions have become part of the standard template for U.S. FTAs. The chief U.S. negotiator on the TPP, Assistant USTR Barbara Weisel, reportedly indicated that the current TPP participants are open to allowing developing countries in the TPP to have longer phase-in periods for rules- based commitments. She stated that those countries would eventually have to adhere to all of the obligations of the agreement.[82]

Intellectual Property Rights (IPR)

The United States has sought increased intellectual property rights (IPR) protection in its FTAs. IPR negotiating objectives in the last U.S. trade promotion authority (P.L. 107-210) in effect between 2002 and 2007 included, among others, (1) the application of existing IPR protection to digital media and (2) negotiation of trade agreements in terms of IPR that "reflect a standard of protection similar to that found in U.S. law." This phrase opened the door to the negotiation of provisions that go beyond the level of protection provided in the WTO Trade Related Aspects of Intellectual Property (TRIPS) Agreement, most recently with the TPP negotiations. For example, the United States has sought to have its partner countries sign the World Intellectual Property Organization's (WIPO's) Performances and Phonograms Treaty, an agreement to which Brunei, Malaysia, New Zealand, and Vietnam are not parties. For its part, New Zealand reportedly floated a discussion document that favors a "TRIPS-aligned" position, one that would be consistent with, but not go beyond, international standards already found in the TRIPS Agreement. In contrast, U.S. business groups have favored the TRIPS-plus provisions found in the KORUS FTA as a baseline for future negotiations.[83]

Enforcement

The U.S. text, parts of which have been released unofficially, call for criminal penalties for "willful" trademark counterfeiting and copyright piracy on a "commercial scale." Commercial scale includes acts that result in no direct or financial gain, such as file sharing. It would also require criminal penalties for importing counterfeit labeling and packaging whether done willfully or not, and it would requires criminal penalties for cam-cording in movie theatres.

Some countries, notably Australia, New Zealand, and Singapore, reportedly have sought to replace U.S. text on criminal enforcement with that of the Anti-Counterfeiting Trade Agreement (ACTA), which was signed last year.[84] Although both ACTA and the U.S. proposal, which largely track the IPR provisions in the U.S.-Korea FTA, provide stricter criminal enforcement measures than the World Trade Organization (WTO) Trade-Related Intellectual Property Agreement (TRIPS), ACTA provides greater flexibility than what is reportedly contained in the U.S. text regarding a country's enforcement of IPR. For example, in ACTA, financial gain is necessary to be considered commercial scale for prosecution, and willfulness is required for importation of trademark infringing goods.

Internet Providers

One area where traditionally there has been a difference of opinion among U.S. stakeholders relates to copyright enforcement and the Internet, especially between Internet service providers (ISP) and traditional content providers. Internet providers and other activists are seeking to provide a more explicit balance in the agreement text between the rights of content providers and users of copyright material. The United States reportedly proposed such language to the IPR chapter at the San Diego round of negotiations concluded in July 2012.[85] The proposal places certain limitations on the copyrights consistent with the so-called "three-step test": that the exception (1) is consistent with domestic copyright law; (2) does not conflict with the normal exploitation of the work; and (3) does not unreasonably prejudice the interest of the rights holder. The proposal also reportedly obligates each country to provide for such exceptions in their domestic copyright laws.

Access to Medicines

The debate over the IPR provisions in the TPP relating to pharmaceuticals and access to medicines, some of the more controversial provisions in U.S.-negotiated FTAs in recent years, revolves around whether to assert the more far-reaching IPR provisions of the KORUS FTA or to adopt the somewhat looser "May 10th Agreement" provisions found in the Colombia, Peru, and Panama FTAs.[86] Based on published reports, it appears that U.S. negotiators are trying to develop an approach that would build on the May 10th agreement, which sets different standards for developed countries (as found in the KORUS FTA) than developing countries (as in the Colombia, Panama, and Peru FTAs) for certain intellectual property provisions.[87]

In late November 2013, USTR reportedly introduced a revised proposal that would attempt to balance the provision of certain patent protections with the ability of developing countries in the TPP to access needed medicines.[88] The new proposal tracks the intent of the May 10th provisions by reportedly providing options to developing countries in the TPP concerning certain patent protections, at least as long as they remained a developing country based on some agreed-upon benchmark. According to reports, the proposal would allow developing countries to follow the provisions of the U.S. Peru FTA, under which:

- Patent term extensions, which allow for the extension of a patent term in cases of "unreasonable" delay in market approval, would be optional;

- Patent linkages—preventing regulators from extending market approval to a generic drug without determining an existing patent would not be violated— would be optional provided a rights-holder would otherwise be able to defend the patent; and
- Data exclusivity, the prohibition of use by generics of clinical test data (usually supplied by the original patent holder), would be for five years after marketing approval for the patented product. However, the Peru FTA permitted the clock to start on the exclusivity period at the time of first-country market approval if the second country approved the product within six months of the date of first market approval.

Countries reportedly would be eligible for these provisions based on an economic indicator such as per capita gross national income (GNI) or product (GDP). If the World Bank benchmark of $12,161 per capita GNI was used, Malaysia, Mexico, Peru, and Vietnam would qualify as developing in the TPP. Other countries would have to adhere to as yet undetermined standards based on language contained in the Australia, Chile, and Singapore FTAs with the United States.[89]

The U.S. proposal also supports pre-grant opposition procedures, which allows third parties to object to patents at their initial application to challenge frivolous or substandard patent applications. Prior to this proposal, the United States reportedly favored eliminating pre-grant opposition.[90]

Biologics

The United States reportedly is seeking a 12-year period of data exclusivity for biologics under the proposed TPP. Biologics are medical preparations derived from living organisms, but generally are not considered distinct from traditional pharmaceuticals in U.S. IP law.[91] Biotechnology groups claim that the development and approval process for large molecule biologics—as opposed to small molecule pharmaceuticals—are more complex and require longer exclusivity periods for a product to be commercially viable. Under the 2010 Affordable Care Act, biologics are given a 12-year exclusivity period. Moreover, USTR, in its blog release, stated "[t]raditionally, the U.S. approach to trade negotiations been to base proposals on existing U.S. law, where the current standard is 12 years."[92] Various groups of Senators, totaling 40 in number, have written to the President supporting the 12-year exclusivity period, as has a group of 40 Representatives.[93] Separately, a letter signed by 7 Representatives requests the President refrain from introducing a 12-year exclusivity provision in the negotiations.[94]

Trade Secrets

The United States is reportedly seeking language to improve protections for trade secrets, especially as USTR describes protection of U.S. trade secrets as a growing challenge in its 2012 Special 301 report on IPR protections abroad.[95] This text responds to the concerns of U.S. business that governments have pressured them to reveal trade secrets or transfer technology to further a country's "indigenous innovation" policies. Companies are also reportedly increasingly victimized by outright theft of their trade secrets, and have decried the often lax remedies available to combat such theft. Penalties for trade secret theft vary widely among TPP countries; one U.S. objective in the negotiations reportedly is to require countries to establish criminal penalties for the theft of trade secrets.[96]

"The May 10th Agreement"

On May 10, 2007, a bipartisan group of congressional leaders and the Bush Administration released a statement on agreed principles in four policy areas: worker rights, environment protection, intellectual property rights, and foreign investment. The principles were to be reflected in provisions in four U.S. FTAs—with Colombia, Panama, Peru, and South Korea. Regarding worker rights, the May 10th Agreement (the Agreement) required the United States and FTA partners to commit to enforcing the five international labor principles enshrined in International Labour Organization's (ILO's) 1998 Declaration on Fundamental Principles and Rights At Work and that the commitment be enforceable under the FTA. These rights are the freedom of association, the effective recognition of the right to collective bargaining, the elimination of all forms of compulsory or forced labor, the effective abolition of child labor, and the elimination of discrimination in respect of employment and occupation.

The Agreement also required FTAs to adhere to seven major multilateral environmental agreements: The seven agreements are the Convention on International Trade in Endangered Species; the Montreal Protocol on Ozone Depleting Substances; the Convention on Marine Pollution; the Inter-American Tropical Tuna Convention; the Ramsar Convention on the Wetlands; the International Convention for the Regulation of Whaling; and the Convention on Conservation of Antarctic Marine Living Resources.

Furthermore, the parties are not to waive or otherwise derogate from their labor or environmental protection laws in a manner that would affect trade or investment with the FTA partner(s). In addition, the labor and environment provisions must be enforceable, if consultation and other avenues fail, through the same dispute settlement procedures that apply to the other provisions in the FTA.

The Agreement also required the FTAs to include provisions related to patents and approval of pharmaceuticals for marketing exclusivity with different requirements for developed and developing countries. Specifically, the Agreement requires provisions dealing with the effective period of data exclusivity—the restrictions on the use of test data produced for market approval by generic drug producers; patent extensions; linkage of marketing approval of generic drugs to determination of possible patent infringement; and reaffirmation of adherence to Doha Declaration on compulsory licensing of drugs to respond to public health crises.

Regarding foreign investment, the Agreement required each of the FTAs to state that none of its provisions would accord foreign investors greater substantive rights in terms of foreign investment protection than are accorded U.S. investors in the United States.

In addition, other chapters in the TPP negotiations may also concern the issue of trade secrets. Such an agenda may involve prohibiting countries from (1) conditioning market access on technology transfer; (2) seeking concessional terms for acquiring or licensing IPR by SOEs; (3) requiring the use of locally owned or developed IPR; (4) promoting the development of local standards to unfairly advantage local firms; and (5) requiring the unnecessary disclosure of confidential business information, or failing to protect that information.[97] In addition, Malaysia reportedly has proposed preventing countries from requiring the disclosure of proprietary formulas for food and food products as a condition for market access.[98] It is not thought that these practices are particularly egregious in any of the countries currently negotiating the TPP, but they may become more salient if other nations accede to the agreement.

Rules of Origin

Rules of origin (ROO) define those goods that originate in the FTA region and therefore are eligible for preferential treatment under the agreement. The negotiating teams are far along in their consideration of product-specific rules, seeking a single TPP rule of origin to the extent possible.[99] The TPP participants have already agreed that the ROO would be "objective, transparent, and predictable." Negotiators reportedly also have agreed that inputs produced in any TPP country may be cumulated so that a product produced with components made in multiple TPP countries can be claimed as originating within the TPP region and therefore be eligible for preferential treatment.

While ROOs have been discussed in terms of market access for automobiles and concerns about supply chains generally, they have proved especially contentious with regard to textiles and apparel.[100] In all previous FTAs, the United States has used the "yarn forward" rule. This rule requires that an apparel product could be considered from within the FTA area, and therefore eligible for preferential treatment, if the entire manufacture of the product, from the spinning of the yarn to final assembly, has occurred within the FTA region. Representatives of the U.S. textile industry have argued for the tighter "yard forward rule" to be included in the TPP.[101] Some U.S. apparel firms, retailers, and distributors, as well as some TPP countries, including Vietnam, seek a less restrictive "cut and sew," or single transformation, rule, which would allow its products manufactured from materials of non-TPP origin to benefit from the TPP. While U.S. negotiators remained committed to the yarn-forward rule, the United States and other TPP partners reportedly have been discussing compromise positions. For example, the United States has proposed "short- supply provisions" to allow a certain amount of non-originating inputs in apparel assembly on a permanent or temporary basis and reportedly tabled an initial list of yarns and fabrics eligible for the short-supply designation during the Lima Round in May 2013.[102] Alternatively, some have proposed regional value content ROOs which would allow for certain non-originating inputs to be used as long as originating inputs made up a certain percentage of the value of the product.[103] However, a more liberalized ROO may be opposed by U.S. FTA partners such as Mexico and Peru, where textile and apparel industries have been oriented to trade with the United States through the yard-forward standard.[104]

Technical Barriers to Trade

Technical barriers to trade (TBT) are standards and regulations that are intended ostensibly to protect the health and safety of consumers and for other legitimate purposes, but through design or implementation, discriminate against imports. In order to minimize trade distortion, WTO members must adhere to the Agreement on Technical Barriers to Trade. The TBT Agreement covers voluntary standards that industries apply, technical regulations that governments impose for health and safety purposes, and assessment procedures that governments employ to determine that a product meets required standards. The TBT Agreement establishes rules and procedures for member countries to follow, including making sure that standards, technical regulations, and conforming assessment procedures are applied non-discriminately and in a manner not more trade restrictive than necessary. It addition, it requires that members practice transparency as regulations are developed and applied, that international standards are used where appropriate, and that the domestic technical regulations of trading partners are recognized as equivalent to domestic regulations when possible. A key provision of the agreement is that WTO members have a central point of inquiry from which firms can ask for information on standards and regulations. U.S. FTAs, including the U.S.-South Korea FTA (KORUS), expanded on the TBT agreement by, among other things, providing opportunities for partner countries to comment on proposed standards and regulations and the implementation of regulations. TPP negotiators are seeking to build on the KORUS FTA as a model in developing TBT provisions and are including annexes on sector-specific TBT commitment to harmonize their approaches to regulations in key areas.

Transparency in Health Care Technology and Pharmaceuticals

Several TPP participants, including Australia, Canada, and New Zealand, administer a national formulary for medicines purchased by the government for its national health service.[105] The United States has expressed concern that the practices and procedures such national healthcare programs, including New Zealand's Pharmaceutical Management Agency (Pharmac), which maintains the formulary, put "innovative pharmaceutical products," often made in the United States, at a disadvantage because access to the country's health care technology markets can be blocked by government's use of procedures that are non-transparent or do not provide due process.[106] In negotiations with Australia over a similar system, the United States and Australia agreed to a series of consultation and transparency mechanisms, designed to afford U.S. manufacturers an opportunity to make their case for inclusion in the formulary. New Zealand reportedly has ruled out changes to PHARMAC absent "reciprocal" concessions by the United States to federal or state-level drug pricing or reimbursement programs such as Medicaid.[107] In Canada, each province maintains its own pharmaceutical formulary.

Foreign Investment

Foreign investment has been a high priority for the United States in its FTA negotiations, especially regarding the right of establishment by foreign goods and services providers in the territory of a partner-country. They are discussing such issues as non-discriminatory treatment of foreign investments and investors; minimum standard of treatment; rules on expropriation; transfer of payments of the foreign investor out of the host territory; exceptions for identified non-conforming measures; state-to-state and investor-state dispute settlement procedures; and prohibitions on performance requirements, such as mandatory export levels and local content stipulations.

One issue that has become contentious is whether to include an investor-state dispute settlement provision, which allows for private foreign investors to seek international arbitration against host governments to settle claims over alleged violations of foreign investment provisions under the agreement. Except for the FTA with Australia, U.S. FTAs have included an investor-state provision. The investor-state provision is designed to protect foreign investors from the vagaries of domestic judicial systems, particularly in developing countries, in such cases as government expropriation of foreign-held assets. Critics have argued that investor-state procedures give foreign investors greater protection than domestic investors and infringes on the sovereignty of the host government in protecting the health and safety of its citizens.[108]

On the other hand, Australia has strongly argued against including an investor-state dispute settlement mechanism—although it too has investor-state provisions in many of its FTAs—thus generating a clash with other TPP partners. Australia's position on ISDS, however, may evolve under the newly elected conservative government of Prime Minister Tony Abbott. Opposition to ISDS may stem in part from an attempt by the Philip Morris Tobacco Company to use an investor state provision in an Australian-Hong Kong bilateral investment treaty to sue the Australian government for its requirement for plain packaging for cigarettes. Philip Morris filed the suit from its Asian operations headquartered in Hong Kong.[109]

Another investment-related issue that has raised some concerns relates to the ability of governments to impose controls on capital outflows, particularly in times of financial crises. Previous U.S. FTAs contain clauses which call for the free flow of capital in order to facilitate trade and investment. They also allow for exceptions where controls are imposed to alleviate short-term balance of payments problems in order to protect the stability of the financial system. Some Members of Congress have raised concerns that in light of global financial crises, that the language in FTAs might not adequately preserve governmental discretion to impose controls when they see fit.[110] A new approach to capital controls by the International Monetary Fund (IMF), which has pointed to usefulness of capital controls in ameliorating the effects of capital volatility during periods of economic instability, may also affect the outcome of the negotiations.[111]

Competition Policies

National competition laws and regulations are intended to protect consumers by ensuring that one firm does not so dominate a sector of the economy as to inhibit market entry and stifle competition. Some U.S. FTAs have included provisions to limit the trade-distorting effects of such laws. Among other things, U.S. FTAs require that the United States and the partner country(ies) inform persons from a partner country, who may be subject to administrative actions under domestic antitrust laws, of related hearings and provide them the opportunity to make their case. Under these FTAs, the partner countries agree to cooperate in enforcing competition laws through the exchange of information and consultation. In addition, designated monopolies and state-enterprises are to operate in conformance with the agreement and in accordance with commercial considerations.

The November 2011 framework indicates that the TPP partners are discussing language for a chapter on competition policy to "promote a competitive business environment, protect consumers and ensure a level playing field for TPP companies." The text will include language "on the establishment and maintenance of competition laws and authorities, procedural fairness in competition law enforcement, transparency, consumer protection, private rights of action, and technical cooperation." The U.S. business community has indicated that the provisions on competition policy will be critical in dealing with state-owned enterprises (SOEs), particularly in addressing issues concerning their financing, regulation, and transparency, to ensure that they are not provided an unfair competitive advantage.[112]

Trade Remedies

Trade remedies are measures designed to provide relief to domestic industries that have been injured or threatened with injury by imports. They are regarded by many in Congress as an important trade policy tool to mitigate the adverse effects of unfairly traded imports and import surges on U.S. industries and workers.

The three most commonly used trade remedies are (1) *antidumping* (AD) remedies, which are designed to provide relief from the adverse price effects of imports sold at less than fair-market value; (2) *countervailing duty* (CVD) remedies, which are used to counter the adverse effects of foreign government subsidies to imports; and (3) *safeguard* actions, which are employed to permit temporary relief so that domestic industries can adjust to the adverse effects of surges in fairly traded imports. These actions are sanctioned by the WTO as long as they are undertaken in a fair manner and are consistent with rules specified in WTO agreements.

Congress has insisted that the United States retain the right to use trade remedies to counter unfair trade practices and import surges and has expressed this requirement as a priority in trade negotiating authority legislation. It is also reflected in existing U.S. FTAs.

TPP participants are discussing the possibility of including such provisions in the TPP that make trade remedy investigations and actions more transparent and provide due process in their implementation.

Labor

One of the more controversial issues that the TPP partner countries are addressing pertains to the scope and depth of provisions on worker rights. Supporters of strong worker rights, such as labor unions and certain non-government organizations (NGOs), are concerned that failure to promote and implement these rights, including collective bargaining, could lead to the imposition of low wages and poor conditions for workers by firms in those countries. In so doing, U.S. workers would be placed at a competitive disadvantage as they compete against low-cost, low-standard labor practices.

The November 2011 TPP framework for negotiations indicates that the agreement will have a separate labor chapter. The language in the framework is ambiguous, stating only that the chapter would "include commitments on labor rights protection and mechanisms to ensure cooperation, coordination, and dialogue on labor issues of mutual concern." The original P-4 agreement includes commitments to cooperate on labor issues.

The scope and depth of worker rights provisions in U.S. trade agreements have evolved over time.[113] The North American Free Trade Agreement (NAFTA), included labor provisions in a side letter requiring all Parties to enforce their own labor standards. The provisions are enforced under a special dispute settlement procedure attached to, but outside of, the main agreement. Based on the 2002 Trade Act, all subsequent FTAs, included a similar provision, but within the body of the agreement. Their provisions are enforceable under the agreement's dispute settlement mechanism and violations are subject to potential trade sanctions.

Under the May 10th Agreement, new labor principles were included in FTAs with Peru, Panama, South Korea, and Colombia (see text box above). The agreement stipulated that the four FTAs would require each of the Parties to adopt and to maintain five internationally accepted labor rights that are contained in the ILO Declaration on Fundamental Principles and Rights at Work and Its Follow-Up (1998) (ILO Declaration)—the freedom of association; the effective recognition of the right to collective bargaining; the elimination of all forms of compulsory or forced labor; the effective abolition of child labor; and the elimination of discrimination in respect of employment and occupation. These provisions are enforceable under FTA dispute settlement procedures.

The issue of the treatment of worker rights in the TPP has provoked debate among TPP partners and among U.S. stakeholders. In late December 2011, the United States reportedly submitted a proposal on labor issues to the other TPP partners. According to one report, the proposal largely reflects the requirements contained in the May 10th Agreement that countries should uphold core ILO principles. The proposal reportedly would go further by indicting how these principles would be implemented by requiring countries to have labor laws related to minimum wage requirements, work time, and occupational health and safety. The U.S. proposal reportedly would also require TPP countries to take measures to reduce trade in products made through forced or child labor and to apply labor laws to export processing zones and free trade zones.[114] To date, none of this information has been corroborated publically by U.S. officials.

In a December 21, 2011, letter to then USTR Ambassador Ron Kirk, the chairmen of the House Ways and Means Committee and Trade Subcommittee and the ranking Members of the Senate Finance Committee and Trade Subcommittee raised concerns about expanding labor-related obligations in the TPP and, instead, argued for "improving the labor-related capacity building provisions in past trade agreement." Referring to the May 10th Agreement, the letter states:

> While some of us still have serious doubts about the approach followed in the Peru, Colombia, Panama, and South Korea agreements, we recognize that it reflected a careful balancing of interests. We caution that any move to further expand the scope of the labor provisions would seriously undermine support for the TPP negotiations.
>
> Moreover, further expanding the scope of obligations could unduly expose the United States to potential unwarranted litigation and trade sanctions on a new and broader array of its labor laws and policies in this new forum.

On the other hand, representatives of the labor community have called the proposal a "move in the right direction," but have said it does not meet all of their demands. For example, labor groups have called for the elimination of the requirement, included in the four most recent U.S. FTAs (and noted above), that the worker rights obligations only apply to the ILO 1998 Declaration and not to the ILO conventions.[115]

Worker rights may also be controversial among the TPP partners. For example, Vietnam and Brunei reportedly have expressed opposition to having worker rights provisions subject to binding dispute settlement procedures. At the Lima Round, Canada tabled its approach modeled after its Canada-Panama labor cooperation agreement, which does not allow for the suspension of trade concessions. Instead, a dispute settlement panel would be limited to mandating the development of an "action plan" to remedy a dispute, and if the offending party fails to implement it, a monetary penalty capped at $15 million could be assessed.[116] This issue is likely to continue to evolve as the negotiations proceed.

Environment

Like the U.S. position on worker rights, environmental provisions in U.S. FTAs have evolved. As with worker rights, environmental provisions were originally placed in side letters in the NAFTA agreement, and "enforce your own laws" provisions were placed in subsequent FTAs with limited dispute settlement based on Trade Act of 2002. The May 10, 2007, understanding added an affirmative obligation to adhere to multilateral environmental agreements (MEA), backed by potential resort to the dispute settlement provisions of the agreement, as well as a binding commitment to prevent countries from relaxing their environmental standards to promote trade or investment.

The U.S. environment proposal was tabled at the Chicago negotiating session in September 2011. It reportedly contains three main components: conservation, core commitments, and public participation. The first component reportedly contains specific new provisions on illegal logging, marine fisheries, and endangered species, as well as obligations to enforce domestic laws or regulations on illegal trade in plants and wildlife. The second proposal would require the parties to uphold their commitments to any of the MEAs they have signed. The third proposal would allow for stakeholder participation to challenge member state's adherence to the provisions— including the possibility of binding dispute settlement across the disciplines.[117] Subjecting the provisions of the environmental chapter to binding dispute settlement has proved controversial, reportedly even among countries that have signed FTAs with—albeit narrower—environmental chapters with dispute settlement provisions.[118]

In addition to the U.S. proposals, New Zealand and Chile reportedly have tabled trade and climate change submissions. New Zealand and Chile have tabled marine fisheries and fishing subsidies proposals, respectively. Australia has proposed the full removal of tariffs on environmental goods and green technology, a goal the United States supports and which received broad support among APEC members at the November 2011 APEC summit.[119]

NEW AND CROSS-CUTTING ISSUES

In addition to treating certain existing issues in new or different ways, the TPP also seeks disciplines on certain activities not heretofore addressed in FTAs. These include not only horizontal or cross-cutting issues that address best practices in several negotiations, such as with regulatory coherence, but also issues not generally addressed in previous U.S. FTAs, such as regulatory coherence, supply chain competitiveness, and small- and medium-sized enterprises. While some of the commitments relating to these issues are in stand-alone chapters, others are included, as appropriate, in other chapters of the agreement.

Regulatory Coherence

The issue of regulatory coherence represents one of the new cross-cutting trade issues added to the TPP negotiations. The goal of regulatory coherence is to ease the conditions and costs of trade between TPP countries while affirming the rights of TPP countries to regulate their economies to promote legitimate policy objectives. According to the USTR, this initiative stems from the proliferation of regulatory and non-tariff barriers, which have become a major hurdle for business gaining access to foreign markets. Some of the goals of the effort are to "improve regulatory practices, eliminate unnecessary barriers, reduce regional divergence in standards, promote transparency, conduct regulatory processes in a more trade-facilitative manner, eliminate redundancies in testing and certification, and promote cooperation on specific regulatory issues."[120]

Issues related to regulatory coherence are covered in various chapters, including a stand-alone chapter on regulatory coherence as well as in SPS, TBT, and other chapters. The regulatory coherence chapter recommends that TPP partner countries "endeavor" to establish domestic regulatory structures similar to the U.S. Office of Information and Regulatory Affairs in the Office of Management and Budget, a venue to vet proposed regulations, and their compliance with domestic law and policy, as well as with trade agreements and other international obligations. Aside from seeking to assure regulatory consistency among various domestic agencies, the proposed mechanism would be encouraged to conduct regulatory impact assessments (RIA) that would assess the need for a given regulation, conduct cost-benefit analysis, and assess alternatives to regulation. The established body, process, or mechanism would also seek to assure transparency and openness in the rule-making process. The draft also recommends the establishment of a regulatory coherence committee among TPP members. It is unclear, how much, if any, of these provisions would be subject to dispute settlement.[121]

State-Owned Enterprises

Broadly speaking, state-owned enterprises (SOEs) are businesses directly or indirectly owned or influenced by a government. As such, governments may provide these businesses with advantages—such as subsidies, low cost credit, preferential access to government procurement, and trade protection—not enjoyed by their private counterparts, thereby hindering competition. Such advantages may also be directed toward companies not owned but significantly favored or supported by the government. This concern over potential anti-competitive behavior and restrictive trade has shaped texts by the United States regarding SOEs in the proposed TPP agreement. In the context of the current TPP negotiations, the SOE presence in Vietnam—estimated to represent 40% of output—may warrant particular attention, although Malaysia and Singapore also have important SOE sectors.[122] In addition, as the TPP could become a template for a larger Asia-Pacific FTA or future WTO negotiations, wider applicability of these provisions to SOEs in other countries, particularly China, may be envisioned.

In light of these concerns about fair competition, SOEs are addressed, though not extensively, in several existing U.S. FTAs. NAFTA and subsequent U.S. FTAs with Australia, Chile, Colombia, Peru, and South Korea have similar language on SOEs. Though the specific details vary among these agreements, most contain national treatment, non-discrimination, and transparency provisions, while upholding the prerogative of countries to establish and maintain SOEs. The U.S.-Singapore FTA includes somewhat more extensive provisions on SOEs, but they largely apply only to Singapore and not the United States.[123]

Though some business groups, government officials, and labor groups have all expressed an interest in strong SOE provisions in the TPP, it remains unclear what form such provisions may take.[124] Such measures may include provisions that seek to ensure that SOEs operate on a commercial basis, and to address potential trade and investment barriers. SOE disciplines may be enforced based on a harm test similar to that used in the WTO subsidies agreement.[125] Broadly, these provisions will likely seek to achieve competitive neutrality with regard to SOEs. Competitive neutrality, a concept supported by both U.S. government and business groups, refers to an environment in which SOEs receive no competitive advantages beyond those enjoyed by private sector companies.[126]

Not all policy observers, however, agree on the appropriate strength or even necessity of SOE provisions in the TPP. Though the scale and the nature of their behavior differ, SOEs exist in some form in all TPP countries. In the United States for example, organizations such as the Federal National Mortgage Association (Fannie Mae), and the U.S. Postal Service are operated by the government and provide market-oriented products.[127] Therefore, as with most trade negotiations, the U.S. position on SOEs likely seeks to balance both U.S. defensive and offensive interests.[128] Some observers suggest that existing regulations may already adequately temper advantages of SOEs (e.g., subsidies, financing), while others maintain that additional provisions, particularly regarding transparency, will only make existing disciplines more effective.[129]

The United States first tabled its SOE proposal in late 2011. USTR negotiators have suggested that TPP countries generally support the idea of SOE provisions in the FTA, but all parties have not yet agreed on specific language.[130] Some reports suggest that TPP countries may be pressing the United States to extend the coverage of its SOE proposal to include sub-federal SOEs such as those at the state and municipal level.[131] As with government procurement, smaller countries with little activity at the sub-federal level argue that they receive little benefit from such exclusions.

More recently, in the Lima round of negotiations in May 2013, Australia reportedly tabled a proposal on SOE provisions.[132] Australia has a domestic procedure which attempts to achieve competitive neutrality between private and state-owned enterprises in its own economy. Some speculate that Australia's TPP proposal on SOEs is similar to its domestic policy and have raised concerns that such a system would be challenging to enforce in an international environment.[133] They argue it may not be effective in preventing all types of SOE benefits, such as different regulatory standards for private and state-owned firms.[134] Press reports suggest that although the United States and Australia have narrowed the differences in their proposals, the SOE chapter remains a challenging issue in the negotiations.[135]

E-Commerce

According to the November 2011 framework, the TPP partners are negotiating provisions that would establish rules and procedures for trade in goods and services conveyed by the Internet and other electronic means. The text of the framework states that the provisions would address impediments to such trade, including customs duties, the digital environment, authentication of electronic transactions, consumer protection, localization requirements, and other provisions to ensure the free flow of information.

The United States considers these provisions important with the growth of the use of electronic commerce in an increasingly globalized economy. Recently concluded U.S. FTAs, such as the U.S.-South Korea FTA, included e-commerce provisions. They are designed to ensure that services distributed electronically benefit from the same protections as services distributed by other means. In addition, no customs duties are to be imposed on digital products, whether distributed electronically or via a physical medium, such as a disk, and digital products are to be treated in a non-discriminatory manner. The agreement also includes provisions prohibiting unnecessary barriers to the free flow of information.

In the TPP talks, the U.S. proposals reportedly contain language that would prohibit countries from blocking cross-border flows of data over the Internet.[136] If adopted, these provisions could also have implications for a member state's ability to engage in censorship of the Internet. U.S. high technology groups have supported unfettered cross-border data flows and opposed localization requirements for data storage or server location in order to promote Internet-based services and cloud-computing. They claim that companies already have their own mechanisms in place to protect privacy and that privacy would not be undermined by open borders on data flows.[137]

However, TPP partners, such as Australia and New Zealand, reportedly have expressed concern that prohibitions on local data storage could run up against their national privacy laws. Australia reportedly has argued that private-sector based controls would not be sufficient to protect privacy and has suggested alternative language to the U.S. proposal that would give governments more discretion on controlling data flows across borders.[138] Vietnam and Malaysia reportedly have local content restrictions, either for mercantile or censorship reasons.

Competitiveness and Supply Chains

Trade in intermediate goods is an increasingly important component of international trade for many firms. These intermediate goods, which serve as inputs in the production of final goods, accounted for more than half of all non-fuel merchandise traded in 2009.[139] Such intermediate goods represent stages along a global supply chain—the path a good takes as it is transformed from its basic components into a final product used by consumers. This path often crosses multiple international borders, sometimes more than once. U.S. imports from China, for example, may contain components sourced from other parts of East Asia, Europe, Latin America, and elsewhere, including from the United States. The U.S. International Trade

Commission (USITC) estimates that 8.3% of the value of U.S. imports is actually U.S. components that have been incorporated into other goods abroad and re-imported into the United States.[140]

It is unclear exactly how the TPP will address supply chains, although the issue will be addressed in a stand-alone chapter as well as in other chapters covering issues related to supply chains. The broad range of issues affecting supply chains involve many chapters already included in U.S. FTAs. Business groups have encouraged negotiators to consider several aspects that may affect the flow of goods into and out of TPP countries, and, hence the competitiveness in global supply chains of firms in TPP countries. These include harmonization of standards, adequate infrastructure (ports, roads, etc.) to facilitate trade; simplification of rules of origin; and greater customs efficiency.[141]

Competitive supply chains and strong rules of origin may not always be mutually consistent goals. As a regional FTA, some international supply chains may be entirely encompassed by the current negotiating partners. Other supply chains, however, may incorporate intermediate goods that have moved into TPP countries at some point in the production process. These supply chains that incorporate goods originating outside TPP countries, such as apparel production in Vietnam that uses Chinese fabric, may present a challenge to negotiators as they try to develop rules of origin that balance a desire for a TPP that ensures competitiveness and cost efficiency with concerns over outside countries benefitting from the TPP agreement without adhering to its requirements.

Small- and Medium-Sized Enterprises

Small- and medium-sized enterprises (SMEs) (firms with less than 500 employees by the U.S. definition) account for the majority of firms involved in international trade (about 97%), but they account for a much smaller share of the value of U.S. trade (about 30%).[142] In fact, in 2009, eight firms alone accounted for more than 10% of all U.S. exports.[143] SMEs, however, also participate in trade indirectly as suppliers, feeding parts and components into the supply chain of larger, finished products that can be exported. Though SMEs represent a relatively small share of U.S. trade, they employ approximately half of the U.S. workforce in the non-farm private sector.[144] In addition, academic studies have shown that small businesses create disproportionately more jobs than large businesses, though this may be due more to their age than their size—small firms are typically also young firms.[145]

The characteristics of SMEs and their relatively small presence in U.S. trade have led to government efforts to improve SME access to international markets. The USTR commissioned a series of reports from the ITC regarding the role of SMEs in U.S. exporting activities.[146] Those reports identified barriers limiting SME access to foreign markets, and surveyed SMEs for suggestions on policy changes that could ease SME exporting activities. An increased focus on FTAs and other trading agreements was among the top three most frequent responses provided.[147]

The proposed TPP agreement includes a stand-alone chapter on SMEs, although provisions related to SMEs are included in other chapters. This chapter may focus on SME's capacity to take advantage of the enhanced trading opportunities gained through the potential FTA. Though details of the agreement remain sparse, the TPP country trade ministers' statement suggests that the agreement will address concerns SMEs "have raised about the difficulty in understanding and using FTAs."[148] For example, a representative from USTR suggested that the agreement will attempt to address informational challenges SMEs have cited, such as access to foreign country tariff schedules and regulations affecting imports.[149] The negotiations on the SME chapter were concluded during the Dallas round in May 2012.[150] The quick conclusion on this topic may represent both a broad consensus among the negotiating partners and relatively uncontroversial provisions.

INSTITUTIONAL ISSUES

The proposed TPP likely will contain provisions related to dispute settlement and governance of the agreement. Given that the proposed TPP is being touted as a "living agreement," being open to new members, formal procedures may be established for new members to accede to the agreement.

Secretariat

The existence or characteristics of a secretariat for the proposed TPP may be under consideration during the negotiations. Generally, U.S. FTAs have had minimal structures. From NAFTA onward, they have included a free trade commission co-chaired by USTR and trade ministers of the respective parties. Primarily, they have been tasked with (1) supervising the implementation of the agreement; (2) resolving disputes arising from its interpretation or application (see dispute settlement, below); and (3) supervising work of committees established under the agreement. The commission meets regularly once a year, and by special session at the request of a party. The agreements often have created committees on specific issues. The U.S. Korea FTA has committees on outward processing zones and fisheries. However, U.S. agreements do not have free-standing secretariats, and activities are carried out by staff in member's respective trade ministries.[151] Similarly, the P-4 agreement has a commission, but does not have a standing secretariat, although New Zealand serves a repository of documents. However, other economic organizations in the Asia-Pacific region, such as ASEAN and APEC, do have secretariats that engage in trade capacity building and technical assistance activities, as well as conduct studies for and about their members. Negotiators may debate the question of whether having a formal secretariat is necessary or desirable to implement this agreement.

Dispute Settlement

Previous U.S. FTAs as well as the P-4 agreement provide options to resolve disputes arising under the agreement. These are in addition procedures with regard to investor-state dispute resolution (discussed above), or specialized provisions for certain disputes—for example, motor vehicles in the U.S.-Korea FTA.[152] In general, these agreements are designed to resolve disputes in a cooperative manner. A party first seeks redress of a grievance through a request for consultation with the other party. These steps include

- initial consultations,
- meeting of the joint committee representing cabinet level trade officials of each parties,
- establishment of a dispute settlement panel.

In previous agreements, panels have been composed of three arbiters, of which each side appoints one and the third is appointed by mutual consent, or failing that, by lot from a list of individuals not nationals of either side. After the panel makes its decision, the unsuccessful party would be expected to remedy the measure or practice under dispute. If it does not, compensation, suspension of benefits, or fines have been traditional remedies. In addition, WTO dispute settlement may also be used in instances where the dispute is common to both WTO and FTA rules. Although State-State dispute settlement has been infrequent under U.S. FTAs, the size of the potential agreement, the inclusion of new members, and the negotiation of new provisions may cause negotiators to scrutinize existing models of FTA dispute settlement to meet the challenges this agreement may bring.

One question is whether dispute settlement will cover all the provisions of the agreement. The May 10th Agreement stipulated that labor and environmental provisions would be fully enforceable under U.S. FTAs, and dispute settlement to those provisions in the Colombia, Peru, Panama, and South Korea FTAs. Whether these provisions apply to the TPP have proven controversial both domestically, and among TPP partners in the negotiations.

A "Living Agreement"

The TPP has been envisaged as a "living agreement," one that is both open to new members willing to sign up to its commitments and open to addressing new issues as they evolve. Thus far, the manner in which new members are added while the negotiations are still under way, as with the case of Canada, Mexico, and Japan, has followed a process agreed by current members informally, with each aspiring candidate being approved with the consensus of the other parties. In practice, the aspiring participant must not only agree to negotiate saying that "everything is on the table," but must show in words, deeds, or perception that there is a genuine willingness to negotiate on issues sensitive to others and to commit to a high-standard agreement overall. This has led to months of bilateral consultations on issues of interest to the other parties and confidence building measures in areas of the greatest sensitivity.

In the case of Canada, the United States, Australia, and New Zealand had concerns about Canada's supply management system for dairy and poultry. The United States was also interested in leveraging action on Canada's long-languishing legislation to modernize its copyright laws. In return for entry in the talks, Canada and Mexico reportedly agreed not to seek to reopen chapters already agreed in the TPP, or possibly, sub-chapters that contained areas of agreement. Japan, meanwhile, agreed to commitments regarding its beef, auto, and insurance sectors, in order to become a negotiating partner in the TPP talks.

While the expansion of the group has been publicly contemplated, as a trans-Pacific agreement, to date it has focused first on APEC countries. Of these, there are many potential candidates, from relatively advanced economies such as Taiwan, to middle-income states with dynamic economies and youthful populations like Thailand or Philippines. Other countries beyond APEC, such as Colombia and Costa Rica, have expressed interest, and it is conceivable that additional countries or trade blocs beyond the Pacific shores could link up to the agreement in the future.

No new members are expected to join the negotiations at this stage, but may accede later to the final agreement. For example, South Korea recently expressed interest in participating in the talks, but U.S. Administration officials made clear that if they were to join it would be after existing negotiations conclude.[153] Such an accession process raises the question of whether a country, especially one with political or economic heft, can be expected to simply join an agreement already negotiated or whether it should have input on the existing agreement, especially if the goal is to produce a free trade area for the Asia-Pacific, or beyond. Yet, reopening the agreement's substantive provisions with each new entrant—as opposed to its market access provisions which presumably would need to be negotiated with each existing member anyhow— offers up its own difficulties.

The "Noodle Bowl"

Differences of opinion exist among the participants as to how best and to what extent the TPP will serve to harmonize trade rules among the parties. They have agreed to pursue a single set of TPP rules of origin, which will be key to achieving this goal. However, they are pursuing different approaches to developing a TPP tariff schedule. The United States has maintained that it is negotiating market access bilaterally and only with the TPP participants with which it does not have FTAs: Brunei, Japan, Malaysia, New Zealand, and Vietnam. Other participants have sought to negotiate plurilateral market access schedules. While the participants have agreed to conduct the tariff negotiations as they choose, they have agreed to develop a single TPP tariff schedule that will support the goal of facilitating trade. However, it is known that some participants seek to reopen the market access provisions of their prior FTAs with the United States or others. For example, Australia is known to seek a better market access for its sugar in the United States than it received in its FTA. Through TPA, or other vehicle, Congress may wish to make its views known about the architecture of the agreement.

ISSUES FOR CONGRESS

Congress has already taken a strong interest in the TPP negotiations even before a substantive agreement has been reached. Hearings have been held, and some Members have expressed views on the negotiations. As the negotiations proceed, a number of issues important to Congress are emerging.

EXCHANGE RATES AND THE TPP[155]

Some Members of Congress are calling for "currency manipulation" to be addressed in the proposed TPP. In June 2013, 230 Representatives sent a letter to President Obama urging the Administration to address unfair exchange rate policies in the TPP.[156] In September 2013, 60 Senators sent a letter to the Treasury Secretary, Jacob Lew, and the U.S. Trade Representative, Michael Froman, asking them to address currency manipulation in the TPP and all future free trade agreements.[157] Both letters cite a December 2012 study by the Peterson Institute for International Economics (PIIE), which estimates that "currency manipulation" has caused the U.S. trade deficit to increase by $200 billion to $500 billion per year and the U.S. economy to lose between 1 million and 5 million jobs.[158] Congressman Levin released a specific proposal to address unfair exchange rate practices in the TPP.[159] To date, TPP negotiators have yet to take up currency issues.[160]

Generally, Member concerns about currency issues focus on the claim that certain countries are using, or have used in the past, various economic policies to lower the value of their currency in order to unfairly boost exports at the expense of other countries, including the United States. Traditionally, concerns have been raised about countries that have prolonged, sustained interventions in foreign exchange markets to artificially weaken the value of their currency, meaning that they are selling domestic currency in exchange for foreign currency. More recently, concerns have also been raised about the effects of expansionary monetary policy on exchange rate levels.

In the context of the TPP, congressional concerns appear to be focused on Japan. In 2013, the Central Bank of Japan embarked on a package of expansionary monetary policies, as part of a larger economic reform program nicknamed "Abenomics," that aims to grow Japan's economy and eliminate deflation (falling prices). Most economists agree that Japan's expansionary monetary policies are focused on increasing aggregate demand, similar to the motivations for quantitative easing in the United States, rather than targeting a specific exchange rate value. That said, the change in monetary policy has contributed to a weakening in Japan's currency, the yen, which fell by more than 25% against the dollar between mid-2012 and mid-2013. Additionally, Japan has a history of intervening in currency markets, meaning it has sold yen in exchange for foreign currencies in order to decrease the value of the yen. Japan is believed to have last intervened in currency markets in 2011.

Although congressional concerns have been focused on Japan, analysts have also voiced concerns about the exchange rate practices of other TPP member countries. The PIIE study identifies two TPP countries—Malaysia and Singapore—as among the most significant "currency manipulators."[161]

Given the effect that exchange rates can have on trade, some policy makers argue that addressing unfair exchange rate policies should be an integral part of a trade agreement to create a "level playing field," even if such provisions would be novel in the context of a free trade agreement.

The U.S. auto industry in particular has been supportive of efforts to address currency manipulation in TPP.[162] Proponents of including currency provisions in TPP argue that other efforts to address currency manipulation, such as through the International Monetary Fund (IMF), have not been fruitful and that other avenues, like trade agreements, need to be pursued.

Others argue that seeking to include currency issues in a trade agreement is not a straight-forward process and could make the agreement more difficult to conclude. For example, there are different views about how currency issues could or should be addressed in trade agreements. Some have called for enforceable provisions, but there may be disagreement over how exchange rate disputes would be adjudicated, while others have called for cooperative frameworks to examine currency issues. There is also disagreement among economists about how to define currency manipulation and what benchmarks should be used.

Still others caution that there may be a number of reasons to refrain from taking action on exchange rate disputes. A key reason is that U.S. imports from countries with weak currencies may be less expensive than they would be otherwise, benefitting U.S. consumers and U.S. businesses that rely on inputs from abroad.

Note: This section prepared by Rebecca M. Nelson. For more information about current debates over exchange rates, see CRS Report R43242, *Current Debates over Exchange Rates: Overview and Issues for Congress*, by Rebecca M. Nelson

Negotiating a Comprehensive, High-Standard Agreement

An issue for U.S. policy makers in general, and Congress in particular, is whether the United States will be able to achieve its objective of creating a comprehensive, high-standard agreement that encompasses a broad spectrum of trade and trade-related issues. As the largest FTA negotiated by the United States, it brings together a large and expanding group of countries representing various levels of development. Likewise, with 29 chapters under negotiations, it is the most comprehensive agreement in terms of breadth and depth of commitment undertaken by the United States. At the same time, the United States and the other TPP partners are aiming for a high-standard agreement to provide a structure for trade within the Asia-Pacific region in the 21st century. Members of Congress have already presented differing views on which countries should be included in a TPP, and on what constitutes "high-standards" in such areas as worker rights, intellectual property rights, protection for pharmaceuticals, and investor rights. In addition, some Members of Congress have expressed an interest in broadening the negotiations to include issues such as exchange rates, which the Administration acknowledges as important, but has to date preferred to address through other venues.[154] Likewise, outside the United States, the course of the negotiations has revealed differences on the meaning of "high-standard" among the negotiating partners. This emerging debate may presage a vigorous debate within Congress on the TPP as the process proceeds and Members weigh in with their views.

The Role of Trade Promotion Authority (TPA) and Congressional Trade Negotiating Objectives

Any trade agreement that the United States reaches with TPP partners would have to be approved by Congress through the passage of implementing legislation, presumably under TPA procedures (see text box on TPA). The latest TPA expired on July 1, 2007, although the Obama Administration has proceeded to negotiate the proposed TPP as if TPA were in effect. It has consulted with Congress and followed TPA's procedural steps. For example, U.S. Trade Representative Ron Kirk formally notified Congress of the Administration's intention to enter into negotiations with the TPP countries on December 14, 2009, 90 days prior to beginning the negotiations, as stipulated under the expired TPA. Nevertheless, some observers, including Members of Congress, have asserted that TPP partners will not engage in serious negotiations on sensitive issues without the assurance that U.S. commitments are credible and cannot be amended by Congress, although negotiators have not experienced this problem to date.[163]

In addition, even though the Administration has been consulting Members and congressional staff, Congress, as a whole, formally has yet to weigh in on the form of negotiating objectives embedded in TPA authorizing statutes. In the past, these objectives have included reducing barriers to various types of trade (e.g., goods, services, agriculture, electronic commerce); protecting foreign investment and intellectual property rights; encouraging transparency, fair regulatory practices, and anti-corruption; ensuring that countries protect environment and worker rights; providing for an effective dispute settlement process; and protecting the U.S. right to enforce its trade remedy laws. However, over the years, Congress has revised and expanded the negotiating objectives as policy issues have evolved and the global trading system has become more complex. In any renewal of TPP, Congress may wish to establish new negotiating objectives to reflect 21st-century trade policy, including issues currently under negotiation such as state- owned enterprises, regulatory coherence, digital technology, and trade in green technologies, among other areas. At the same time, the objectives would likely have to be flexible enough to allow the Administration to negotiate a "living agreement" that can change and be kept current with an evolving international trading system. It is unclear at this time if and when the Administration and Congress will take up the issue of TPA renewal.

Institutional Issues

In addition, Congress may wish to consider the institutional structure of a future TPP agreement. It may wish to consider the manner in which the agreement can be expanded, or upon the terms to which it is willing to agree to expand new members. As well as attracting new members, new content may be negotiated, or existing content renegotiated. In the manner of accession of new members, Congress may consider whether it would approve each new member, or whether U.S. approval would be handled in a manner similar to WTO accessions. In terms of content, Congress may also wish to consider whether the TPP, if concluded, would have a Secretariat or other body that could serve as a venue for continuing negotiations.

Relationship with the Multilateral System

A successfully concluded TPP agreement may shape the future course of multilateral trade liberalization. After 10 years of negotiations, the Doha Round of multilateral trade negotiations is at an impasse, and WTO members are developing new approaches to address global trade issues.[164] TPP may offer an opportunity for a group of countries dedicated to concluding a comprehensive, high-standards FTA to break new ground on issues thus far not negotiated at the multilateral level.

Past FTAs, such as NAFTA, incorporated new trade policy ideas, such as dispute settlement and intellectual property rights, that were concurrently being negotiated in the Uruguay Round. NAFTA was approved first, and the approval of NAFTA among Canada, Mexico and the United States helped push the Uruguay Round to conclusion. Today, the approval of a comprehensive, high-standard TPP agreement could signal to recalcitrant members of the WTO that trade liberalization can proceed without them and might spur action at the multilateral level.

However, the world trading system is much different than it was in the early 1990s when NAFTA signatories (United States and Canada) made up half of the so-called "Quad-countries" (United States, Canada, the European Union, and Japan) that decided the Uruguay Round. Developing countries, such as Brazil, India, and China, that now exercise their interests in the WTO, may be more assertive in pursuing their own interests. Yet, as an alternative venue promoting trade liberalization at the time when the WTO is not seen to be doing so, it may attract additional countries to the negotiations.

The Potential Impact of the TPP on U.S. Trade Policy

The U.S. pursuit of the TPP and the possible outcome of the negotiations raises other questions regarding its possible impact on the status and shape of current and future U.S. trade policy. For example, how will the TPP talks and potential final agreement relate to the recently launched U.S.-EU FTA negotiations (Trans-Atlantic Trade and Investment Partnership or TTIP)?[165] If both negotiations concluded successfully could they be eventually be merged?

Similarly, the TPP raises the issue of the United States and the future of the WTO as a major force for trade liberalization. Some may argue, for example, that the United States has signaled the death knell of future rounds of multilateral agreements in favor of regional pacts. Others might assert that the TPP could serve as a building block for a more viable multilateral trade system that responds to trade challenges of the 21st century. Some may even say that the TPP may become the predominant force for trade liberalization going forward, that is, if it can agreed to by the current parties.

Another issue for possible consideration is: What would be the impact on U.S. trade policy if the TPP negotiations are not completed successfully or are delayed indefinitely? Some could argue that such an outcome would indicate that it is not feasible to negotiate a comprehensive set of rules with a diverse group of countries and that the United States would have to tailor its ambitions. In addition, some might assert that such an outcome would signify a temporary, if not permanent setback to the notion of a Free Trade Area of the Asia-

Pacific (FTAAP). Still others may conclude that such result could force the United States to retreat from negotiating trade agreements altogether.

CONCLUSION

The potential Trans-Pacific Partnership agreement may have a large impact on U.S. trade and trade policy, but much of its substance and its future remains undecided. The agreement is ambitious in at least three ways: (1) in terms of its size—it would be the largest U.S. FTA by trade flows and could expand in a region that represents over half of all U.S. trade; (2) the scope and scale of its liberalization—the negotiating partners have expressed an intent to comprehensively reduce barriers in goods, services, and agricultural trade as well as rules and disciplines on a wide range of topics including new policy issues that neither the WTO nor existing FTAs yet cover; and (3) its flexibility—this "living agreement" has been and may continue to be expanded in terms of its membership and its trade and investment disciplines.

Due to this level of ambition, however, achieving such an agreement may be difficult. Differences in opinion exist, both domestically and among the negotiating partners, on precisely what form the agreement's provisions should take. A broad range of U.S. interests groups view the TPP as a way to "correct" flaws in previous U.S. FTAs, but changes that some groups consider improvements to U.S. trade policy others see as unwarranted intrusions into public policy, or as factors that contribute to economic insecurity for some Americans. Even challenges with "20th- century" trade issues, such as market access for goods, have yet to be resolved among the TPP partners.

Yet, the partner countries have expressed their commitment to achieving this ambitious agreement and the negotiators remain positive about the progress being made. This group of countries has self-selected into the negotiations presumably because it sees the TPP as a catalyst to greater economic growth and prosperity, especially if it is expanded to include other countries. In addition, the large network of existing FTAs among the members could be seen as an indicator of their willingness to cooperate on trade issues and may imply that some of the challenging issues have already been addressed.

APPENDIX

Table A-1. U.S. Goods Trade with TPP Countries, 2012 (in millions of U.S. dollars, ordered by total trade)

Country	Exports	Imports	Total	Balance
Canada	291,758	324,246	616,004	-32,488
Mexico	216,331	277,653	493,984	-61,322
Japan	70,046	146,388	216,434	-76,342
Singapore	30,561	20,224	50,785	10,337
Australia	31,208	9,536	40,744	21,672
Malaysia	12,854	25,934	38,788	-13,080
Chile	18,886	9,381	28,267	9,505

Country	Exports	Imports	Total	Balance
Vietnam	4,623	20,266	24,889	-15,643
Peru	9,357	6,426	15,783	2,931
New Zealand	3,223	3,439	6,662	-216
Brunei	157	86	243	71
Total	689,004	843,579	1,532,583	-154,575

Source: U.S. International Trade Commission.

Notes: Rank based on total trade (imports + exports); U.S. general imports, U.S. total exports.

Table A-2. U.S. Services Trade with TPP Countries, 2012 (in millions of U.S. dollars, ordered by total trade)

Country	Exports	Imports	Total	Balance
Canada	61,213	29,779	90,992	31,434
Japan	46,479	26,916	73,395	19,563
Mexico	27,350	15,128	42,478	12,222
Australia	17,179	6,778	23,957	10,401
Singapore	12,250	4,931	17,181	7,319
Chile	3,238	1,375	4,613	1,863
Malaysia	2,047	1,898	3,945	149
New Zealand	2,456	1,363	3,819	1,093
Total	172,212	88,168	260,380	84,044

Source: Bureau of Economic Analysis, Survey of Current Business, 2012.

Notes: Rank based on total trade (imports + exports); BEA does not collect services trade data from every partner country.

End Notes

[1] Remarks of President Obama at Suntory Hall, Tokyo, Japan, November 14, 2009.

[2] Although TPA expired in 2007, both the Bush and Obama Administrations have continued to adhere to its notification and consultation requirements.

[3] The United States now has FTAs in force with 19 countries. These countries include Australia, Bahrain, Canada, Chile, Colombia, Costa Rica, Dominican Republic, El Salvador, Guatemala, Honduras, Israel, Jordan, Mexico, Morocco, Nicaragua, Oman, Panama, Peru, South Korea, and Singapore.

[4] For more information, see CRS Report RL33743, *Trade Promotion Authority (TPA) and the Role of Congress in Trade Policy*, by J. F. Hornbeck and William H. Cooper.

[5] See CRS Report R42344, *Trans-Pacific Partnership (TPP) Countries: Comparative Trade and Economic Analysis*, by Brock R. Williams.

[6] The 10 ASEAN members are Brunei, Burma (Myanmar), Cambodia, Indonesia, Laos, Malaysia, the Philippines, Singapore, Thailand, and Vietnam.

[7] APEC consists of Australia, Brunei, Canada, Chile, China, Hong Kong (officially Hong Kong, China), Indonesia, Japan, Malaysia, Mexico, New Zealand, Papua New Guinea, Peru, the Philippines, Russia, Singapore, South Korea, Taiwan (officially, Chinese Taipei), Thailand, the United States, and Vietnam.

[8] This organization was famously described as "four adjectives in search of a noun" by former Australian Foreign Minister Gareth Evans, as quoted in "APEC: Successes, Weaknesses, and Future Prospects," by John McKay, *Southeast Asian Affairs*, 2002, pp. 42-53.

[9] Asia-Pacific Economic Cooperation, *2010 Leaders' Declaration*, November 2010, http://www.apec.org/Meeting-Papers/Leaders-Declarations/2010/2010_aelm.aspx.

[10] A recent quantitative study by the East-West Center and the Peterson Institute considers the possibility of TPP and ASEAN+ agreements simultaneously expanding in the Asia-Pacific and models the welfare gains from each agreement eventually leading to an FTAAP. Due to the assumption that the TPP agreement would

involve greater liberalization, the model predicts greater welfare benefits from an FTAAP based on the TPP. See Peter A. Petri, Michael G. Plummer, and Fan Zhai, *The Trans-Pacific Partnership and Asia-Pacific Integration: A Quantitative Assessment*, Peterson Institute for International Economics, Policy Analyses in International Economics, November 2012.

[11] "Froman Welcomes Korean Interest in TPP, Says Entry Would Follow Initial Agreement," *BNA International Trade Daily*, December 2, 2013.

[12] Susan E. Rice, "America's Future In Asia," November 30, 2013, http://www.whitehouse.gov/the-press-office/2013/11/21/remarks-prepared-delivery-national-security-advisor-susan-e-rice.

[13] These arguments regarding FTAs have been placed in a TPP context, but are drawn largely from Jeffrey J. Schott, "*Free Trade Agreements: Boon or Bane of the World Trading System," in Free Trade Agreements US Strategies and Priorities*, ed. Jeffrey J. Schott (Institute for International Economics, 2004).

[14] This is the so-called "spaghetti bowl" effect of FTAs put forward by Jagdish Bhagwati, Professor of Economics and Law at Columbia University. His view on the TPP agreement is expressed in his op-ed article on the Project Syndicate website at http://www.project-syndicate.org/commentary/bhagwati20/English.

[15] USTR, "Outlines of the Trans-Pacific Partnership Agreement," fact sheet, November 2011, http://www.ustr.gov/about-us/press-office/fact-sheets/2011/november/outlines-trans-pacific-partnership-agreement.

[16] For more information, see CRS Report R42448, *Pivot to the Pacific*? The Obama Administration's "Rebalancing" Toward Asia, coordinated by Mark E. Manyin.

[17] For more information, see CRS Report R42344, *Trans-Pacific Partnership (TPP) Countries: Comparative Trade and Economic Analysis*, by Brock R. Williams.

[18] Vietnam's GDP growth has slowed somewhat relative to the high rates it achieved during the past decade. In 2012 its growth rate was 5.0%, according to the International Monetary Fund's World Economic Outlook, compared to an average growth rate of 7.3% in the period 2001-2010.

[19] The data for this section comes from the International Trade Commission's trade database and the World Trade Organization's Country Trade Profiles.

[20] For more information on AUSFTA, see CRS Report RL32375, *The U.S.-Australia Free Trade Agreement: Provisions and Implications*, by William H. Cooper.

[21]

[22] U.S. Trade Representative, 2012 Special 301 Report, http://www.ustr.gov/sites/default/files/2012%20Special%20301%20Report_0.pdf. Brunei, p. 42. Placement of a trading partner on the Priority Watch List or Watch List indicates that particular problems exist in that country with respect to IPR protection, enforcement, or market access for persons relying on intellectual property. Countries placed on the Priority Watch List are the focus of increased bilateral attention concerning IPR protection, enforcement, or market access for persons relying on intellectual property.

[23] For additional information, see CRS Report RL33087, *United States-Canada Trade and Economic Relationship: Prospects and Challenges*, by Ian F. Fergusson.

[24] *2012 Special 301 Report*, Canada, p. 25.

[25] For more information on this agreement, see CRS Report RL31144, *The U.S.-Chile Free Trade Agreement: Economic and Trade Policy Issues*, by J. F. Hornbeck.

[26] *2012 Special 301 Report*, Chile, p. 26.

[27] Rosalba O'brien and Anthony Esposito, "Bachelet triumps in Chile election but faces runoff," Reuters, November 18, 2013.

[28] For more information, see CRS Report R42676, *Japan Joins the Trans-Pacific Partnership: What Are the Implications*?, by William H. Cooper and Mark E. Manyin.

[29] For more information, see CRS Report RL33445, *The Proposed U.S.-Malaysia Free Trade Agreement*, by Michael F. Martin.

[30] USTR, *2012 Special 301 Report*, Malaysia, p. 8.

[31] Malaysian Ministry of International Trade and Industry, *Brief on the Trans-Pacific Partnership (TPP)*, August 2013, http://www.miti.gov.my/cms/storage/documents/1ed/com.tms.cms.document.Document_c5ada311c0a8156f-72160910-3ecfcd41/1/TPP%20-%20Briefing%20Notes%20-%20Website%20%28FINALrev1%29.pdf.

[32] See CRS Report RL32934, *U.S.-Mexico Economic Relations: Trends, Issues, and Implications*, by M. Angeles Villarreal.

[33] For more information on NAFTA issues related to Mexico, see CRS Report RL34733, *NAFTA and the Mexican Economy*, by M. Angeles Villarreal.

[34] For more information, see CRS Report RL34108, *U.S.-Peru Economic Relations and the U.S.-Peru Trade Promotion Agreement*, by M. Angeles Villarreal.

[35] "USTR Says New TPP IPR Approach Still Achieves Goals Of 'May 10' Deal," *Inside U.S. Trade*, October 28, 2011.

[36] USTR, 2012 *Special 301 Report*, Peru, p. 48.

[37] For more information, see CRS Report RL31789, *The U.S.-Singapore Free Trade Agreement*, by Dick K. Nanto, and CRS Report RL34315, *The U.S.-Singapore Free Trade Agreement: Effects After Five Years*, by Dick K. Nanto.

[38] "U.S. SOE Proposal Raises Ire of Singapore State-Owned Investment Firm," Inside U.S. Trade, May 13, 2012.

[39] For more information, see CRS Report R41550, *U.S.-Vietnam Economic and Trade Relations: Issues for the 113th Congress*, by Michael F. Martin.

[40] "Vietnam Rejects U.S. Push on State Firms in Trade Talks," *The Financial Express*, October 30, 2011.

[41] USTR, *2012 Special 301 Report*, Vietnam, p. 50.

[42] *World Trade Online*, March 5, 2012.

[43] For more information, see CRS Report R42772, *U.S. Textile Manufacturing and the Trans-Pacific Partnership Negotiations*, by Michaela D. Platzer.

[44] Regarding insurance, the FTA's coverage would be limited to cross-border trade in marine, aviation, and transit insurance; reinsurance; services auxiliary to insurance, such as consultancy, risk assessment, and actuarial and claim settlement services; and insurance intermediation services such as brokerage and agency services. Regarding banking and securities, the agreement's coverage in cross-border trade would be limited to providing financial information and data processing, advisory, and other auxiliary financial services.

[45] "Press Release: NZ to Join WTO's Government Procurement Agreement," August, 15, 2012, http://www.beehive.govt.nz/release/nz-join-wto%E2%80%99s-govt-procurement-agreement.

[46] Letter available at http://donnaedwards.house.gov/uploads/Buy%20American%20TPP%20Ltr%20to%20Admin.pdf.

[47] "Canada to Push Opening U.S. Government Procurement Contracts at TPP-Source," *Wall Street Journal*, February 21, 2013.

[48] Briefing Note: Government Procurement Agreement, http://www.wto.org/english/thewto_e/minist_e/min11_e/brief_gpa_e.htm.

[49] "U.S. Seeks Delay in Addressing Sub-Central Procurement in TPP Talks," *World Trade Online*, May 14, 2012.

[50] "In TPP, Canada May Seek Bilateral Deals with U.S. On Procurement, Visas," *Inside U.S. Trade*, March 15, 2013.

[51] *World Trade Online*, "Japan Opts To Submit Bilateral Tariff Offers With Differing Schedules," August 26, 2013.

[52] *The Asahi Shimbun*, "Japan to propose lifting tariffs on 85% of items under TPP, but not farm produce," August 19, 2013; Jiji Press, "Japan Mulling Import Quotas for "Sensitive" Items Under TPP," November 13, 2013; Dow Jones Newswires, "Japan Cannot Make Further Concessions to US in TPP Talks: Minister –Kyodo," November 14, 2013; Nikkei Report, "US turns up heat on Japan in TPP talks," November 14, 2013; Kyodo World Service, "Biden Hints Japan Needs to Compromise for TPP Free Trade Deal,' December 3, 2013. For background on the politics in Japan surrounding the issue of agricultural trade liberalization, see "Japanese Politics and the TPP" in CRS Report R42676, *Japan Joins the Trans-Pacific Partnership: What Are the Implications?,* by William H. Cooper and Mark E. Manyin.

[53] *Inside U.S. Trade*, "Malaysian Cabinet Directs Negotiators To Refrain From Endorsing TPP Deadline," August 23, 2013.

[54] Dairy Farmers of Canada (DFA), "Trade talks," March 11, 2013, http://www.dairyfarmers.ca/farmers-voice/farm-policy/trade-talks; "Maintaining Supply Management during Trade Negotiations," http://www.dairyfarmers.ca/what-we-do/international-trade/maintaining-supply-management-during-trade-negotiations; Egg Farmers of Canada, "Pillars of Supply Management," http://www.eggfarmers.ca/international-trade/trade-updates/; DFA, "Stop the CETA Giveaway," October 16, 2013.

[55] *Inside U.S. Trade*, "Business Groups Urge USTR To Offer Australia More Sugar Access In TPP," May 4, 2012, p. 15; U.S. Business Coalition for TPP, "48 U.S. Associations Call for Further Liberalization Across All Sectors in the TPP Negotiations," July 23, 2013.

[56] The NMPF is the trade association that represents dairy farmers and their marketing cooperatives. The USDEC's objective is to help promote dairy exports by helping member firms increase sales or reduce their costs of doing business. Its membership includes milk producers, dairy cooperatives, proprietary processors, export traders and industry suppliers.

[57] Comments by the National Milk Producers Federation and the U.S. Dairy Export Council to USTR Concerning Negotiating Objectives with respect to Japan's Participation in the Trans-Pacific Partnership Trade Agreement, June 9, 2013; Office of Congressman Reid Ribble, "Dairy Trade Letter to Secretary Vilsack and Ambassador Froman," July 26, 2013, http://ribble.house.gov/dairy-trade-letter-secretary-vilsack-and-ambassador-froman.

[58] For background, see CRS Report 96-397, *Canada-U.S. Relations*, coordinated by Carl Ek and Ian F. Fergusson, *Canada-U.S. Relations*, 'Canada's Supply Management Programs for Dairy, Poultry, and Eggs,' pp. 49-51 (pdf).

[59] *Inside U.S. Trade*, "Australia Seeks Broad Market Access To Offset TPP Rules Commitments," November 1, 2013; *Australian Financial Review*, "Robb tells US a trade deal needs sweetener," November 7, 2013; Minister for Trade and Investment, "Robb to advance Australia's trade interests in Bali and Singapore," December 1, 2013, http://www.trademinister.gov.au/releases/2013/ar_mr_131201.html; American Sugar

Alliance, "No Additional Sugar Access for Australia in TPP," August 8, 2012, http://www.sugaralliance.org/newsroom/no-additional-sugar-access-for- australia-in-tpp.html.

[60] For background on how U.S. sugar policy operates, see CRS Report R42535, *Sugar Program: The Basics*, by Remy Jurenas.

[61] American Sugar Alliance, Submission to the USITC, Investigation Nos. TA-131-034 and TA 2104-026 on the "U.S.- Trans-Pacific Free Trade Agreement: Advice on Probable Economic Effect of Providing Duty-Free Treatment for Imports," March 2, 2010, pp. 3, 5-6.

[62] Sweetener Users Association, "Pre-Hearing Brief Submitted to the U.S. International Trade Commission [USITC]," Investigation Nos. TA-131-034 and TA 2104-026 on the "U.S.-Trans-Pacific Free Trade Agreement: Advice on Probable Economic Effect of Providing Duty-Free Treatment for Imports," February 18, 2010, p. 3.

[63] "New U.S. SPS Text Includes Consultative Mechanism, RRM Provisions," *Inside U.S. Trade*, May 24, 2013; "Food, Agriculture Groups Blast U.S. Approach to SPS Disputes in TPP," *Inside U.S. Trade*, May 10, 2013.

[64] Letter to USTR Ron Kirk from Members of the House Agriculture and Ways and Means Committees, August 3, 2012; "TPP's Biggest Benefit for Agriculture is Binding SPS Rules, Stallman Says," *Inside U.S. Trade*, November 16, 2012.

[65] "Canada, Mexico's Inclusion in 15th Round Brings Momentum, U.S. TPP Negotiator Says," *Bloomberg BNA International Trade Daily*, December 11, 2012.

[66] "SPS Group Won't Meet in Malaysia; Issues To Be Resolved At Higher Level," *Inside U.S. Trade*, July 19, 2013.

[67] Office of the United States Trade Representative, "Fact Sheet: TPP Tobacco Proposal," May 2012, at http://www.ustr.gov/about-us/press-office/fact-sheets/2012/may/tpp-tobacco-proposal.

[68] For a brief summary of the Tobacco Control Act, see CRS Report R41304, *FDA Final Rule Restricting the Sale and Distribution of Cigarettes and Smokeless Tobacco*, by C. Stephen Redhead and Jane M. Smith. More information is available on FDA's tobacco products website at http://www.fda.gov/TobaccoProducts/default.htm.

[69] "USTR Prepares To Table Revised TPP Tobacco Proposal, Briefs Congress," *Inside U.S. Trade*, August 16, 2013; USTR, "Fact Sheet: New U.S. Proposal on Tobacco Regulation in the Trans-Pacific Partnership," August 21, 2013, http://www.ustr.gov/about-us/press-office/fact-sheets/2013/august/fact-sheet-tobacco-and-tpp.

[70] Statement of Campaign for Tobacco-Free Kids, American Cancer Society Cancer Action Network, American Heart Association, American Lung Association and American Academy of Pediatrics, "USTR Abandons Plan to Protect Tobacco Control Measures under Trans-Pacific Partnership Trade Agreement," August 19, 2013, http://www.tobaccofreekids.org/press_releases/post/2013_08_19_trade.

[71] See footnote 69.

[72] Article 22.1 of the Uruguay Round Agreement on Trade-Related Aspects of Intellectual Property Rights (TRIPS) refers to a GI as a mark or label that "identifies a good as originating in the territory of a country, or a region or locality in that territory, where a given quality, reputation or other characteristic of the good is essentially attributable to its geographical origin." For background, see CRS Report RS21569, *Geographical Indications and WTO Negotiations*, by Charles E. Hanrahan.

[73] World Trade Online, "U.S., NZ, Australian Industry Demand More Protection from GIs Than USTR," May 14, 2012. Background on this group—Consortium for Common Food Names—can be accessed at http://www.commonfoodnames.com/.

[74] *Inside U.S. Trade*, "TPP Countries Aiming To Table Remaining Proposals Soon, USTR Says," January 11, 2013, p. 21; "Groser: NZ Seeking Reasonable Compromises On PHARMAC, GIs", December 7, 2012, pp. 7-8.

[75] *Inside U.S. Trade*, "Australia, New Zealand Seek to Address Export Competition in TPP Deal," May 25, 2012, pp. 1, 20-21.

[76] *Inside U.S. Trade*, "Australian TPP Proposal Could Impact U.S. GSM 102, Food Aid Programs," October 12, 2012, pp. 1, 18.

[77] For background, see "Export Competition" in CRS Report RS22927, *WTO Doha Round: Implications for U.S. Agriculture*, by Randy Schnepf and Charles E. Hanrahan.

[78] *Inside U.S. Trade*, "Australia, New Zealand Seek to Address Export Competition in TPP Deal," May 25, 2012, pp. 1, 20-21.

[79] *Inside U.S. Trade*, "U.S. To Consult on Ag Export Competition; Next TPP Round in Auckland," September 21, 2012.

[80] "USTR Says It Will Oppose Inclusion Of Food Aid Disciplines In TPP Talks," *Inside U.S. Trade*, December 7, 2012, pp. 10-11.

[81] *Inside U.S. Trade*, "Australian Opposition on Key U.S. Priorities Emerges as Hurdle in TPP," September 21, 2012.

[82] *World Trade Online*, July 4, 2012.

[83] "New Zealand IPR Stance in TPP at Odds with Past U.S. FTA Provisions," *Inside U.S. Trade*, December 10, 2010.

[84] "Countries Offer ACTA Language to Replace U.S. IPR Proposal," *Inside U.S. Trade*, May 14, 2012.

[85] "U.S. Tables New Proposal in TPP Outlining Broad Copyright Exceptions," Inside U.S. Trade, July 6, 2012.

[86] The May 10th provisions, which applied to the Colombia, Peru, and Panama FTAs, among other issues, relaxed IPR provisions on patent term extensions, patent linkages, and data exclusivity. For more information about these provisions, see CRS Report RL34292, *Intellectual Property Rights and International Trade*, by Shayerah Ilias Akhtar and Ian F. Fergusson.

[87] "U.S. Discussing Tailored Approach to IPR for Medicines in Trans-Pacific Partnership," Bloomberg BNA, November 29, 2013;

[88] "Stakeholder Input Sharpens, Focuses U.S. Work on Pharmaceutical Intellectual Property Rights in the Trans-Pacific Partnership," USTR Release, 11/27/2013. http://www.ustr.gov/about-us/press-office/blog/2013/November/stakeholder-input-sharpens-focuses-us-work-on-pharmaceutical-IP-in-TPP. This proposal replaces a prior U.S. offer known as the Trade Enhancing Access to Medicines (TEAM) initiative, which would have encouraged companies to market innovative drugs in TPP markets more quickly by making stronger patent term extensions, data exclusivity, and patent linkage provisions conditional to firms who apply for marketing approval for their products in an expedited fashioned. This proposal reportedly was roundly criticized by other TPP participants.

[89] "In TPP, U.S. Floats 12-year Data Period for Biologics, Flexibilities for Developing Countries," *Inside U.S. Trade*, November 29, 2013.

[90] Public Citizen, "Briefing Memo: Analysis of Leaked U.S. Paper on Eliminating Patent Pre-Grant Opposition," July 7, 2011 http://www.citizen.org/analysis-of-leaked-US-paper-on-eliminating-patent-pre-grant-opposition

[91] For more information on biologics, see CRS Report R41483, *Follow-On Biologics: The Law and Intellectual Property Issues*, by Wendy H. Schacht and John R. Thomas.

[92] USTR Release, 11/27/2013

[93] Hatch-Kerry Letter to Ambassador Ron Kirk, September 12, 2011, http://www.finance.senate.gov/newsroom/ranking/release/?id=9fc0a1bb-e420-418a-835c-14512434a436; House letter of July 27, 2011, available at http://infojustice.org/wp-content/uploads/2011/07/40-Members-of-Congress-07272011.pdf.

[94] "Waxman Wants Biologic Drugs Kept Out of Trade Talks," *The Hill*, August 4, 2011.

[95] USTR, 2012 Special 301 Report, pp. 17-19. available at http://www.ustr.gov/sites/default/files/2012%20Special%20301%20Report_0.pdf.

[96] "TPP Members Reluctant To Adopt Criminal Sanctions For Trade Secret Theft," *Inside U.S. Trade*, July 22, 2013.

[97] This non-exclusive list of possible negotiating objectives was drawn from the U.S. Trade Representative's 2012 Special 301 Report section of trade secrets and forced technology transfer, pp. 17-18.

[98] "Civil Society Groups Air Worries About Malaysian TPP Formula Proposal," *Inside U.S. Trade*, March 8, 2013.

[99] Conversation with Assistant U.S. Trade Representative Barbara Weisel.

[100] For more information, see CRS Report R42772, *U.S. Textile Manufacturing and the Trans-Pacific Partnership Negotiations*, by Michaela D. Platzer.

[101] Textile and Apparel Alliance for TPP, letter to USTR Ambassador Ron Kirk, February 29, 2012.

[102] TPP Short Supply Presentation, USTR, Department of Commerce, http://www.tppapparelcoalition.org/uploads/Short_Supply_Power_Point.pdf; "TPP Partners Need Time To Evaluate U.S. 'Short-Supply' List for Textiles," *Inside U.S. Trade*, May 30, 2013.

[103] "Negotiators Signal Start of Process for Resolving Apparel Rules of Origin," *Inside U.S. Trade*, December 14, 2012.

[104] Jeffrey J. Schott, *et al*, *Understanding the Trans-Pacific Partnership*, Peterson Institute of International Economics, Policy Analysis #99, January 2013, p. 24.

[105] A formulary is a list of medicines approved for prescription under a medical plan.

[106] *FTB report*, New Zealand, p. 263.

[107] "U.S. Leaked TPP Proposal on Drug Pricing Sets Up Fight with New Zealand," *Inside U.S. Trade*, November 3, 2011.

[108] Proponents argue that these provisions are modeled after U.S. laws and an interpretation of the "takings clause" of the U.S. Constitution.

[109] *International Trade Daily*, March 6, 2012.

[110] *International Trade Daily*, May 29, 2012.

[111] "New IMF View on Capoital Controls Raises Questions for U.S. Approach in TPP," *Inside U.S. Trade*, January 4, 2013.

[112] Briefing by members of the Emergency Committee for American Trade (ECAT).

[113] For more information, see CRS Report RS22823, *Overview of Labor Enforcement Issues in Free Trade Agreements*, by Mary Jane Bolle.

[114] *World Trade Online*, January 5, 2012.

[115] Ibid.

[116] "Canada Tables Alternative Enforcement Mechanism In TPP Labor Chapter," *Inside U.S. Trade*, May 23, 2013.

[117] "USTR Green Paper on Conservation and the Trans-Pacific Partnership," (http://www.ustr.gov/about-us/press-office/fact-sheets/2011/ustr-green-paper-conservation-and-trans-pacific-partnership); "ÚSTR Touts TPP Environmental Proposal, But Acknowledges Challenges," *Inside U.S. Trade*, December 9, 2011

[118] "USTR Confirms Objections On Enforceability In TPP Environmental Talks," *Inside U.S. Trade*, June 29, 2012.

[119] "Marantis Says TPP Advances Conservation; USTR Releases TPP Environmental Provision," *International Trade Daily*, December 9, 2011; "U.S. Pushes Conservation Initiatives for Proposed Trans-Pacific Pact, Bridges Weekly Trade News Digest, December 7, 2011.

[120] "Trans-Pacific Partnership (TPP) Trade Ministers' Report to Leaders," November 12, 2011, available at http://www.ustr.gov/about-us/press-office/press-releases/2011/november/trans-pacific-partnership-tpp-trade-ministers%E2%80%99-re.

[121] The draft text is available at http://www.citizenstrade.org/ctc/wp-content/uploads/2011/10/ TransPacificRegulatoryCoherence.pdf; See also " U.S. Proposal for TPP Regulatory Coherence Chapter Mostly Non- Binding," November 4, 2011.

[122] Economist Intelligence Unit, *Vietnam Country Report*, March 2012, p. 12.

[123] For instance, the agreement states that Singapore's government must ensure that any government enterprise "acts solely in accordance with commercial considerations in its purchase or sale of goods or services" and that Singapore must make public a listing of organizations that satisfy the agreement's definition of a "covered entity," essentially any company organized in Singapore above a certain size and with a sufficient level of government influence. This list is also to include the ownership structure of the organization, members of government that serve on the board of directors, and total revenue or assets; USTR, *United States-Singapore Free Trade Agreement*, May 2003, pp. 133-140, http://www.ustr.gov/sites/default/files/uploads/agreements/ fta/ singapore/asset_upload_file708_4036.pdf.

[124] Labor groups are particularly concerned with SOE investment in the United States and potential unfair competition in the domestic market. "Brown, Kyl Urge Disicplines on SOE U.S. Investments as Part of TPP Deal," *World Trade Online*, August 17, 2011.

[125] "USTR Expected to Clarify Provision in SOE Proposal on 'Harm Test' Soon," *Inside U.S. Trade*, March 22, 2012.

[126] Deborah A. McCarthy, Principal Deputy Assistant Secretary, Bureau of Economic and Business Affairs, U.S. Department of State, "State Capitalism and Competitive Neutrality" (speech, APCAC 2012 U.S.-Asia Business Summit, March 2, 2012), http://www.state.gov/e/eb/rls/rm/2012/181520.htm; and Coalition of Service Industries; U.S. Chamber of Commerce, *State-Owned Enterprises: Correcting a 21st Century Market Distortion*.

[127] For more information, see CRS Report RL30365, *Federal Government Corporations: An Overview*, by Kevin R. Kosar.

[128] "U.S. Fixes Future-SOE 'Loophole,' Sends TPP Partners Proposed Text," *Inside U.S. Trade*, October 20, 2011.

[129] "Stakeholders Urge USTR to Make Changes to SOE Proposal in TPP Talks," *Inside U.S. Trade*, September 29, 2011.

[130] Amy Tsui, "Some TPP Groups Finish Talks in San Diego; Other Groups Beginning to Meet Mid-Round," *International Trade Daily*, July 9, 2012.

[131] "Australia Eyes Enforceable SOE Rules That Extend To Sub-Central Level," *Inside U.S. Trade*, March 14, 2013.

[132] "Australia Tables Alternative SOE Proposal at Peru TPP Negotiating Round," *Inside U.S. Trade*, June 7, 2013.

[133] Derek Scissors, *Why the Trans-Pacific Partnership Must Enhance Competitive Neutrality*, The Heritage Foundation, June 6, 2013.

[134] Ibid.

[135] "U.S., Australia Narrow Differences on SOEs, But Challenges Still Remain," *Inside U.S. Trade*, August 8, 2013.

[136] "Internet Companies, Copyright Holders Clash Over Free Flow of Data Principles," *Inside U.S. Trade*, October 20, 2011.

[137] See, for example, letter from the Coalition of Services Industries and other business groups to USTR Kirk on June 9, 2012.

[138] *World Trade Online*, July 5, 2012.

[139] World Trade Organization and the Institute of Developing Economies, *Trade Patterns and Global Value Chains in East Asia: From Trade in Goods to Trade in Tasks*, 2011.

[140] USITC, *The Economic Effects of Significant U.S. Import Restraints*, Investigation No. 332-325, Publication 4253, August 2011, p. xv, http://www.usitc.gov/publications/332/pub4253.pdf.

[141] Emergency Committee for American Trade, *ECAT 2011 Agenda*, June 14, 2011, p. 76.

[142] In the U.S. the typical definition for an SME is a firm with fewer than 500 employees. Other countries use different employment cutoffs or other metrics to delineate SMEs.

[143] The trade statistics in this section come from: U.S. Census Bureau, Department of Commerce, *A Profile of U.S. Importing and Exporting Companies, 2008-2009*, CB11-60, April 12, 2011, p. 25, http://www.census.gov/ foreign- trade/Press-Release/edb/2009/text.pdf. Not all U.S. exports and imports can be matched to specific companies. In 2009, this "unidentified" trade accounted for 11% of exports and 13% of imports.

[144] Firm and employment share data from U.S. Census Bureau, Department of Commerce, *Statistics of U.S. Businesses: Statistics about Business Size*, http://www.census.gov/econ/smallbus.html#RcptSize.

[145] David Neumark, Brandon Wall, and Junfu Zhang, "Do Small Businesses Create More Jobs? New Evidence for the United States from the National Establishment Time Series," *Review of Economics and Statistics*, vol. 93, no. 1 (February 2011), pp. 16-29; John C. Haltiwanger, Ron S. Jarmin, and Javier Miranda, *Who Creates Jobs? Small vs. Large vs. Young*, National Bureau of Economic Research, NBER Working Paper 16300, August 2010, http://www.nber.org/papers/w16300.

[146] These reports can be found at http://www.usitc.gov/research_and_analysis/small_med_enterprises.htm.

[147] USITC, *Small and Medium-Sized Enterprises: U.S. and EU Export Activities, and Barriers and Opportunities Experienced by U.S. Firms*, Investigation No. 332-509, USITC Publication 4169, July 2010, p. 3-27.

[148] USTR, "Outlines of the Trans-Pacific Partnership Agreement," fact sheet, November 2011, http://www.ustr.gov/about-us/press-office/fact-sheets/2011/november/trans-pacific-partnership-tpp-trade-ministers'-re.

[149] Comments from Ambassador Demetrios Marantis at the Wilson Center event, *The Trans-Pacific Partnership and the Future of International Trade*, August 8, 2012.

[150] Amy Tsui, "Good Progress Being Made in TPP Dallas Round, U.S. Negotiator Says," *International Trade Daily*, May 5, 2012.

[151] The NAFTA Commissions for Labor Cooperation and on Environmental Cooperation are an exception as they do have free-standing secretariats.

[152] For more detailed information on the U.S.-South Korea FTA dispute settlement process, see CRS Report R41779, *Dispute Settlement in the U.S.-South Korea Free Trade Agreement (KORUS FTA)*, by Brandon J. Murrill.

[153] USTR, "Statement by U.S. Trade Representative Michael Froman on Korea's Announcement Regarding the Trans- Pacific Partnership," press release, November 29, 2013, http://www.ustr.gov/about-us/press-office/press- releases/2013/November/Froman-statement-TPP-Korea.

[154] *Washington Trade Daily*, October 17, 2013, p. 3.

[155] For more information about current debates over exchange rates, see CRS Report R43242, *Current Debates over Exchange Rates: Overview and Issues for Congress*, by Rebecca M. Nelson.

[156] Representative Mike Michaud, "Majority of House Members Push Obama to Address Currency Manipulation in TPP," Press Release, June 6, 2013, http://michaud.house.gov/press-release/majority-house-members-push-obama- address-currency-manipulation-tpp.

[157] Senator Debbie Stabenow, "Sixty Senators Urge Administration to Crack Down on Currency Manipulation in Trans-Pacific Partnership Talks," Press Release, September 24, 2013, http://www.stabenow.senate.gov/?p=press_release&id=1171.

[158] C. Fred Bergsten and Joseph E. Gagnon, "Currency Manipulation, the US Economy, and the Global Economic Order," Peterson Institute for International Economics Policy Brief 12-25, December 2012, http://www.iie.com/publications/interstitial.cfm?ResearchID=2302.

[159] U.S. Representative Sander Levin, "U.S.-Japan Automotive Trade: Proposal to Level the Playing Field," http://www.piie.com/publications/papers/levin20130723proposal.pdf.

[160] Don Lee, "Currency Manipulation at Issue in Pacific Free-Trade Talks," *Los Angeles Times*, September 26, 2013.

[161] C. Fred Bergsten and Joseph E. Gagnon, "Currency Manipulation, the US Economy, and the Global Economic Order," Peterson Institute for International Economics Policy Brief 12-25, December 2012, http://www.iie.com/publications/interstitial.cfm?ResearchID=2302.

[162] For example, see Michael Stumo, "American Auto Industry Applauds Senate Currency Letter," *Trade Reform*, September 25, 2013.

[163] Conversation with Assistant U.S. Trade Representative Barbara Weisel, September 27, 2012.

[164] Preliminary discussions for a plurilateral agreement to update the commitments in the General Agreement on Trade in Services have been held.

[165] For more information on the TTIP negotiations, see CRS Report R43158, *Proposed Transatlantic Trade and Investment Partnership (TTIP)*: In Brief, by Shayerah Ilias Akhtar and Vivian C. Jones.

In: Free Trade Agreements
Editor: Jenell Gallo
ISBN: 978-1-63117-366-0

Chapter 4

FREE TRADE AGREEMENTS: IMPACT ON U.S. TRADE AND IMPLICATIONS FOR U.S. TRADE POLICY*

William H. Cooper

SUMMARY

Free trade areas (FTAs) are arrangements among two or more countries under which they agree to eliminate tariffs and nontariff barriers on trade in goods among themselves. However, each country maintains its own policies, including tariffs, on trade outside the region.

In the last few years, the United States has engaged or has proposed to engage in negotiations to establish bilateral and regional free trade arrangements with a number of trading partners. Such arrangements are not new in U.S. trade policy. The United States has had a free trade arrangement with Israel since 1985 and with Canada since 1989, which was expanded to include Mexico and became the North American Free Trade Agreement (NAFTA) effective in January 1994.

U.S. interest in bilateral and regional free trade arrangements surged, and the Bush Administration accelerated the pace of negotiations after the enactment of the Trade Promotion Authority in August 2002. U.S. participation in free trade agreements can occur only with the concurrence of Congress. In addition, FTAs affect the U.S. economy, with the impact varying across sectors.

The 112th Congress and the Obama Administration faced the question of whether and when to act on three FTAs pending from the Bush Administration—with Colombia, Panama, and South Korea. Although the Bush Administration signed these agreements, it and the leaders of the 110th Congress could not reach agreement on proceeding to enact them. No action was taken during the 111th Congress either.

After discussion with congressional leaders and negotiations with the governments of Colombia, Panama, and South Korea to assuage congressional concerns regarding treatment

* This is an edited, reformatted and augmented version of a Congressional Research Service Publication, CRS Report for Congress RL31356, dated April 2, 2013.

of union officials (Colombia), taxation regimes (Panama), and trade in autos (South Korea), President Obama submitted draft implementing legislation to Congress on October 3, 2011. The 112th Congress approved each of the bills in successive votes on October 12, along with legislation to renew an aspect of the Trade Adjustment Assistance (TAA) program. President Obama signed the bills into law on October 21, 2011.

In the meantime, on November 14, 2009, President Obama committed to work with the current and partners in the negotiations to form a Trans-Pacific Partnership (TPP) Agreement. The TPP is a free trade agreement that includes nations on both sides of the Pacific. The TPP negotiations emerged from an FTA that included Brunei, Chile, New Zealand, and Singapore and that entered into force in 2006. Besides the United States, Australia, Canada, Malaysia, Peru, Mexico, and Vietnam have joined the negotiations. In addition, Japan has expressed interest in joining. Furthermore, the United States has announced its intention to launch negotiations with the European Union for form an FTA—the Transatlantic Trade and Investment Partnership (TTIP).

FTAs raise some important policy issues: Do FTAs serve or impede U.S. long-term national interests and trade policy objectives? Which type of an FTA arrangement meets U.S. national interests? What should U.S. criteria be in choosing FTA partners? Are FTAs a substitute for or a complement to U.S. commitments and interests in promoting a multilateral trading system via the World Trade Organization (WTO)? What effect will the expiration of TPA have on the future of FTAs as a trade policy strategy?

In the last few years, the United States has considered bilateral and regional free trade areas (FTAs) with a number of trading partners. Such arrangements are not new in U.S. trade policy. The United States has had a free trade arrangement with Israel since 1985 and with Canada since 1989. The latter was suspended when the North American Free Trade Agreement (NAFTA) that included the United States, Canada, and Mexico went into effect in January 1994.

U.S. interest in bilateral and regional free trade arrangements surged, and the Bush Administration accelerated the pace of negotiations after the enactment of the Trade Promotion Authority in August 2002. U.S. participation in free trade agreements can occur only with the concurrence of Congress. In addition, FTAs affect the U.S. economy, with the impact varying across sectors.

The 112th Congress and the Obama Administration faced the question of whether and when to act on three pending FTAs—with Colombia, Panama, and South Korea. Although the Bush Administration signed these agreements, it and the leaders of the 110th Congress could not reach agreement on proceeding to enact them. No action was taken during the 111th Congress either. In addition, the Trade Promotion Authority (TPA) expired on July 1, 2007, meaning that any new FTAs agreed to would not likely receive expedited legislative consideration, unless the authority is renewed.

After discussion with congressional leaders and negotiations with the governments of Colombia, Panama, and South Korea to assuage congressional concerns regarding treatment of union officials (Colombia), taxation regimes (Panama), and trade in autos (South Korea), President Obama submitted draft implementing legislation to Congress on October 3, 2011. The 112th Congress approved each of the bills in successive votes on October 12, along with legislation to renew an aspect of the Trade Adjustment Assistance (TAA) program.

In the meantime, on November 14, 2009, President Obama committed to work with the current and prospective partners to form the Trans-Pacific Partnership (TPP) Agreement. The

TPP is a free trade agreement that includes nations on both sides of the Pacific. The TPP grew out of an FTA that included Brunei, Chile, New Zealand, and Singapore. Besides the United States, Australia, Canada, Malaysia, Mexico, Peru, and Vietnam have also joined the negotiations, and Japan has expressed interest in participating as well. Furthermore, The United States has announced its intention to launch negotiations with the European Union to form an FTA—the Transatlantic Trade and Investment Partnership (TTIP).

FTAs raise some important policy issues: Do FTAs serve or impede U.S. long-term national interests and trade policy objectives? Which type of an FTA arrangement meets U.S. national interests? What should U.S. criteria be in choosing FTA partners? Are FTAs a substitute for or a complement to U.S. commitments and interests in promoting a multilateral trading system via the World Trade Organization (WTO)? What effect will the expiration of TPA have on the future of FTAs as a trade policy strategy?

WHAT ARE FREE TRADE AREAS?

Free trade areas are part of the broad category of trade arrangements under which member-countries grant one another preferential treatment in trade. Preferential trade arrangements include the following:

- **free trade areas** (FTAs), under which member countries agree to eliminate tariffs and nontariff barriers on trade in goods within the FTA, but each country maintains its own trade policies, including tariffs on trade outside the region;
- **customs unions**, in which members conduct free trade among themselves and maintain common tariffs and other trade policies outside the arrangement;
- **common markets**, in which member countries go beyond a customs union by eliminating barriers to labor and capital flows across national borders within the market; and
- **economic unions**, where members merge their economies even further by establishing a common currency, and therefore a unified monetary policy, along with other common economic institutions. The European Union is the most significant example of a group of countries that has gone from a customs union to an economic union.[1]

The process of forming an FTA usually begins with discussions between trading partners to ascertain the feasibility of forming an FTA. If they agree to go forward, then the countries undertake negotiations on what the FTA would look like. At a minimum, participants in an FTA agree to eliminate tariffs and some other nontariff trade barriers and agree to do so over a specific time period. In addition, the partner countries usually agree on rules of origin, that is, a definition of what constitutes a product manufactured within the FTA and, therefore, one that is eligible to receive duty-free and other preferential trade treatment. Rules of origin prevent products from nonmembers entering an FTA market over the lowest tariff wall. Most FTAs also include procedures on the settlement of disputes arising among members and rules on the implementation of border controls, such as product safety certification and sanitary and phytosanitary requirements. Most recent FTAs contain rules on economic activities besides trade in goods, including foreign investment, intellectual property rights protection, treatment of labor and environment, and trade in services. The size and complexity of the FTA will largely reflect the size and complexity of the economic relations among the participating countries. U.S. FTAs with Israel and Jordan are relatively basic, while the NAFTA (the United States, Canada, and Mexico) is very complex.

WHY COUNTRIES FORM FTAS

Countries form free trade areas for a number of economic and political reasons. Most basically, by eliminating tariffs and some nontariff barriers, FTAs permit the products of FTA partners easier access to one another's markets. The 1989 FTA between the United States and Canada was formed arguably for this purpose. Developed countries have also formed FTAs with developing countries to encourage them toward trade and investment liberalization.

FTAs may be used to protect local exporters from losing out to foreign companies that might receive preferential treatment under other FTAs. For example, some supporters of the U.S.-Chile FTA argued that U.S. firms were at a disadvantage vis-à-vis their Canadian competitors whose exports face no Chilean tariffs under the Canada-Chile FTA. Slow progress in multilateral negotiations has been another impetus for FTAs. For example, when the 1986-1994 Uruguay Round negotiations got bogged down, the impetus for the United States, Mexico, and Canada to form NAFTA seemed to increase. Arguably, the surge in FTA formation worldwide in the past few years has been a result of the difficulties encountered in launching and implementing the Doha Development Agenda round of negotiations in the WTO.

Political considerations are also a motivation to form FTAs. The United States formed FTAs with Israel and with Jordan to reaffirm American support of those countries and to strengthen relations with them.

FTAS IN THE CONTEXT OF U.S. TRADE POLICY

Post-World War II trade policy under various presidential administrations has had several interrelated objectives. One has been to secure open markets for U.S. exports. A second has been to protect domestic producers from foreign unfair trade practices and from rapid surges in fairly traded imports. A third has been to control trade for foreign policy and national security reasons. A fourth objective has been to help foster global trade to promote world economic growth.

In fulfilling these objectives, U.S. political leaders have formed and conducted trade policy along three tracks. One track has been the use of multilateral negotiations to establish and develop a rules-based trading system. The United States was a major player in the development and signing of the General Agreement on Tariffs and Trade (GATT) in 1947. It was a leader in nine rounds of negotiations that have expanded the coverage of GATT and that led to the establishment in 1995 of the World Trade Organization (WTO), the body that administers the GATT and other multilateral trade agreements. The United States has continued this approach as a leader in the latest round—the Doha Development Agenda (DDA).

U.S. policymakers have used a second track, which can be labeled the "unilateral" track. Under this approach, the United States threatens retaliation, usually in the form of restricting trade partners' access to the vast U.S. market, in order to get the partner to open its markets to U.S. exports or to cease other offensive commercial practices and policies. The United States has employed this approach primarily against foreign practices not covered by GATT/WTO rules or because the multilateral dispute settlement process proved too slow and ineffective to meet U.S. needs. For several decades, especially in the 1970s and 1980s, the United States conducted its trade policy with Japan "unilaterally" to get Japan to amend domestic laws, regulations, and practices that prevented U.S. exporters from securing what they considered to be a fair share of the Japanese market.

More and more, however, U.S. trade policy is becoming dominated by a third track—bilateral and regional negotiations to establish FTAs. The United States completed its first FTA with Israel in 1985 under President Reagan. It completed its second with Canada in 1989 under President Bush, whose Administration was involved in the process of expanding it to Mexico, a process that was completed by the Clinton Administration in 1993. However, even after the completion of NAFTA, it was still unclear whether bilateral and regional FTAs had become a fixture in U.S. foreign trade policymaking or anomalies to cement already strong economic relationships.

By 1994 it seemed apparent that FTAs were indeed becoming a fixture when the United States, under the Clinton Administration, led a group of trade ministers from 33 other Western Hemispheric countries in agreeing to work toward establishing a Free Trade Area of the Americas (FTAA) by 2005. In the same year, political leaders from the United States and other member- countries of the Asian-Pacific Economic Cooperation (APEC) forum signed a declaration in Bogor, Indonesia, to work toward free trade and investment in the region by 2010 for developed countries and by 2020 for all member-countries. Both of those efforts have flagged.

The pursuit of FTAs continued when, on June 6, 2000, President Clinton and Jordanian King Abdullah announced that their two countries would begin negotiations on establishing a free trade area. An agreement was quickly reached and was signed on October 24, 2001. Similarly, President Clinton and Singapore Prime Minister Goh Chok Tong announced, somewhat unexpectedly, on November 16, 2000, that their two nations would launch negotiations to complete a free trade agreement. And on December 6, 2000, the United States and Chile started negotiations to establish an FTA. Chile had long been mentioned as a potential addition to NAFTA or as a partner in a stand-alone FTA.

In the meantime, many countries, including the other major trading powers, were actively negotiating free trade agreements. The WTO has reported that more than 200 FTAs are in force. For example, Canada formed an FTA with Chile, as did Mexico. The EU has formed FTAs with a number of countries. Japan, which had shunned the use of FTAs, formed an FTA with Singapore and is exploring the possibility of forming an FTA with Korea, although those negotiations have been suspended.

The Bush Administration had affirmed the strategy of pursuing U.S. trade policy goals through the multilateral trade system but gave strong emphasis to building bilateral and regional trade ties through free trade agreements through a policy called a *competition in liberalization*.

The Bush Administration continued negotiations that the Clinton Administration initiated. At the end of 2002, the Bush Administration completed FTA negotiations with Chile and Singapore first begun by the Clinton Administration in 2000. The FTAs with Chile and Singapore entered into force on January 1, 2004.

Perhaps encouraged by the passage and enactment of legislation granting the President trade promotion authority (TPA), as contained in the Trade Act of 2002 (P.L. 107-210—signed into law on August 6, 2002), the Bush Administration moved ahead with a trade agenda that contained an unprecedented number of FTAs. In 2004, agreements with Australia and Morocco were signed, approved by Congress. The agreement with Australia entered into force on January 1, 2005, and the one with Morocco on January 1, 2006. An agreement with Central American countries and one with the Dominican Republic were also signed and combined into one agreement, the DR- CAFTA. The President sent Congress draft implementing legislation on June 23, 2005. The House and Senate passed the legislation (H.R. 3045) on July 27 and 28, 2005, respectively, and President Bush signed it into law on August 2, 2005 (P.L. 109-53). The agreement with El Salvador entered into force on March 1, 2006, with Honduras and Nicaragua on April 1, 2006, with Guatemala on July 1, 2006, with the Dominican Republic on March 1, 2007, and with Costa Rica on January 1, 2009.

An agreement with Bahrain was signed on September 14, 2004, for which Congress passed and the President signed implementing legislation (H.R. 4340/P.L. 109-169, January 11, 2006). The agreement entered into force on August 1, 2006. Congress passed and the President signed implementing legislation (P.L. 109-283) for an FTA with Oman, which entered into force on January 1, 2009. Under the Bush Administration, the United States signed FTAs with Colombia, Peru, Panama, and South Korea (see **Table 1**).[2] The House passed (285-132) on November 8, 2007, and the Senate passed on December 4, 2007, implementing legislation (H.R. 3688) for the U.S.-Peru FTA. The President signed the bill into law (P.L. 110-138) on December 14, 2007. The FTA entered into force on February 1, 2009.

After several months of negotiations, on May 10, 2007, congressional leaders and the Bush Administration reached an agreement on new policy priorities that are to be included in pending FTAs. These priorities included the enforcement of five core labor standards that are part of the International Labor Organization's Declaration on Fundamental Principles and Rights of Work; commitment to enforce seven multilateral environmental agreements to which FTA partners are parties; the availability of affordable generic pharmaceuticals; port security; and foreign investor rights in investor-state disputes.

Obama Administration Policy and Recent Developments

President Obama and his Administration had expressed support for three pending FTAs from the Bush Administration—with Colombia, Panama, and South Korea—but with the understanding that some outstanding issues needed to be addressed. Specifically, regarding Colombia, critics, particularly labor unions, remain concerned about the treatment of union leaders and other labor activists. While supporters cited data showing that violence against union leaders had decreased, critics charged that the violence was still unacceptably high.[3]

Regarding Panama, the primary concerns raised pertained to Panamanian tax policy, which, critics charged, allowed Panama to be a haven for companies and individuals to avoid taxes.[4]

Table 1. U.S. Free Trade Agreements

FTAs in Force	
U.S.-Israel FTA	Implemented by P.L. 99-47 (June 11, 1985). Entered into force September 1, 1985.
U.S.-Canada FTA	Implemented by P.L. 100-449 (September 28, 1988). Entered into force January 1, 1989. Suspended with implementation of NAFTA.
North American Free Trade Agreement (NAFTA)	Implemented by P.L. 103-182 (December 8, 1993). Entered into force January 1, 1994.
U.S.-Jordan FTA	Implemented by P.L. 107-43 (September 28, 2001). Entered into force December 17, 2001.
U.S.-Singapore FTA	Implemented by P.L. 108-78 (September 3, 2003). Entered into force January 1, 2004.
U.S.-Chile FTA	Implemented by P.L. 108-77 (September 3, 2003). Entered into force January 1, 2004.
U.S.-Australia FTA	Implemented by P.L. 108-286 (August 3, 2004). Entered into force on January 1, 2005.
U.S.-Morocco FTA	Implemented by P.L. 108-302 (August 17, 2004). Entered into force on January 1, 2006.
U.S.-Bahrain FTA	Implemented by P.L. 109-169 (January 11, 2006). Entered into force on August 1, 2006.
U.S.-Dominican Republic-Central American FTA (DR-CAFTA)	President signed implementing bill (H.R. 3045) on August 2, 2005 (P.L. 109-53). Entered into force with El Salvador (March 1, 2006), Honduras and Nicaragua (April 1, 2006), Guatemala (July 1, 2006), the Dominican Republic (March 1, 2007), and Costa Rica (January 1, 2009).
U.S.-Oman FTA	President signed implementing bill on September 26, 2006 (P.L. 109-283). Entered into force on January 1, 2009.
U.S.-Peru FTA	Agreement with Peru signed April 12, 2006. President signed implementing bill (H.R. 3688) on December 14, 2007 (P.L. 110-138). Implemented on February 1, 2009.
U.S.-Colombia FTA	Agreement signed November 22, 2006. Congress approved implementing legislation (H.R. 3078) on October 21, 2011, and the President signed it into law on October 21, 2011 (P.L. 112-42). Entered into force on May 15, 2012.
U.S.-South Korea FTA	Agreement signed on June 30, 2007. Congress approved implementing legislation (H.R. 3080) on October 21, 2011, and the President signed it into law on October 21, 2011 (P.L. 112-41). Entered into force on March 15, 2012.
U.S.-Panama FTA	Agreement signed on June 28, 2007. Congress approved implementing legislation (H.R. 3079) on October 12, and the President signed it into law on October 21, 2011 (P.L. 112-43). The agreement entered into force on October 31, 2012.
FTAs Under Negotiation	
Trans-Pacific Partnership Agreement (TPP)	Negotiations underway.
Transatlantic Trade and Investment Partnership (TTIP)	Negotiations set to be launched

The South Korean agreement was the most challenging case. Some Detroit-based car manufacturers, especially Ford and Chrysler, had opposed the agreement because, they asserted, the agreement did not adequately address South Korean barriers to auto imports. (GM had taken a neutral position on the KORUS FTA.) However, as a result of the modifications agreed to in December 2010, most of which pertain to autos, both Ford and Chrysler support approval of the KORUS FTA, as does the United Auto Workers (UAW) union. U.S.-based steel manufacturers have also opposed the agreement because, they argued, it would weaken U.S. trade remedy (antidumping, countervailing duty) laws. Other major labor unions, including the AFL-CIO, oppose the agreement.[5]

On April 6, 2011, the Obama Administration announced that Colombia had agreed to an "Action Plan Related to Labor Rights" laying out steps it was prepared to take to resolve the labor rights issues.[6] Panama and the United States came to a resolution on the tax transparency issue by agreeing to a Tax Information and Exchange Agreement (TIEA), which Panama ratified on April 13, 2011. The TIEA permits either country to request information on most types of federal (U.S.) or national (Panama) taxes. To address the tax haven issue, Article 7 specifically allows for tax information exchange "under the existing Treaty on Mutual Legal Assistance in Criminal Matters," which covers money laundering among other illicit financial activities.

Eventually, President Obama submitted draft implementing legislation to Congress on October 3, 2011, for each of the FTAs. The 112th Congress approved each of the bills in successive votes on October 12, along with legislation to renew an aspect of the Trade Adjustment Assistance (TAA) program, and the President signed them into law on October 21, 2012. The U.S.-South Korean agreement entered into force on March 15, 2012, the U.S.-Colombia FTA entered into force on May 15, 2012, and the U.S.- Panama FTA entered into force on October 31, 2012.

In the meantime, on November 14, 2009, President Obama committed to work with the current and prospective members of the Trans-Pacific Strategic Economic Partnership Agreement (TPP). The TPP is a free trade agreement that includes nations on both sides of the Pacific. Negotiations on the TPP, which grew out of a FTA among four countries—Brunei, Chile, New Zealand, and Singapore—now includes, besides the United States, Australia, Malaysia, Mexico, Peru, and Vietnam.[7] Japan has also expressed interest in joining. Furthermore, the United States and the European Union have expressed their intention to negotiate an FTA—the Transatlantic Trade and Investment Partnership (TTIP).

Economic Impact of FTAs

The surge in U.S. interest in FTAs and in the formation of FTAs worldwide raises the question of their impact on the countries included in an FTA and on the rest of the world. It is an issue that economists have long studied and debated. Interest in the issue has peaked at various times in the post-World War II period. The first time was the formation of the European Common Market. Interest has peaked again with the current trends in FTAs. The debate has relied largely on theory since empirical data are scarce save for the experience of the European Union. The debate has also divided economists between those who strongly oppose FTAs as an economically inefficient mechanism and those who support them as a means to build freer trade.

Economists usually base their analysis of the impact of FTAs on the concepts of trade creation and *trade diversion*. These concepts were first developed by economist Jacob Viner in 1950.[8] Viner focused his work on the economic effects of customs unions, but his conclusions have been largely applied to FTAs and other preferential trade arrangements. His analysis was also confined to static (one-time) effects of these arrangements.

Trade creation occurs when a member of an FTA replaces domestic production of a good with imports of the good from another member of the FTA, because the formation of the FTA has made it cheaper to import rather than produce domestically. The creation of the trade is said to improve economic welfare within the group because resources are being shifted to more efficient uses. Trade diversion occurs when a member of an FTA switches its import of a good from an efficient nonmember to a less efficient member because the removal of tariffs within the group and the continuation of tariffs on imports from nonmembers make it cheaper to do so. Trade diversion is said to reduce economic welfare because resources are being diverted from an efficient producer to a less efficient producer.

In most cases, it appears that FTAs lead to both trade diversion and trade creation with the net effects determined by the structure of the FTA. Therefore, even if two or more countries are moving toward freer trade among themselves in an FTA, the FTA could make those countries and the world as a whole worse off if the FTA diverts more trade than it creates, according to economic theory.[9] (See box below for illustrative examples of trade diversion and trade creation.)

TRADE CREATION OR TRADE DIVERSION?

Economist Robert Z. Lawrence has provided the following example to illustrate the difference between trade creation and trade diversion:

Assume that prior to implementing a free trade agreement with the United States, all television sets purchased in Mexico are subject to a tariff of 10%. Assume that Japan produces TVs under competitive conditions, which it sells at a cost of $100, but the United States could only produce such sets at $105. Initially, all TVs sold in Mexico and elsewhere would be Japanese. These would be imported at a price of $100 from Japan and sold to Mexican consumers for $110, with the additional $10 representing the tariff that would be paid by Mexican consumers to the Mexican government. Assume now that a free trade agreement is signed between Mexico and the United States which removes tariffs between Mexico and the United States but retains Mexican tariffs on other countries. Mexican consumers will now have a choice between buying American TVs, which will sell in Mexico at $105, or Japanese TVs, which will sell at $110. They will buy the U.S. TVs and be better off. However, the Mexican economy as a whole will be worse off. Before the agreement, Mexico bought TVs from Japan. Although consumers paid $110, $10 was just a transfer from Mexican consumers to the Mexican government. The economy as a whole, therefore, spent $100 per TV. After the agreement, however, Mexico is spending $105 per TV. TV prices in Mexico do not reflect their social opportunity costs. The impact of the agreement is to expand TV production in the United States, which is relatively less efficient, and to reduce it in Japan, which is relatively more efficient.

Of course, not all of the increased trade between partners will represent expansion from a less efficient source. Pure trade creation would also result. Assume in the example that initially Mexico could produce TV sets for $107. In this case, prior to the agreement Mexico would not have imported them from Japan, instead it would have supplied these TV sets domestically. In this case, Mexico would benefit from the agreement, which would allow it [to] pay only $105 per TV, although of course it would have done better by liberalizing fully and buying the sets from Japan.

Source: Lawrence, Robert Z. *International National Economies: Regionalism, Multilateralism, and Deeper Integration.* Brookings Institution. Washington. 1996. pp. 24-25.

Trade policymakers encounter circumstances much more complicated than those depicted in economic theory. Many functioning and proposed FTAs encompass more than two countries and involve a range of products, both goods and services, making it much more challenging to evaluate their economic impact. To provide an analytical framework, some economists have developed sets of conditions under which, they have concluded, an FTA would create more trade than it diverts. They state that trade creation is likely to exceed trade diversion—

- the larger the tariffs or other trade barriers among members before the FTA is formed;
- the lower the tariffs and other barriers in trade with nonmembers;
- the greater the number of countries included in the FTA;
- the more competitive or the less complementary the economies joining the FTA; and
- the closer the economic relationship among the members before the FTA was formed.[10]

Economists also have determined that, along with the immediate, static effects of trade diversion and creation, FTAs generate long-term dynamic effects that might include the following:

- increased efficiency of production as producers face increased competition with the removal of trade barriers;
- economies of scale, that is, decreased unit costs of production as producers can have larger production runs since the markets for their goods have been enlarged; and
- increased foreign investment from outside the FTA as firms seek to locate operations within the borders of the FTA to take advantage of the preferential trade arrangements.[11]

Until recently not many FTAs were in operation; therefore, available data on their impact have been limited to the experience of the formation of the European Common Market and subsequently the European Union. Most studies have concluded that the European Community has resulted in more trade creation than trade diversion. However, in some sectors, such as agriculture, the net effect has been trade diversion because the EU's Common Agricultural Policy raised barriers to agricultural trade outside the EU.[12]

FTAs and the WTO

A basic principle of the General Agreement on Tariffs and Trade (GATT) that is administered by the WTO is the most-favored nation (MFN) principle. Article I of GATT requires that "any advantage, favor, privilege, or immunity granted by any contracting party to any product originating in or destined for any other country shall be accorded immediately and unconditionally to the like product originating in or destined for the territories of all other contracting parties." FTAs, by definition, violate the MFN principle, since products of FTA member countries are given preferential treatment over nonmember products. However, the original GATT signatories recognized that FTAs and customs unions, while violating the MFN principle, improve economic welfare of all members, if certain conditions are met to minimize trade diversion.

Article XXIV of the GATT requires that FTA members shall not erect higher or more restrictive tariff or nontariff barriers on trade with nonmembers than existed prior to the formation of the FTA. Furthermore, Article XXIV requires the elimination of tariffs and other trade restrictions be applied to "substantially all the trade between the constituent territories in products originating in such territories." In addition, Article XXIV stipulates that the elimination of duties and other trade restrictions on trade within the FTA be accomplished "within a reasonable length of time," meaning a period of no longer than 10 years, according to the "Understanding of the Interpretation of Article XXIV of the General Agreement on Tariffs and Trade" reached during the Uruguay Round. Member countries are required to report to the WTO their intention to form FTAs. In addition to Article XXIV, the "Enabling Clause," agreed to by GATT signatories in 1979, allows developing countries to form preferential trading arrangements without the conditions under Article XXIV.

Article V of the General Agreement on Trade in Services (GATS), the agreement that governs trade in services under the WTO, provides for the preferential treatment of trade in services within FTAs or similar regional trading arrangements. Article V lays out requirements of substantial coverage of the elimination of trade restrictions and the prohibition on the *ex post facto* imposition of higher restrictions on services trade with nonmember countries.

The WTO formed the Committee on Regional Trade Agreements (CRTA) in 1996 to review pending and operating FTAs and customs unions to determine whether they conform to WTO rules under the GATT and the GATS. However, the rules are sufficiently ambiguous as to be subject to continuing debate within the CRTA. For example, the members have been unable to agree on what constitutes "substantially all trade" under Article XXIV (GATT) or "substantially all sectors" under Article V (GATS).[13] The number of FTAs and customs unions worldwide has increased at a rapid rate. As of July 2010, 474 FTAs and customs unions had been notified to the GATT/WTO. Some 283 FTAs and customs unions are in force. The remaining FTAs and customs unions were largely superseded by other agreements involving the same participants.[14]

Yet, none of the reports of notifications has been completed because CRTA members have not been able to reach a consensus on any of them. Nevertheless, the vast majority of the FTAs have gone into operation. For example, the CRTA has not completed its report on NAFTA, which went into effect in January 1994. The proliferation of FTAs and disagreements on rules have crippled the WTO review process and led WTO members to place review of the rules on regional agreements on the agenda of the Doha Development Agenda round. The Doha Ministerial Declaration, which established the agenda for the new round, states that the negotiations will strive at "clarifying and improving disciplines and procedures under the existing WTO provisions applying to regional trade agreements."

THE DEBATE OVER FTAS

The surge in the number of FTAs worldwide has been driving a spirited debate among experts, policymakers, and other observers over whether they promote or damage U.S. economic interests and the economic interests of the world at large. The differing views can be categorized into three main groups. One group consists of those who oppose FTAs because, they assert, FTAs undermine the development of the multilateral trading system and act as a "stumbling block" to global trade liberalization. A second group supports FTAs because, they believe, FTAs act as a "building block" to multilateral trade liberalization. The third category are those individuals and groups that are opposed to trade liberalization in general because they believe its impact on workers in import-sensitive sectors or on the environment is unacceptable, or because, they assert, it undermines U.S. sovereignty.

Among representatives of the first group of experts are international economists Jagdish Bhagwati and Anne O. Krueger, who have strongly advocated that the United States and other national governments should not pursue FTAs at the expense of multilateral negotiations in the WTO. Bhagwati has concluded that FTAs are by definition discriminatory and therefore trade diverting. He argues that tariffs remain high on many goods imported into developing countries and even on some labor-intensive goods (such as wearing apparel and agricultural products) imported into developed countries. Consequently, he asserts, trade diversion will likely result when an FTA is formed.[15]

Both Bhagwati and Krueger cite the "rules of origin" and other conditions of an FTA's establishment for strong criticism. Bhagwati claims, for example, that the rules of origin in one FTA more than likely do not coincide with the rules of origin in many of the other FTAs. Furthermore, he argues, the schedule of implementation of the tariff reductions and other conditions for one FTA will not match the schedule of other FTAs. The incongruity of these regulations across FTAs has created what Bhagwati sees as a customs administration nightmare and calls the "spaghetti-bowl" phenomenon.[16]

In her criticism, Krueger claims that in order to meet the input thresholds of rules of origin requirements, producers in one FTA partner will be encouraged to purchase as many inputs as possible from other partner countries, even if a non-FTA member can produce and sell the inputs more cheaply and even if the tariff rate on inputs from non-FTA producers is zero. Importing inputs from within the FTA to meet the rules of origin threshold allows the producer to sell the final product within the FTA duty free. Under such circumstances imports of inputs are diverted from efficient producers outside the FTA to less efficient producers inside the FTA. A corollary to Krueger's conclusion is that the higher the threshold established in the rules of origin, the greater the chance that trade diversion will take place.[17]

A range of economists, policymakers, and other experts embrace a second view that FTAs can enhance trade and should be pursued. Economist Robert Z. Lawrence argues, for example, that recent FTAs involve much more economic integration than the elimination of tariffs. NAFTA, he points out, has led to the reduction in barriers on services trade, foreign investment, and other economic activities not covered by the GATT/WTO. In addition, under NAFTA, Mexico has affirmed its commitment to economic reform, making its economy more efficient. Lawrence asserts that the theory traditionally applied to FTAs (by Bhagwati, Krueger, and others) does not take into account these dynamic welfare enhancing characteristics of FTAs, which he believes are likely to outweigh any trade diversion that results from the elimination of tariffs.[18]

A CATO Institute study by economist Edward L. Hudgins argues that while it may be preferable to liberalize trade multilaterally, countries should take any available avenue, including bilateral or regional FTAs, even if they lead to some trade diversion. Furthermore, Hudgins asserts that FTAs can be more efficient vehicles for addressing difficult trade barriers than the WTO, where the large membership requires compromise to the least common denominator to achieve consensus. FTAs have also have provided momentum for GATT/WTO members to move ahead with new trade rounds, he claims.[19]

Economist C. Fred Bergsten holds a position similar to the one expressed in the CATO study, that in lieu of multilateral trade negotiations, FTAs are the next best thing and promote global trade liberalization. Bergsten has advocated establishing U.S. FTAs with New Zealand and with South Korea. Economist Jeffrey Schott argues that some U.S. firms are being discriminated against because FTAs are rapidly forming in which the United States is not a participant; therefore, in his review, the United States must negotiate FTAs.[20]

Bergsten and others have also advocated structuring FTAs in a manner that could serve as building blocks of a global free trade system. Using the APEC plan as a model, Bergsten argues for an FTA based on "open regionalism," that is, establishing the road map for free trade and investment in the Asian-Pacific region for 2010/2020 among the members but allowing other countries to join if they agree to accede to the conditions. In order to minimize trade diversion, he suggests that trade and investment could be implemented on an MFN principle, perhaps conditional MFN in order to limit the "free rider" effects. Other countries, and other regional groupings, Bergsten presumes, would be willing to accept the conditions having been enticed by the trade and investment opportunities until most of the membership of the WTO would be engaged in forming a free trade area.[21] A Heritage Foundation report draws up a similar proposal for a "Global Free Trade Association."[22]

A third group opposes FTAs but also trade liberalization or "globalization" in general. Included in this group are representatives of import-sensitive industries, for example labor unions, and representatives of social action groups such as some environmentalists, who question the wisdom of trade liberalization whether done through multilateral negotiations or through bilateral and regional trading arrangements. They assert that trade liberalization unfairly affects workers by exporting jobs to countries with lower wages and undermines the nation's ability to protect the environment by allowing companies to relocate to countries with less stringent environmental regulations.[23] For example, the United Auto Workers (UAW) union has stated the following position regarding the Free Trade Area of the Americas (FTAA):

> Such an agreement would provide broader protections for the rights of corporations, further undermine the ability of governments in the region to regulate their economies in the interests of their citizens and intensify the downward pressure on workers' incomes through competition for jobs and investments. All of this would take place in the absence of any counter-balancing protections for workers, consumers or the environment. This is why the UAW has consistently opposed the direction of these negotiations, the positions taken by the U.S. government, and worked closely with other organizations in the region to oppose the creation of an FTAA.[24]

CONCLUSIONS AND IMPLICATIONS FOR CONGRESS

Free trade agreements are viewed by many as a significant trade policy vehicle for the United States and for other major trading nations. Over the last 10-15 years, the debate in U.S. trade policy has shifted from, "Should the United States form FTAs?" to "Should the United States form any more FTAs and, if so, with whom, when, and under what conditions?" Congress has a direct role in addressing those questions. Before any FTA can go into effect, Congress must review it as part of implementing legislation.

A number of questions regarding FTAs could arise as the Obama Administration pursues the TPP, and Congress oversees and evaluates overall U.S. trade policy strategy. One question pertains to the economic impact of an FTA. As with any trade liberalizing measure, an FTA can have positive effects on some sectors and adverse effects on others. An FTA may create trade for one sector of the U.S. economy but divert trade away from others. A Member of Congress is placed in the position of weighing the effects on his/her constituency versus the overall impact on the United States and other trading partners. Because conditions can differ radically from one FTA to another, the evaluation will likely differ in each case. Furthermore, Members might take into account not only the immediate static effects of FTAs but also the long-term, dynamic effects, which could play an important role in evaluating their contribution to U.S. economy.

A second, broader question is whether bilateral and regional FTAs are the appropriate trade policy strategy to promote U.S. national interests. Economic specialists differ sharply on this question, with some viewing the proliferation of FTAs as leading to confusion and serving as stumbling blocks to the development of a rules-based multilateral trading system. Other specialists consider FTAs as appropriate trade policy vehicles for promoting freer trade, as building blocks to a multilateral system, and as necessary to protect U.S. interests against the FTAs that other countries are forming without the United States. Still others oppose trade liberalization in any form as counter to U.S. interests.

A third question is whether the Office of the United States Trade Representative and other trade policy agencies have sufficient time and human resources to negotiate a number of FTAs simultaneously while managing trade policy in the WTO and other fora. Others might find some U.S. interests being short-changed.

A fourth question is to what degree, if any, should non-trade concerns be included in FTAs? This issue has emerged in a number of completed and ongoing FTA negotiations.

A fifth overarching question is what criteria should the United States employ in determining which countries would make appropriate FTA partners. For example, to what degree should political factors be given weight over economic factors?

End Notes

[1] Besides the arrangements described above under which member countries extend *reciprocal* preferential treatment, there are trade arrangements under which one party agrees to extend nonreciprocal preferential treatment to the imports of a country or group of countries unilaterally. Such arrangements involve primarily developed countries extending nonreciprocal preferential treatment to the imports from developing countries. For example, the United States employs the Generalized System of Preferences (GSP), the Andean Trade Preferences Act (ATPA), the Caribbean Basin Initiative (CBI), and the Africa Growth and Opportunity Act (AGOA). The main objective of these nonreciprocal arrangements is to encourage economic development in developing countries.

[2] The President submitted implementing legislation for the U.S.-Colombia Free Trade Agreement which was introduced in the 110th Congress (H.R. 5724/S. 2830) on April 8, 2008. However, the House voted (H.Res. 1092) to make certain expedited procedures, including established deadlines under section 151 of the Trade Act of 1974, not applicable to the bill. The 110th Congress took no further action on the legislation.

[3] CRS Report RL34470, *The U.S.-Colombia Free Trade Agreement: Background and Issues*, by M. Angeles Villarreal.

[4] CRS Report RL32540, *The U.S.-Panama Free Trade Agreement*, by J. F. Hornbeck.

[5] CRS Report RL34330, *The U.S.-South Korea Free Trade Agreement (KORUS FTA): Provisions and Implications*, coordinated by William H. Cooper.

[6] For more information see, CRS Report RL34470, *The U.S.-Colombia Free Trade Agreement: Background and Issues*, by M. Angeles Villarreal.

[7] For more information on the TPP, see CRS Report R42694, *The Trans-Pacific Partnership Negotiations and Issues for Congress*, coordinated by Ian F. Fergusson.

[8] Viner, Jacob. *The Customs Union Issue*. Carnegie Endowment for International Peace. 1950. New York.

[9] This conclusion is called the General Theory of the Second Best and was developed by economists Richard Lipsey and Kelvin Lancaster. Lipsey, Richard and Kelvin Lancaster. The General Theory of the Second Best. *Review of Economic Studies*. vol 24. p. 11-32. Cited and discussed in Lawrence, Robert Z. *International National Economies: Regionalism, Multilateralism, and Deeper Integration. Brookings Institution*. Washington, DC. 1996. p. 22.

[10] Salvatore, Dominick. *International Economics*. Fifth Edition. Englewood Cliffs, NJ: Prentice-Hall, 1995, pp. 305-306.

[11] Ibid, p.307.

[12] CRS Report 97-663. *Regional Trade Agreements: Implications for U.S. Trade Policy*, by George Holliday.

[13] The CRTA meets several times during the year.

[14] http://www.wto.org.

[15] Bhagwati, Jagdish. *The Wind of the Hundred Days: How Washington Mismanaged Globalization*. The MIT Press. Cambridge, MA. 2000. p. 240-245.

[16] Ibid.

[17] Krueger, Anne O. "Free Trade Agreements As Protectionist Devices: Rules of Origin," in Melvin, James R., James C. Moore, and Raymond Riezman (eds.). *Trade, Theory, and Econometrics: Essays in Honor of John C. Chipman*. Routledge Press. New York. 1999. pp. 91-101.

[18] Lawrence, Robert Z. *Regionalism, Multilateralism, and Deeper Integration: Changing Paradigms for Developing Countries*. in Mendoza, Miguel Rodriquez, Patrick Low, and Barbara Kotschwar (eds.). *Trade Rules in the Making*. Organization of American States/Brookings Institution Press. Washington, DC. 1999. p. 41-45.

[19] Hudgins, Edward. L. Regional and Multilateral Trade Agreements: Complementary Means to Open Markets. *Cato Journal*. Vol. 15. No. 23. Fall/Winter 1995/96.

[20] Schott, Jeffrey J. *Free Trade Agreements: The Cost of U.S. Nonparticipation*. Testimony before the Subcommittee on Trade. House Ways and Means Committee. March 29, 2001. http://www.iie.com.

[21] Bergsten, C. Fred. *Open Regionalism*. Working paper 97. Institute for International Economics. 1997.

[22] Hulsman, John C. and Aaron Schavey. *The Global Free Trade Association: A New Trade Agenda*. The Heritage Foundation Backgrounder No. 1441. May 16, 2001.

[23] For more information, see for example, the United Auto Workers positions on trade policy at http://www.uaw.com and the positions of Public Citizen's Global Trade Watch at http://www.citizen.org.

[24] http://www.uaw.com.

In: Free Trade Agreements
Editor: Jenell Gallo
ISBN: 978-1-63117-366-0

Chapter 5

OVERVIEW OF LABOR ENFORCEMENT ISSUES IN FREE TRADE AGREEMENTS*

Mary Jane Bolle

SUMMARY

Since 1993, the Administration has negotiated and Congress has approved 13 free trade agreements (FTAs) that contain labor provisions with different degrees of enforceability. This report identifies two types of labor enforcement issues: (1) those that relate to the FTA provisions themselves, including their definitions and their enforceability, and (2) those that relate to executive branch responsibilities, such as resource availability and determining dispute settlement case priorities. This report does not address other labor issues in the various free trade agreements, including cooperative consultation provisions.

BACKGROUND

The inclusion of enforceable labor provisions—that is, those subject to dispute resolution procedures—in various trade agreement authorities and related reciprocal trade agreements has evolved over time.[1] At first, U.S. trade policy focused on lowering tariffs on goods. It was later extended to various types of nontariff barriers.

Labor principles and standards are not subject to World Trade Organization (WTO) rules and disciplines. The International Labor Organization (ILO), an arm of the United Nations founded in 1919, is the multilateral organization with responsibility for labor issues. For nearly 90 years, the ILO has been working to create, through adoption at its annual International Labor Conferences of Member countries, *Conventions*, which set international standards.

---

* This is an edited, reformatted and augmented version of a Congressional Research Service Publication, CRS Report for Congress RS22823, dated January 31, 2013.

The ILO has adopted at least 183 Conventions, eight of which define four "core labor" principles. This occurred when first, a U.N. Social Summit in Copenhagen Denmark in 1995 declared that four categories of principles and rights at work are fundamental: (1) freedom of association and collective bargaining; (2) the elimination of forced labor; (3) the elimination of child labor; and (4) the elimination of discrimination in respect of employment and occupation.[2] The ILO then responded by pulling these together as the 1998 *ILO Declaration on Fundamental Principles and Rights at Work and its Follow-Up*. The *Declaration* commits all ILO Member States, whether or not they have ratified the specific conventions, to respect the labor principles in these four key areas. The *Follow-Up*, among other things, calls for reports by developing countries that have not ratified one or more of the core Conventions, on the status of their implementation of the various rights.[3]

The United States had unilaterally promoted the development of "internationally recognized worker rights," principles similar to those in the *ILO Declaration*, through its trade preference laws for developing countries. These trade preference laws cover five main programs: the *Generalized System of Preferences* (GSP), 1975; the *Caribbean Basin Initiative* (CBI), 1983; the *Andean Trade Preference Act* (ATPA), 1991; and the African Growth and Opportunity Act (AGOA), 2000; and the Haiti Opportunity through Partnership Act (HOPE), 2006. These laws all require that as a condition of obtaining and maintaining program eligibility, beneficiary countries must take steps to afford their workers "*internationally recognized worker rights*." These rights are listed in *Trade Act of 1974*, as amended, (Section 507), as similar to ILO core labor principles listed above, except the U.S. list substitutes for the fourth principle listed above: "acceptable conditions of work with respect to minimum wages, hours of work, and occupational safety and health.[4]

In 1996, backed by the United States and other developed countries, the then-124-member WTO debated whether to form a committee to look into the relationship between trade and labor standards. Developing countries, in the majority, argued that the issue had no place in the WTO framework; was little more than a smokescreen for protectionism; and was a bid by industrial nations to undermine the comparative advantage of lower-wage trading partners.[5] Ultimately they prevailed. The Singapore Ministerial Declaration, reporting on what they decided, stated that the ILO (rather than the WTO) would be the "competent body to set and deal with ... internationally recognized core labor standards."[6] The ILO has no enforcement tools, but rather promotes labor standards through consensus, moral suasion, and technical assistance.

Inclusion of labor provisions in bilateral U.S. trade agreements has evolved. The first two U.S. FTAs with Israel, 1985, and Canada, 1988, did not include labor provisions. This pattern began to change after 1993, when a number of factors came into play. First, the United States began to undertake FTA negotiations with lesser-developed countries. Second, it became increasingly accepted that labor issues were related to trade and trade policy. Third, consensus broadened that globalization had both costs and benefits. The benefits tend to be broadly dispersed and include relatively higher economic growth and productivity and greater access to lower-priced goods. The costs tend to be concentrated in import-competing sectors where there may be downward pressure on wages and job displacement. In developing countries, pressures to become a low-cost producer can lead to diminished working conditions and diminished worker rights. Fourth, business groups have increasingly been willing to make some concessions to labor groups in order to promote trade agreements and pave the way for greater trade with and investment in developing countries.

LABOR ENFORCEMENT IN U.S. FREE TRADE AGREEMENTS

Since 1993, the United States has negotiated 13 FTAs that include 19 countries. These are, chronologically, the North American Free Trade Agreement (NAFTA) with Mexico and Canada; bilateral agreements with Jordan, Chile, Singapore, Australia, Morocco, Bahrain, and Oman; a regional agreement known as CAFTA-DR, with the Dominican Republic and the five Central American Countries (Costa Rica, El Salvador, Guatemala, Honduras, and Nicaragua); and bilateral FTAs with Peru, Colombia, Panama, and South Korea. The last four agreements reflect a bipartisan compromise on labor language as delineated in the "Bipartisan Trade Deal" (popularly known as the "May 10th Agreement,") jointly agreed to between the leadership in Congress and the Administration on May 10, 2007. This agreement calls for, among other things, two additional labor provisions in FTAs: (1) a fully enforceable commitment that FTA countries will adopt, maintain, and enforce in their laws and practice, the basic international labor standards as stated in the 1998 *ILO Declaration*; and (2) the use of identical enforcement provisions for labor and the other provisions in the agreements. Labor and enforcement provisions in these various trade agreements can be categorized into four different models.

Model 1

For *NAFTA*, labor provisions are included in the *North American Agreement on Labor Cooperation (NAALC)*, a side agreement, rather than in the main agreement. Under NAALC, countries agree to enforce their own labor laws and standards. However, under NAALC, the only provision enforceable with sanctions is a Party's "persistent pattern of failure ... to effectively enforce its occupational safety and health, child labor or minimum wage technical standards," where that failure is trade-related and covered by mutually recognized labor laws (Article 29). By comparison, all provisions relating to commercial operations are enforceable under the *NAFTA*. Furthermore, the labor side agreement has different enforcement procedures than does the main agreement, and places limits on monetary enforcement assessments, with suspension of benefits for noncompliance. There are no monetary assessments under the *NAFTA*.

Model 2

In the *U.S.-Jordan Free Trade Agreement*, labor provisions and commercial provisions share the same dispute resolution procedures. Among labor provisions, each Party agrees to "not fail to effectively enforce its labor laws ... in a manner affecting trade" (Article 6.4). Under the Jordan agreement, labor laws are defined as U.S. *internationally recognized worker rights*. All labor provisions and commercial provisions are equally enforceable. If the dispute is not resolved under procedures specified, the affected Party shall be entitled to take "any appropriate and commensurate measure" (Article 17.2(b)). However, in an exchange of letters between the USTR Robert Zoellick and Jordanian Ambassador Marwan Muasher before

Congress considered the implementing legislation in 2001, the governments reportedly agreed to resolve any potential disputes without resorting to trade sanctions.[7]

Model 3

Seven trade agreements with 12 different countries (Chile, Singapore, Australia, Morocco, Bahrain, Oman, and the six CAFTA-DR countries) include only one enforceable labor provision: each country "shall not fail to effectively enforce its labor laws ... in a manner affecting trade between the Parties." The agreements define *labor laws* as "a Party's statutes or regulations ... that are directly related to" the list of U.S. *internationally recognized worker rights*. All provisions in these agreements relating to commercial operations are enforceable. The seven trade agreements share many of the same procedures for labor and commercial disputes. Procedures for labor disputes place limits on monetary penalties, whereas those for commercial disputes do not. Suspension of benefits is a "last recourse" option for both types of disputes.

Model 4

On May 10, 2007, the bipartisan leadership in Congress and the Administration agreed to a *Bipartisan Trade Deal* to include, among other things, provisions in pending FTAs: with Peru, Colombia, Panama, and South Korea. These are (1) a fully enforceable commitment that Parties to free trade agreements would adopt and maintain in their laws and practices the *ILO Declaration*; (2) a fully enforceable commitment prohibiting FTA countries from lowering their labor standards; (3) new limitations on "prosecutorial" and "enforcement" discretion (i.e., countries cannot defend failure to enforce laws related to the five basic core labor standards on the basis of resource limitations or decisions to prioritize other enforcement issues); and (4) the same dispute settlement mechanisms or penalties available for other FTA obligations (such as commercial interests).[8]

The four concepts were incorporated into all four agreements in virtually identical form. The language appears to limit item (1) in the May 10th Agreement, described above, by including two footnotes to the key provision: that each Party shall adopt and maintain in its statutes, regulations, and practices, the *rights* as stated in the *ILO Declaration and its Follow-Up*. The first footnote limits obligations of Parties to those specified in the *ILO Declaration* (i.e., without also including the *Follow-Up*). The second footnote requires that a party seeking to challenge violations must demonstrate that the failure to adopt or maintain ILO core labor principles has been "in a manner affecting *either* trade *or* investment between the two countries,"[9] In Model 4 resolution of disputes may involve monetary assessments (with no dollar limits) and, if they are not paid, suspension of benefits until the non-conformity is eliminated. The most recent agreements were approved by Congress in the following implementing bills: with Peru, in 2007 (P.L. 110-138); with South Korea in 2011 (P.L. 112-41); with Panama in 2011 (P.L. 112-43); and with Colombia in 2012 (P.L. 112-42).

ENFORCEMENT ISSUES

Based on the differences between labor and commercial FTA provisions articulated in the four models, policy issues can be divided into two categories: the differences in labor vs. commercial provisions themselves (issues 1-3 below); and the differences stemming from the agencies charged with that enforcement (issues 4 and 5 below).

1. Only Some Labor Provisions Are Enforceable

Under Models 2 and 4, all labor provisions in trade agreements are technically enforceable.[10] In Models 1 and 3, only certain labor provisions in trade agreements are enforceable. All commercial provisions in trade agreements are fully enforceable under all models. Under NAFTA, covered by Model 1, the labor side agreement, *NAALC*, as mentioned, includes one enforceable provision: a country must enforce a few of its labor standards—those relating to child labor, minimum wages, and occupational safety and health. A country is not required to enforce its laws relating to the most basic core labor rights—the right to organize and bargain collectively—issues which account for the majority of the labor submissions filed with *NAALC*.[11] The FTAs covered by Model 3 also include only one enforceable labor provision, but it is broader in scope than that in the NAALC: countries must enforce *all* of their own laws relating to *internationally recognized worker* rights in a manner affecting trade between the Parties.

2. Different Enforcement Procedures for and Caps on Penalties for Labor Provisions

Model 1 has separate and dissimilar enforcement procedures for violation of labor as opposed to other provisions. Model 3 has relatively similar procedures for violations under both types of provisions. However, both Models 1 and 3 place caps on potential maximum monetary penalties for violation of labor provisions, but place no caps on penalties for violations of other provisions. Models 2 and 4 have a single set of enforcement procedures covering labor and other provisions and place no caps on penalties. However, as mentioned, under the Model 2, U.S.-Jordan FTA, the Parties agree to make every attempt to arrive at a mutually agreeable resolution through consultations and without application of the FTA's dispute settlement procedures.

3. Limits Placed on Scope of Definition of a Term in Labor Provisions

Labor provisions in Model 4 agreements are "fully enforceable" through the same dispute resolution procedures available for other disputes. However, a footnote limits a key labor provision—that countries adopt and maintain in their laws and practices, the rights as stated in the *ILO Declaration*. The footnote limits the scope of the definition, as mentioned, by saying,

"The obligations set out in Article 17.2, as they relate to the ILO, refer only to the *ILO Declaration*." This would suggest that trading Partners could be held to the principles of the *Declaration*, but not the details of the Conventions and not the Follow-Up procedures.[12] Some observers have raised concerns that some of the details in some of the ILO core labor standard conventions conflict with some U.S. labor laws, particularly state laws.

4. Differentials in Procedures for Considering Disputes on Labor vs. Other Provisions

Differences in the way that commercial and labor disputes are considered by the Department of Commerce (DOC) and the Department of Labor (DOL) can be summarized as follows: The DOC receives complaints about compliance with trade agreements from the Market Access and Compliance Office (MAC)'s Trade Compliance Center (TCC) "hotline," industry groups, trade associations, Congress, U.S. Foreign Commercial Service officers, the USTR *National Trade Estimates Report*, and other sources. It uses its many resources to conduct research on compliance cases.[13] The DOL does not have a comparable "hotline," but does have procedures for receiving complaints about labor violations under a free trade agreement.[14] The DOL also states (1) that its core mission is primarily to protect the needs of U.S. workers, rather than those of other countries, which is where complaints about labor conditions related to trade agreements typically arise; and (2) that its international responsibilities include ensuring compliance with labor provisions of trade agreements and trade preference programs. The DOL receives information on foreign labor conditions from a number of sources including trade unions, Congress, Department of State labor officers at U.S. embassies, and the State Department's *Country Reports on Human Rights Practices*. The DOL, like the DOC, may take action to resolve an issue at any stage prior to dispute resolution.[15] Any case not so resolved, may be referred by the respective agency to the Office of the USTR.

5. Priorities for Disputes to be Pursued by the USTR

Labor submissions have been filed with the DOL alleging violations of the labor provisions of the FTAs involving a number of countries, including Guatemala, Bahrain, Honduras, the Dominican Republic, Mexico, and Peru. However, to date, none of these disputes has resulted in formal consultation between the USTR and a foreign government, potentially leading to dispute resolution. Two cases currently pending are: one involving Guatemala, on which negotiations are still proceeding short of formal consultation; and another involving Bahrain, on which the Department of Labor has recommended to the USTR that the United States launch formal consultations.[16]

Should a case not be resolved short of dispute resolution, the USTR must decide which cases it will pursue based on priorities. The USTR is a small operation. Entering into the dispute resolution process is a lengthy, involved, expensive process in terms of both personnel and resources. The USTR typically chooses cases to pursue based on a number of factors. These may include cases that involve clear violations, could clarify particular issues and/or be cases the USTR believes it can win, based on evidence and facts.

End Notes

[1] Trade promotion authority refers to presidential authority to enter into trade agreements that Congress considers under expedited procedures (most recently in Title XXI of the *Trade Act of 2002*, P.L. 107-210). For more information, see CRS Report RL33743, *Trade Promotion Authority (TPA) and the Role of Congress in Trade Policy*, by J. F. Hornbeck and William H. Cooper.

[2] United Nations World Summit for Social Development, Copenhagen. March 6-12. 1995.

[3] *ILO Declaration on Fundamental Principles and Rights at Work and its Follow-Up: About the Declaration.* From the ILO website, at http://www.ilo.org.

[4] See Trade Act of 1974 (P.L. 93-618 as amended), Sec. 507 (4)(E).

[5] World Trade Organization, *Singapore Ministerial Declaration*, adopted December 13, 1996, Sec. 4, Core Labour Standards.

[6] See WTO press brief on Trade and Labour Standards, http://www.wto.org/english/thewto_ e/ minist_e/ min96_e/labstand.htm.

[7] Governments: "would not expect or intend to apply the Agreement's dispute settlement enforcement procedures … in a manner that results in blocking trade." Jordan Free Trade Agreement Approved by Finance and Ways and Means, *Inside U.S. Trade*, July 27, 2001.

[8] Text: Congress Administration Trade Deal, *Inside U.S. Trade*, May 11, 2007; and *Trade Facts: Bipartisan Trade Deal*. Office of the USTR. Bipartisan Agreement on Trade Policy, May 2007.

[9] Labor chapter of each of the four FTAs, footnote 2.

[10] Under the two-page dispute settlement section in the U.S.-Jordan FTA, which includes much less detail in its procedures than do Model 4 FTAs, if the Joint Committee does not resolve the dispute within 30 days after the presentation of the panel report, the affected Party shall be entitled to take "any appropriate and commensurate measure." However, the dispute settlement, begins with language specifying that "the Parties shall make every attempt to arrive at a mutually agreeable resolution through consultations," and, as mentioned earlier, this provision was reinforced by a mutual exchange of letters between the two countries before Congress considered the implementing legislation.

[11] U.S. Department of Labor, Office of Trade and Labor Affairs.

[12] The United States has ratified only two of the eight ILO core labor principles, although most of their substance is covered by U.S. law.

[13] Phone conversation with Commerce Department officials February 15, 2008.

[14] Procedural guidelines for submitting complaints to the DOL, Office of Trade and Labor Affairs (OTLA) under a labor chapter of a free trade agreement are located in the Federal Register, Vol. 7, p. 245. December. 21, 2006.

[15] Phone conversation with USTR officials, April 4, 2008.

[16] *World Trade Online*, U.S., Guatemala Takes Another Stab at Resolving CAFTA Labor Fight, December 22, 2011; and DOL Report Recommends Bahrain Consultations Over FTA Labor Violation, January 3, 2013.

INDEX

#

A

B

D

I

J

L

Q

R

S

T

U

V

W

Y